Fod[illegible]
Toronto

Allan Gould

Fodor's Travel Publications, Inc.
New York and London

 Published in the United States by Fodor's Travel Publications, Inc., a subsidiary of Random House, Inc., New York, and simultaneously in Canada by Random House of Canada Limited, Toronto. Distributed by Random House, Inc., New York.

ISBN 0-679-01837-9

Fodor's Toronto

Editor: Andrew E. Beresky
Art Director: Fabrizio La Rocca
Cartographer: David Lindroth
Illustrator: Karl Tanner
Cover Photograph: Frank Whitney/The Image Bank

Design: Vignelli Associates

About the Author

Allan Gould has had a dozen books published, including an earlier guide to his chosen city, *The Toronto Book*, as well as critically acclaimed biographies of Canadian business people *(The New Entrepreneurs: 80 Canadian Success Stories)* and an award-winning study of the Stratford Festival, coauthored with its founder, Tom Patterson *(First Stage: The Making of the Stratford Festival)*. Gould has taught theater history and the humanities at York University, the University of Toronto, and the Ontario College of Art. He writes for many Canadian magazines and has both written and performed political satire and biographical sketches for radio and TV. He has lived in Toronto since 1968.

Special Sales

Fodor's Travel Publications are available at special discounts for bulk purchases (100 copies or more) for sales promotions or premiums. Special editions, including personalized covers, excerpts of existing guides, and corporate imprints, can be created in large quantities for special needs. For more information write to Special Marketing, Fodor's Travel Publications, 201 East 50th St., New York, NY 10022. Inquiries from the United Kingdom should be sent to Fodor's Travel Publications, 30–32 Bedford Square, London WC1B 3SG.

MANUFACTURED IN THE UNITED STATES OF AMERICA
10 9 8 7 6 5 4 3 2 1

Contents

Maps

Foreword

This is an exciting time for Fodor's, as we continue our ambitious program to rewrite, reformat, and redesign all 140 of our guides. Here are just a few of the new features:

★ Brand-new computer-generated maps locating all the top attractions, hotels, restaurants, and shops

★ A unique system of numbers and legends to help readers move effortlessly between text and maps

★ A new star rating system for hotels and restaurants

★ Restaurant reviews by major food critics around the world

★ Stamped, self-addressed postcards, bound into every guide, give readers a chance to help evaluate hotels and restaurants

★ Complete page redesign for instant retrieval of information

★ FODOR'S CHOICE—Our favorite museums, beaches, cafés, romantic hideaways, festivals, and more

★ HIGHLIGHTS—An insider's look at the most important developments in tourism during the past year

★ TIME OUT—The best and most convenient lunch stops along exploring routes

★ Exclusive background essays create a powerful portrait of each destination

★ A mini-journal for travelers to keep track of their own itineraries and addresses

The publishers thank Steve Johnson of the Metropolitan Toronto Convention & Visitors Association for all his help in gathering information for this book. The author thanks Annette Poizner for her work on the Nightlife chapter; Sandra Bernstein for hers on the Shopping chapter; and his wife, Merle, for all her help and patience.

While every care has been taken to assure the accuracy of the information on this guide, the passage of time will always bring change, and consequently, the publisher cannot accept responsibility for errors that may occur.

All prices and opening times quoted here are based on information available to us at press time. Hours and admission fees may change, however, and the prudent traveler will avoid inconvenience by calling ahead.

Fodor's wants to hear about your travel experiences, both pleasant and unpleasant. When a hotel or restaurant fails to live up to its billing, let us know and we will investigate the complaint and revise our entries where the facts warrant it.

Send your letter to the editors of Fodor's Travel Publications, 201 E. 50th Street, New York, NY 10022.

Highlights '90 and Fodor's Choice

Highlights '90

Visitors to Toronto in 1990 will find two major new attractions: an exciting new hotel and a fabulous new nightclub that even the children may enjoy on occasion.

The 26-floor, 522-room **Chestnut Park Hotel,** located in downtown Toronto just behind City Hall, opened in early 1989. Its special features are especially suitable for business people.

Superstars, the nightclub—really an entertainment center—opened near the airport also in early 1989. Its 1,700 seats make it the largest of its kind in the Metropolitan Toronto area, and its broad selection of entertainment, from rock and jazz to comedy and children's concerts, makes it an important addition to the city's pop culture.

Among other new hotels are the **Novotel,** located on the Esplanade, within walking distance of Lake Ontario and the Harbourfront; the moderately priced **Ibis** (240 Jarvis St.), located a few blocks east of the New City Hall and Eaton Centre, and **Journey's Court,** part of the Journey's End budget chain, also in the Eaton Centre/New City Hall area.

In the realm of dining, Toronto has become more than ever the city of bistros. The restaurant with the most delicious food may also be the most casual. Gone are the excruciatingly formal places that never quite succeeded at imitating Paris. The most interesting recent additions to the Toronto restaurant scene are all owner-run, informal, and multiethnic. There is **Bistro 990,** where chef Chris Klugman serves, according to our dining critic, "Gallic bistro bliss." At **Joso's** you'll have to put up with the tacky decor but you'll enjoy the best seafood served in Toronto. For Italian specialties, chef Claude Bouillet at **Le Bestingo** serves up some of the finest flavors Toronto can offer. Meanwhile, the dishes of Michael Pagliaro at **Barolo** tend toward the nouvelle Italian. If it's Canada's native cuisine you're seeking, **Trapper's** will introduce you to it deliciously.

The Canadian dollar has been surprisingly strong for the past few years, moving steadily upward against the American dollar, from a low of about 70¢ in early 1987 to as much as 85¢ at press time. American visitors can expect to get less for their money than in previous years.

Toronto has been the financial capital of Canada for years now, a fact that has become more visually pronounced as the banks and trust companies of the country continue to build their towers in the downtown area. **Scotia Plaza,** in the heart of the financial district, was completed in 1989. As with the many other major skyscrapers, it is connected to Toronto's subterranean city. Scheduled for completion in

1990 are the two towers of **BCE Place** (the BC referring to Bell Canada, the phone-service company); one at Bay and Front streets, the other on Wellington Street. Canada's five largest banks and two biggest trust companies (the latter being Canada Trust and Royal Trust) will be doing business in these two major buildings. The beautiful 1885 **Bank of Montreal,** now standing at the northwest corner of Front and Yonge streets, will be restored and incorporated into one of the new, modern towers as the home of the Hockey Hall of Fame.

Another major project, which began in late 1988 and should be completed in 1992, is the new $380 million Toronto headquarters for the **Canadian Broadcasting Corporation.** The $1 billion complex, on a 9.3-acre gravel parking lot next door to Roy Thomson Hall, will include two office towers, a hotel, a retail plaza, and a condominium complex.

The most spectacular new building to be built in Toronto in many decades is the **SkyDome,** which was supposed to have had its grand debut on the first day of the 1989 baseball season, last April. But, due to strikes in 1988, it was rescheduled to open in the summer of 1989.

Besides baseball, the SkyDome is slated to provide a home for the city's football team, the Toronto Argonauts, and to host dozens of rock concerts, exhibitions, and musical events every year. The world's first multipurpose stadium with a retractable roof, it is expected to attract over 4 million spectators annually, making it, overnight, the most popular of all of Toronto's main attractions.

In addition to the amazing roof—which opens or closes in only 20 minutes—the SkyDome has the world's largest video-screen scoreboard (115 by 34 feet). Three times the size of the next largest in the world (the one in Miami's Joe Robbie Stadium), the screen was bought from Sony of Canada for $17 million.

The $244-million stadium has slowly grown into a $427.5-million complex, including a 400-room hotel (with 70 suites overlooking the field), a health club, an entertainment center, and six restaurants. One of the SkyDome's greatest assets—its location in the heart of downtown, just steps from the CN Tower and a few blocks from Union Station—could prove a complete disaster. While the stadium seats approximately 54,000 for baseball, 56,000 for football, and up to 70,000 for concerts, there are only 500 parking spaces in the underground garage. This may mean that anyone who drives in the area of Spadina Road and Front Street on the day of a game or major concert should have at least a day's provisions in the car.

In provincial politics, the Liberals, empowered to rule at least until 1991, passed a law in early 1989 that will allow "local municipalities" to decide whether to allow shops to open on Sundays. This means the chances are good that by the time you read this in 1990, most of Toronto and environs will be swinging seven days a week.

In May 1988, the new provincial government raised the sales tax from 7% to 8%, to help pay for a fairly large deficit that had been built up over the years. Hotel and restaurant bills will increase accordingly, but visitors may still apply for a sales tax rebate on goods purchased in the country.

By the early 1990s, some 1,500 of the city's streetcars will be off to the Terminus in the Sky, to be replaced by buses. But the delightful trolleys will remain.

A major production of the blockbuster hit musical *The Phantom of the Opera*—overseen by the London and New York team—was scheduled to open in the fall of 1989 at the newly—and magnificently—refurbished **Pantages Theatre,** where it is expected to run for the next five years or longer. More good news for musical lovers: The fine Canadian production of *Les Misérables*, which opened in March 1989 at the handsome Alexandra Theatre, is scheduled to be held over into the summer of 1990. These two musicals, along with local and regional productions, give visitors who never get to Broadway or London's West End an opportunity to enjoy top-rate theater.

Fodor's Choice

No two people will agree on what makes a perfect vacation, but it's fun and helpful to know what others think. We hope you'll have a chance to experience some of Fodor's Choices yourself while visiting Toronto. For detailed information about each entry, refer to the appropriate chapters within this guidebook.

Sights Worth at Least a Quick Look

Casa Loma
CN Tower
Metro Toronto Library
New City Hall
Roy Thomson Hall
Royal Bank Tower
SkyDome

Sights Worth Two Hours or More

Black Creek Pioneer Village
Eaton Centre
Harbourfront
Metro Toronto Zoo
Ontario Place
Ontario Science Centre
Royal Ontario Museum

Sights Worth a Two-Hour Drive

African Lion Safari
Algonquin Park
Marineland and Niagara Falls

Parks

Bluffers Park and Cathedral Bluffs Park, Scarborough
High Park (including the zoo)
Leslie Street Spit
Riverdale Farm
Toronto Islands and Centreville

Shopping Areas

Eaton Centre
Hazelton Lanes and Yorkville
Kensington Market/Chinatown
Mirvish Village
Queen's Quay Terminal on Lake Ontario
Queen Street West

Theaters and Cultural Events

Canadian Opera Company at the O'Keefe
Concerts and Symphonies at Roy Thomson Hall
National Ballet of Canada at the O'Keefe
Phantom of the Opera at the Pantages Theatre
Shaw Festival (Niagara-on-the-Lake)
Stratford Festival
Theater at the Royal Alexandra
Theater at the St. Lawrence Centre

Seasonal Events

Caravan (June)
Caribana (July)
Canadian National Exhibition (August/September)
Festival of Festivals (September)
Royal Agricultural Winter Fair (November)

Hotels

The Four Seasons Toronto *(Very Expensive)*
The Harbour Castle Westin *(Very Expensive)*
King Edward Hotel *(Very Expensive)*
Sutton Place Hotel *(Very Expensive)*
Royal York *(Expensive)*
Sheraton Centre *(Expensive)*
Novotel Toronto Centre *(Moderate)*

Drives

Cabbagetown
Forest Hill
Rosedale
Toronto Islands (by bike; cars not allowed!)

Restaurants

Le Bestingo *(Very Expensive)*
Le Fave's *(Very Expensive)*
Beaujolais *(Expensive)*
Bistro 990 *(Expensive)*
Centro *(Expensive)*
Palmerston *(Expensive)*
Pronto *(Expensive)*
Bamboo *(Moderate)*
Kensington Kitchen *(Moderate)*
La Fenice *(Inexpensive)*
Pearl Court *(Inexpensive)*
United Bakers *(Inexpensive)*

Toronto Area Orientation

Georgian Bay
Bruce Peninsula
O N
Lake Huron
Owen Sound
Port Elgin
Collingwood
Kincardine
Durham
Shelburne
Wingham
Arthur
Goderich
Listowel
Clinton
Guelph
Waterloo
Kitchener
Stratford
MICHIGAN
Dundas
Lucan
Woodstock
Brantford
Sarnia
Watford
Port Huron
London
St. Thomas
Thames River
Lake St. Clair
Detroit
Chatham
Windsor
Lake Erie
Leamington
Erie
Cleveland
OHIO
26
21
10
6
4
9
6
86
24
23
8
2
3
69
94
75
90
79
80 90
80

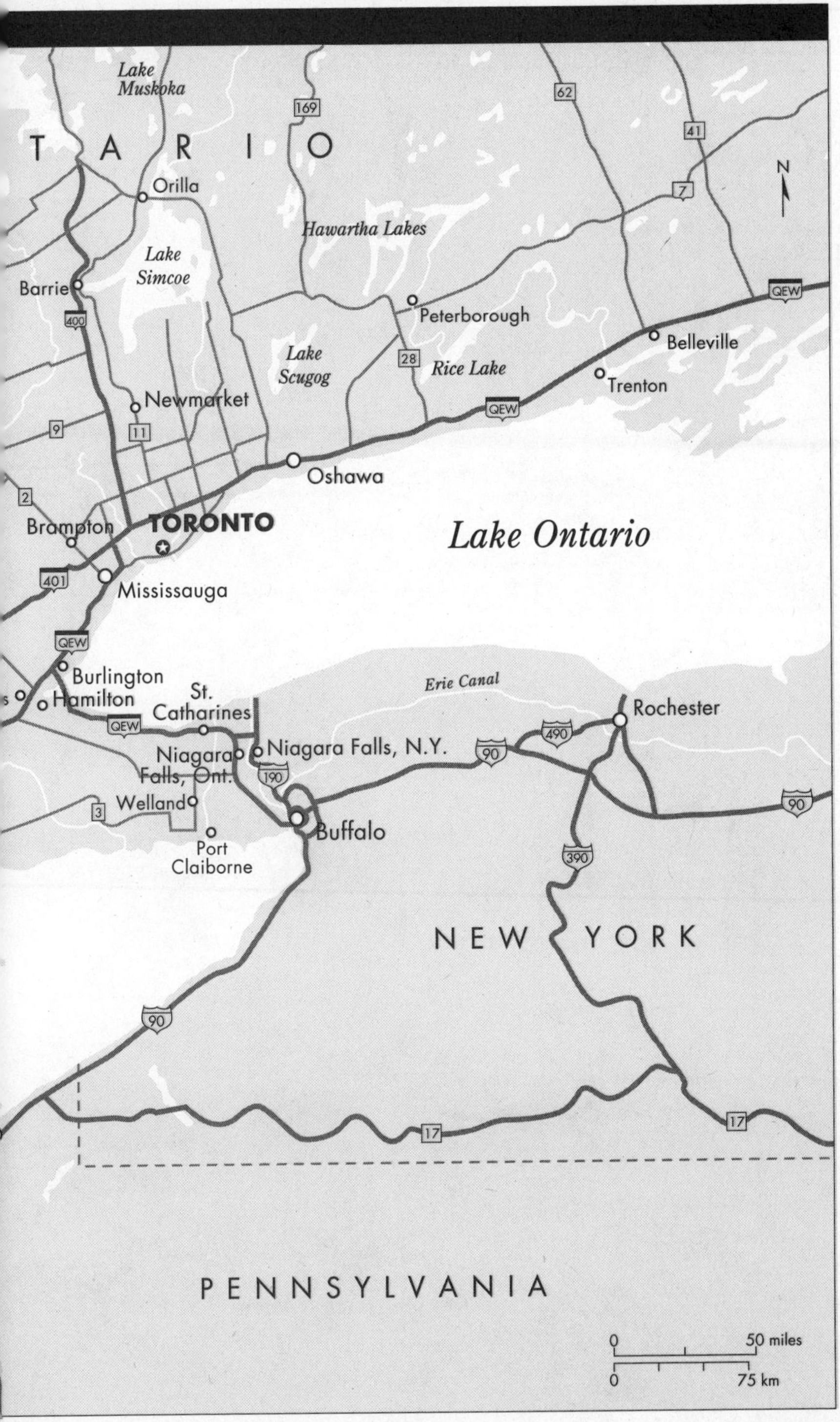
Lake Muskoka
TARIO
169
62
41
Orilla
7
N
Hawartha Lakes
Lake Simcoe
Barrie
400
QEW
Peterborough
Belleville
Lake Scugog
28
Rice Lake
Trenton
Newmarket
9
11
QEW
Oshawa
2
Brampton
TORONTO
Lake Ontario
401
Mississauga
QEW
Burlington
Hamilton
St. Catharines
Erie Canal
Rochester
QEW
490
Niagara Falls, Ont.
Niagara Falls, N.Y.
90
190
Welland
3
90
Buffalo
Port Claiborne
390
NEW YORK
90
17
17
PENNSYLVANIA
0
50 miles
0
75 km

Metropolitan Toronto

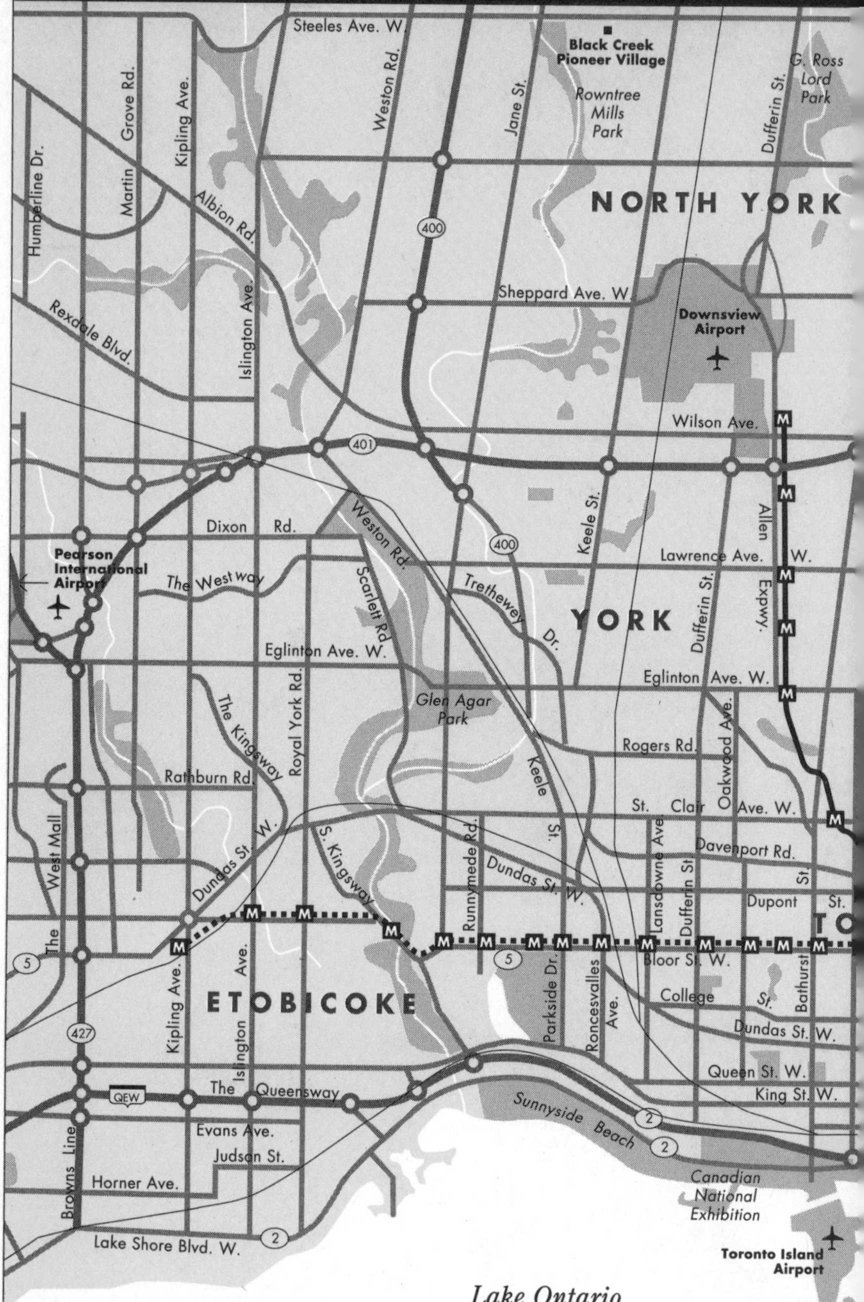

Steeles Ave. W.
Black Creek Pioneer Village
G. Ross Lord Park
Rowntree Mills Park
Weston Rd.
Jane St.
Dufferin St.
Grove Rd.
Kipling Ave.
Martin
Humberline Dr.
Albion Rd.
400
NORTH YORK
Sheppard Ave. W.
Downsview Airport
Rexdale Blvd.
Islington Ave.
Wilson Ave.
401
Dixon Rd.
Weston Rd.
Keele St.
Allen Expwy.
Pearson International Airport
The Westway
Scarlett Rd.
Trethewey Dr.
Lawrence Ave. W.
YORK
Dufferin St.
Eglinton Ave. W.
Eglinton Ave. W.
Royal York Rd.
The Kingsway
Glen Agar Park
Oakwood Ave.
Rogers Rd.
Rathburn Rd.
Keele St.
St. Clair Ave. W.
West Mall
The
Dundas St. W.
S. Kingsway
Runnymede Rd.
Dundas St. W.
Lansdowne Ave.
Davenport Rd.
Dufferin St.
Dupont St.
5
Kipling Ave.
Islington Ave.
ETOBICOKE
Parkside Dr.
Roncesvalles Ave.
Bloor St. W.
College St.
Bathurst St.
Dundas St. W.
427
Queen St. W.
QEW
The Queensway
King St. W.
Sunnyside Beach
2
Evans Ave.
Judson St.
Canadian National Exhibition
Horner Ave.
Browns Line
Lake Shore Blvd. W.
Toronto Island Airport
Lake Ontario
0
2 miles
0
3 km

Bathurst St.
Yonge St.
Finch East Park
Don Mills Rd.
Don Valley Pkwy.
Pharmacy Ave.
Finch Ave W.
Finch Ave.
E.
Finch Ave. E.
Metro Toronto Zoo
11
404
Bayview Ave.
Sheppard Ave.
E.
SCARBOROUGH
Earl Bales Park
401
York Mills
Rd.
Ellesmere Ave.
Avenue Rd.
Leslie St.
Lawrence Ave. E.
Don Mills Rd.
Pkwy.
Wigmore Park
Victoria Park Ave.
Warden Ave.
Birchmount Rd.
Kennedy Rd.
Rd.
Eglinton
Ave. E.
Laird Dr.
Sunnybrook Park
Don Valley
Mount Pleasant
EAST YORK
Pharmacy Ave.
St. Clair Ave. E
O'Connor Dr.
Ave.
Taylor Creek Park
Bayview Ext.
404
Broadview Ave.
Pape Ave.
Greenwood
Coxwell Ave.
Ave.
Dawes Rd.
Danforth Rd.
TORONTO
Bloor St. E.
Parliament St.
Woodbine
Gerrard St. E.
2
Gerrard
St. E.
Dundas
St. E.
Leslie St.
Queen St. E.
Eastern Ave.
N
Lake Shore Blvd. E.
Ashbridges Bay Park
Harbourfront Park
Inner Harbour
Subway Lines
Bloor Danforth Line
Yonge-University Line
Scarborough Rapid Transit
M Subway stop
Railroad lines
Toronto Islands
Aquatic Park

World Time Zones

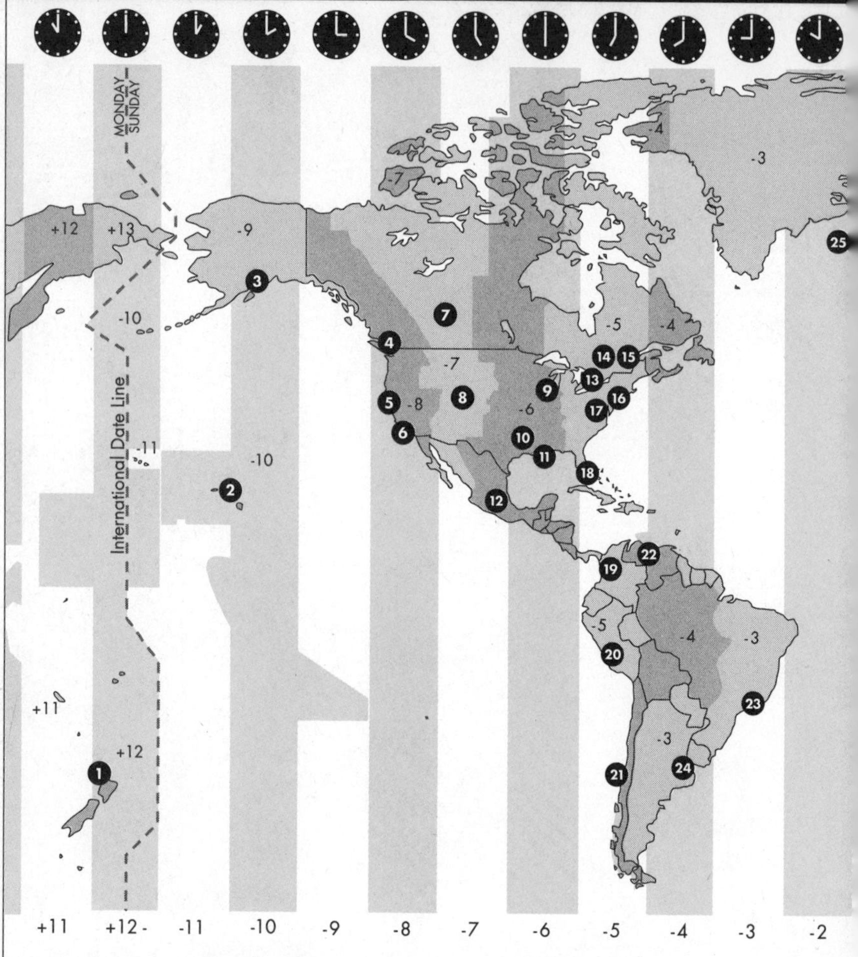

Numbers below vertical bands relate each zone to Greenwich Mean Time (0 hrs.). Local times may differ, as indicated by lightface numbers on the map.

Algiers, **29**
Anchorage, **3**
Athens, **41**
Auckland, **1**
Baghdad, **46**
Bangkok, **50**
Beijing, **54**
Berlin, **34**
Bogotá, **19**
Budapest, **37**
Buenos Aires, **24**
Caracas, **22**
Chicago, **9**
Copenhagen, **33**
Dallas, **10**
Delhi, **48**
Denver, **8**
Djakarta, **53**
Dublin, **26**
Edmonton, **7**
Hong Kong, **56**
Honolulu, **2**
Istanbul, **40**
Jerusalem, **42**
Johannesburg, **44**
Lima, **20**
Lisbon, **28**
London (Greenwich), **27**
Los Angeles, **6**
Madrid, **38**
Manila, **57**

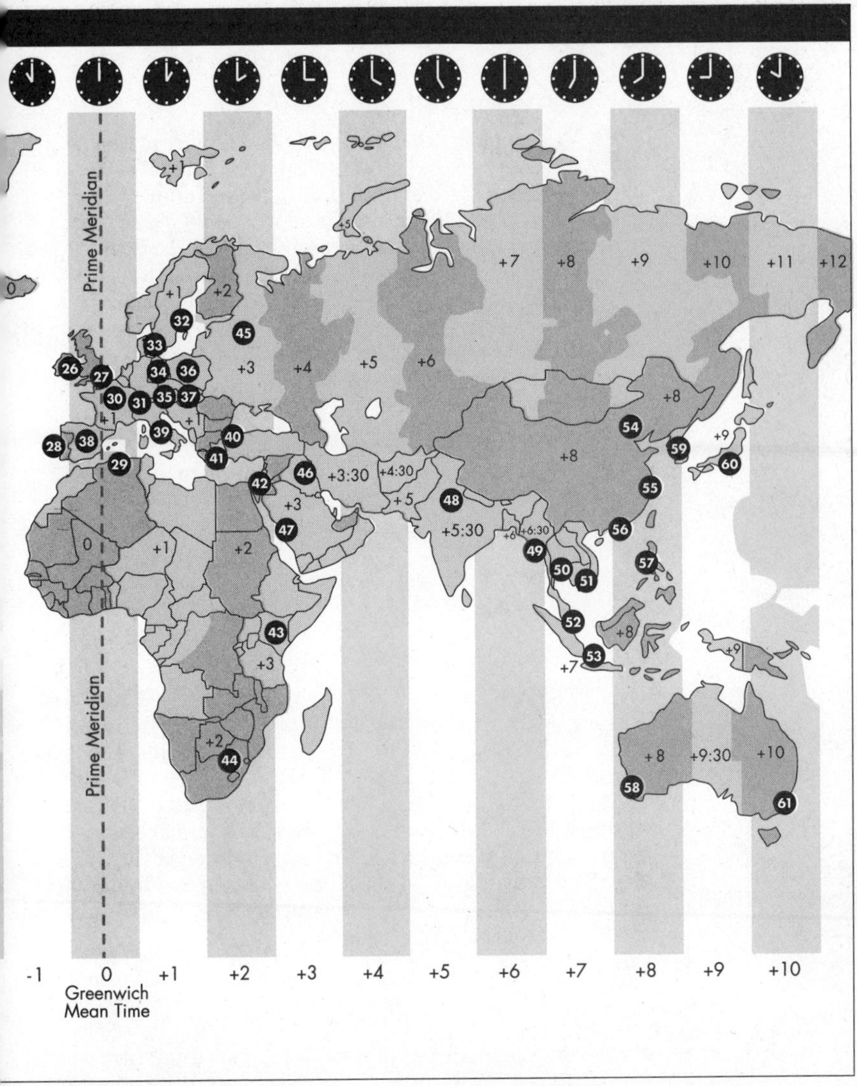

Mecca, **47**
Mexico City, **12**
Miami, **18**
Montreal, **15**
Moscow, **45**
Nairobi, **43**
New Orleans, **11**
New York City, **16**

Ottawa, **14**
Paris, **30**
Perth, **58**
Reykjavík, **25**
Rio de Janeiro, **23**
Rome, **39**
Saigon, **51**

San Francisco, **5**
Santiago, **21**
Seoul, **59**
Shanghai, **55**
Singapore, **52**
Stockholm, **32**
Sydney, **61**
Tokyo, **60**

Toronto, **13**
Vancouver, **4**
Vienna, **35**
Warsaw, **36**
Washington, DC, **17**
Yangon, **49**
Zürich, **31**

Introduction

A joke popular in the neighboring province of Quebec between the wars went "First prize, one week in Toronto. Second prize, two weeks in Toronto. Third prize, three weeks in Toronto." And who could blame them for laughing? Toronto was a deadly city, right into the 1950s, at which time its half-million citizens used to rush off to Detroit (a four-hour drive to the southwest) and Buffalo (90 minutes to the south, around Lake Ontario) for a good time. Today, of course, the rushing is in the opposite direction, for hundreds of reasons that are sprinkled through this volume.

Yet, is not Toronto the city that American novelist John Dos Passos called "a beastly place" in his letter to a friend in 1907? And the city that the great British poet Rupert Brooke, during a visit in 1913, gave halfhearted, one-handed applause to, by writing that "the only depressing thing is that it will always be what it is, only larger"? The city that Ernest Hemingway, while honing his writing craft at *The Toronto Star* in the 1920s, could not wait to escape from, for fear of going mad with boredom?

Even as late as 1960, the witty Irish dramatist Brendan Behan was letting the city have it: "Toronto will be a fine town when it is finished." And in the words of Leopold Infeld, the Polishborn mathematical physicist who worked with Einstein: "It must be good to die in Toronto. The transition between life and death would be continuous, painless and scarcely noticeable in this silent town. I dreaded the Sundays and prayed to God that if he chose for me to die in Toronto he would let it be on a Saturday afternoon to save me from one more Toronto Sunday."

What on earth could have happened in so short a period? And why was no one surprised (in Toronto, at least) when various participants at the 1982 International Conference on Urban Design, in Toronto, ran around spouting such superlatives as "This is the most livable city in North America" and "It is an example of how a city could grow."

Much of Toronto's excitement is explained by its ethnic diversity. Nearly two-thirds of the 3.2 million people who now live in the metropolitan Toronto area were born and raised somewhere else. And that somewhere else was often very far away.

Nearly 500,000 Italians make Metropolitan Toronto the largest Italian community outside of Italy. It is also the home of the largest Chinese community in Canada and the largest Portuguese community in North America. More than 120,000 Jews. Nearly as many Muslims. Tens of thousands of Germans. Greeks. Hungarians. East Indians.

West Indians. Vietnamese. Maltese. South Americans. Ukrainians. More than 70 ethnic groups in all, speaking over 100 different languages. Certainly, a city worthy of inviting the United Nations to consider moving here from Manhattan.

What this has meant to Toronto is the rather rapid creation of a vibrant mix of cultures that has echoes of turn-of-the-century New York City—but without the slums, crowding, disease, and tensions. Toronto undoubtedly would have had this, too, had Canada been decent and wise enough to open her gates wide back then, as the Yanks had. (This fact the city continues to bemoan and tried to atone for by accepting more "boat people" in the 1970s than any other country in the world. Yet, there are still tensions over large immigration to this very day.)

Still, to give to its burgeoning ethnic population all, or even most, of the credit for Toronto's becoming a cosmopolitan, world-class city in just a few decades would be a kind of reverse racism, and not totally correct, either. Much of the thanks must be given to the so-called dour Scots who set up the banks, built the churches, and created the kind of solid base for commerce, culture, and community that would come to such a healthy fruition in the three decades following World War II. Now a minority in the city they helped make, the much-maligned white Anglo-Saxon Protestants had their noses tweaked mercilessly in an issue of *Toronto,* the free monthly magazine that comes with the *Globe and Mail.* In the March 1988 edition, a writer noted that the city was about to hold its first St. Patrick's Day parade ever: "But Toronto—Toronto was for generations known as the Belfast of the North, a city so firmly in the grip of Protestants, Loyalists, and Royalists that a Roman Catholic celebration would have been unthinkable. Well, it's not anymore." In a subsequent issue (*see* Portrait of Toronto) historian William Kilbourn added, "Once, Toronto the Good was embodied by the masters of the Orange Order: defenders of abstinence, Protestantism, and the British race." His closing words are striking: "My own childhood was pure British colonial . . . But I know I couldn't stand living in that kind of Toronto now. Instead, I think of my two Italian grandsons and my Chilean granddaughter, and of this city as a welcoming and exciting place for them, and I celebrate my non-WASP home."

The letters to the editor in the next issue of the magazine were scathing, with many of the WASPs who had built the city screaming (perhaps justifiably), "Racist!" And one might fairly ask, would Toronto be the decent place it is today had it not been for those harshly criticized white Protestants? Who opened the gates to foreigners, if not those same, now-outnumbered, supposedly boring sons and daughters of what was once the British Empire?

The city that once united Canadians from the Atlantic to the Pacific in a shared hatred of Toronto's sanctimoniousness and industriousness now tends to draw their collective envy at how well the place works. Other critics insist that Toronto remains too smug (well, yes); too regulated (they would prefer chaos?); too provincial (actually, it's municipal; Ontario is provincial); too prim and proper (they'd rather be mugged?); too young (as a major city, perhaps, but it was hardly born yesterday).

We have to laugh with the Montrealers—a wildly different culture of primarily French-speaking Catholics—who joke that "Toronto is a city where people go around saying 'Thank God it's Monday.'" To this day, indeed, Torontonians seem to actually enjoy working, and they appear to lack the ability to enjoy themselves doing anything else. But with the prices of houses, who can afford not to work? And as for "having a good time," there have never been more fine restaurants, theaters, movie houses, concerts, and bars to enjoy oneself in—even on Sunday!

The city officially became Toronto on March 6, 1834, barely more than 150 years ago, but its roots go back to 1615. A Frenchman named Etienne Brûlé was sent into the not-yet-Canadian wilderness in 1610 by explorer Samuel de Champlain to see what he could discover. And he discovered plenty: the river and portage routes from the St. Lawrence to Lake Huron, possibly lakes Superior and Michigan, and, eventually, Lake Ontario.

His discoveries surprised the local Indians, who had known about all these places for centuries and had long since named the area between the Humber and Don rivers Toronto, which is believed to mean "a place of meetings." (How prescient!) It was later a busy Indian village named Teiaiagon, a French trading post, a British town named York (if the British hadn't won the Seven Years' War in the late 1700s, you would be reading this in translation from the French), and finally the city we know today, once again bearing the original Indian name of Toronto.

The city had the usual history of colonial towns of the last century: It was invaded by the Americans in 1812; there were many Great Fires; there was a rebellion in 1837; and there was a slow but steady growth of (you guessed it) white Anglo-Saxon Protestants, from about 9,000 in the 1830s to nearly 500,000 before World War II, at which time they outnumbered the non-WASPs by five to two.

And now, as we've noted, it has somehow metamorphosed into a great world city. There are countless reasons why this has happened, and we have touched on but a few. Toronto is clearly this country's center of culture, commerce, and communications—"New York run by the Swiss," according to Peter Ustinov's marvelously witty description of the place—and this is partly by chance. For example,

Mikhail Baryshnikov chose to defect from the Bolshoi in Toronto in 1974 and has returned frequently to work with its ballet corps.

But far more of Toronto's success can be credited to thoughtful and sensitive government actions, such as the limits that the city council set in the 1970s on the number and size of new buildings, and the decision by the Ontario government to put a stop to a major (Spadina) expressway, which would have slashed like a knife through many precious, long-standing neighborhoods. Toronto is a collection of little neighborhoods united by an enlightened metropolitan form of city government.

With occasional lapses, Metropolitan Toronto has encouraged urban renewal, and many of the city's building projects have mixed low-rent housing with luxury condos, restaurants, offices, and businesses. Somehow, Toronto has managed to avoid the situation in many North American cities, where the middle class has fled to the suburbs, taking their taxes and children with them. On the contrary, one can see tens of thousands of young couples eagerly moving back to the same areas in the heart of the city where they grew up, and where they know that they will have fine schools for their kids and a healthy community to live in.

There are a growing number of problems, to be sure. In late 1988, there were 303 vacant apartments available to rent in Toronto, out of a total of 234,568—in other words, a vacancy rate of .1%. And in a single month in late 1988, the average house price shot up $30,000, making the average resale cost of a home in the Metropolitan Toronto area a towering $250,000 and more. In other words, one has to be upper class anywhere else, to live even lower middle class in Toronto.

Toronto has gained the nickname of "Hollywood North," because literally dozens of major films have been made in this city, especially over the past decade, from *The Black Stallion* to *Three Men and a Baby* and from David Cronenberg's *Dead Ringers* to such TV series as *Degrassi Junior High*, *Night Heat,* and many more. Indeed, it is hard to walk about the city nowadays without tripping over a movie crew and a number of famous people. A story is still told about one particular film made in the downtown area in 1987. Since it was a crime movie set in New York City, street signs had to be put up and several tons of garbage trucked in and spread around the city street. After filming all morning, the cast took a lunch break. When they returned barely an hour later, all the garbage had been cleaned up!

That's Toronto, in a nutshell: Clean. Safe. Orderly. Yet somehow dynamic and exciting. Groucho Marx sang an old vaudeville tune back in 1967 that went "It's better to run to

Toronta/Than to stay in a place you don't wanta." And he was right. But nearly a quarter-century later, we can honestly change the words to "It's best that you run to Toronta/ There's no better place that you'd wanta."

Note: Throughout this guide, unless otherwise stated, prices are quoted in Canadian dollars.

1 Essential Information

Before You Go

Government Tourist Offices

The best source of specific information on travel to Toronto is the **Metropolitan Toronto Convention and Visitors Association** (Queen's Quay Terminal, 207 Queen's Quay W, Suite 509, Box 126, Toronto, Ont. M5J 1A7, tel. 416/368–9821).

American and Canadian visitors can also contact the **Ministry of Ontario Tourism/Ontario Travel** (Queen's Park, Toronto, Ont. M7A 2E5, tel. 800/268–3735).

British travelers can visit or write to the **Ontario Ministry of Tourism and Recreation** (21 Knightsbridge, London SW1X 7LY, England, no phone).

Another excellent source of free information on Toronto and all aspects of travel to Canada is the **Canadian Consulate General** offices (ask for their tourism department):

United States 1 CNN Center, Suite 400, South Tower, Atlanta, GA 30303, tel. 404/577–6815; 3 Copley Pl., Suite 400, Boston, MA 02116, tel. 617/536–1730; 310 S. Michigan Ave., 12th floor, Chicago, IL 60604, tel. 312/427–1666; St. Paul Tower, 17th floor, 750 N. St. Paul St., Dallas, TX 75201, tel. 214/922–9815; 300 S. Grand Ave., Suite 1000, Los Angeles, CA 90071, tel. 213/687–7432; 701 4th Ave. S, Minneapolis, MN 55415, tel. 612/333–4641; Exxon Bldg., 16th floor, 1251 Avenue of the Americas, New York, NY 10020, tel. 212/586–4200; 1 Maritime Plaza, Suite 1160, Alcoa Bldg., San Francisco, CA 94111, tel. 415/981–8515; 1211 Connecticut Ave., Suite 300, Washington, DC 20036, tel. 202/223–9710.

United Kingdom Canada House, Trafalgar Sq., London SW1Y 5BJ, England, tel. 01/629–9492.

Tour Groups

When considering an escorted tour, be sure to find out (1) exactly what expenses are included (particularly tips, taxes, sidetrips, additional meals, and entertainment); (2) ratings of all hotels on the itinerary and the facilities they offer; (3) cancellation policies both for you and for the tour operator; and (4) what the single supplement is, should you be traveling alone. Most tour operators request that bookings be made through a travel agent—there is no additional charge for this.

General-Interest Tours **Talmadge Tours** (1223 Walnut St., Philadelphia, PA 19107, tel. 215/923–7100) has a Toronto–Niagara Falls package. It has also put together a unique itinerary that starts with Niagara Falls and Toronto, crosses Georgian Bay by ferry and Agawa Canyon by train, stops at Mackinac Island in Lake Michigan, and ends up in Michigan. **Maupintour** (Box 807, Lawrence, KS 66044, tel. 913/843–1211 or 800/255–4266) offers an eight-day Toronto–Montreal tour. **Four Winds Travel** (175 5th Ave., New York, NY 10010, tel. 212/777–0260) tours Toronto, Ottawa, Quebec City, and Montreal. Four Winds also has a rail tour that starts in Toronto, crosses the width of the country, and returns to Toronto. **Cosmos/Globus Gateway** (150 S. Los Robles Ave., Suite 860, Pasadena, CA 91101, tel. 818/449–0919 or 800/556- 5454) and

American Express Vacations (Box 5014, Atlanta, GA 30302, tel. 800/241–1700, in GA 800/282–0800) both have tours through Toronto and the northeastern United States.

Special-Interest Tours **Toronto For the Arts** (tel. 416/869–3109 or 800/268–3735) is a tour program that began in 1987 and is expected to be running again between January and the end of April 1990. The many packages—which start at U.S. $129—include first-class accommodations and tickets to the Art Gallery of Ontario, the Canadian Opera Company, the National Ballet of Canada, the Toronto Symphony Orchestra, and/or the Royal Ontario Museum.

Package Deals for Independent Travelers

Air Canada (tel. 800/4–CANADA) has two-night packages with a choice of hotels. The cost depends on the hotel rating. **American Express** includes a half-day sightseeing tour in its city package. Also check with **American Fly AAway Vacations** (tel. 817/355–1234 or 800/433–7300) and **United Airlines** (tel. 312/952–4000 or 800/328–6877) for packages.

When to Go

The weather can often fall below freezing from late November into March and can be brutal in January and February (although the snowfalls are almost never heavy). That simple fact alone could repel some visitors while attracting ski and skating enthusiasts. Some of the best theater, ballet, opera, and concerts take place between September and May; both the Stratford and Shaw festivals, each about a 90-minute drive from Toronto, are in full swing from May to October.

There is no single time when the city is unbearably crowded, or disappointingly empty, in the way that Paris, say, can be. But it cannot be denied that Toronto is most pleasant to walk around, and simply enjoy, from late spring through early fall, when there are outdoor concerts and many restaurants open their patios—when the entire city seems to come to life. On the other hand, many hotels drop their prices up to 50% in the off-season, particularly in December and January.

Climate Jokes about Canadian polar bears and igloos notwithstanding, Toronto's climate is really not that harsh, except in December, January, and February. Okay, and March as well. (And sometimes in late November.) Indeed, a look at a map of North America will prove that the city is farther south than about a dozen states and that Toronto is not in the so-called Snow Belt, in which heavy and often brutal storms paralyze cities such as Detroit, Buffalo, Syracuse, and Rochester. Surprising as it may seem—and as heartbreaking as it is to our ski-lift operators—prolonged snowfalls rarely come to the northern shores of Lake Ontario, and many a December and January snowfall soon melts away.

Furthermore, should you arrive during those often-bleak winter months, you will be pleased to discover that the city does not come to a frozen halt with the first sign of a snowflake—or even a snowstorm. Underground shopping concourses allow one to walk through much of the downtown area and avoid the cold.

Spring can be brief, and a (hot) summer can last through much of June, July, and August, even September. And then come the gorgeous autumn colors—seen best just north of the city and throughout our myriad parks—along with more moderate and pleasant fall temperatures, before the much-cursed winter months come blasting and howling in again.

Lake Ontario often cools the city air in the summer and warms it in the winter. At the airport, therefore, being some distance from the lake, the temperature will be warmer in the summer than it is downtown, and colder in the winter.

The following are average daily maximum and minimum temperatures for Toronto.

Climate

Jan.	30F	-1C	**May**	63F	17C	**Sept.**	69F	21C
	16	-9		44	7		51	11
Feb.	30F	-1C	**June**	73F	23C	**Oct.**	56F	13C
	15	-9		54	12		40	4
Mar.	37F	3C	**July**	79F	26C	**Nov.**	43F	6C
	23	-5		59	15		31	-1
Apr.	50F	10C	**Aug.**	77F	25C	**Dec.**	33F	1C
	34	1		58	14		21	-6

Current weather information on 235 cities around the world—180 of them in the United States—is only a phone call away. To obtain the **Weather Trak** telephone number for your area, call 800/247–3282. The local number plays a taped message that tells you to dial the three-digit access code for the destination you're interested in. The code is either the area code (in the U.S.) or the first three letters of the foreign city. For a list of all access codes, send a stamped, self-addressed envelope to Cities, Box 7000, Dallas, TX 75209. For further information, phone 214/869–3035 or 800/247–3282.

Festivals and Seasonal Events

Top seasonal events in Toronto include the International Boat Show in January, the Toronto Sportsman's Show in March, Caravan celebrations in June, Caribana in July, the Festival of Festivals in September, and the city's New Year's Eve Party. For further details, contact the Metropolitan Toronto Convention and Visitors Association (*see* Government Tourist Offices).

Mid-Jan.: Toronto International Boat Show is held annually at Exhibition Place.
Late Jan.: Molson Export Ice Canoe Race and Barrel Jumping Contests take place at Harbourfront.
Late Feb.: C.D.F.A. Championship Dog Shows are at Exhibition Place.
Mid-Mar.: Toronto Sportsmen's Show is set up at Exhibition Place.
Late Mar.: Annual Springtime Craft Show and Sale is held at Exhibition Place.
Apr.–Oct.: African Lion Safari is open.
Mid-Apr.: Stratford Festival Season opens in Stratford.
Apr.–Oct.: Toronto Blue Jays season at the SkyDome.
Mid-June: Metro Toronto International Caravan takes place throughout Toronto. This is a unique celebration of the city's ethnic communities.

Early July: The **Mariposa Festival** takes place in Molson Park, about an hour drive north of Toronto. Bob Dylan and Gordon Lightfoot have appeared in past years.
Mid-July: Toronto Outdoor Art Exhibition is held in Nathan Phillips Square by the New City Hall.
July: Caribana is a Mardi Gras–like festival held by the West Indian communities, with over 500,000 visitors and a striking parade of some 5,000 brightly dressed revelers.
Aug. 15–Sept. 3: Canadian National Exhibition is held at the Canadian National Exhibition Grounds by Lake Ontario and Ontario Place.
Early–mid-Sept.: Festival of Festivals is a film event that attracts cinematographers and stars from many countries.
Late October: The **International Festival of Authors** at Harbourfront brings in major writers from around the world, on the level of Saul Bellow, Jay McInerney, Jan Morris, and, yes, Salman Rushdie (in 1988).
Mid-Nov.: Santa Claus Parade travels through downtown Toronto.
Dec. 31: City of Toronto's New Year's Eve Party is thrown in Nathan Phillips Square.

What to Pack

Pack light because porters and baggage trolleys are scarce and luggage restrictions are tight. Although restrictions may vary from one airline to another, passengers are usually allowed two pieces of check-in luggage and one carry-on piece. On Canadian planes, no piece of check-in luggage can weigh more than 70 pounds. The first piece cannot exceed 62″ (length + width + height), the second piece, 55″ (length + width + height). The carry-on luggage cannot exceed 45″ (length + width + height) and must fit under the seat or in the overhead luggage compartment. These are the requirements of Air Canada for travel between the United States and Canada; other airlines may have slightly different requirements.

What you pack depends more on the time of year than on any specific dress code. Toronto has extremely cold winters; hot, steamy summers; and lots of rain in between. Winter can extend from November through April. For winter, you'll need your warmest clothes, in many layers, and waterproof boots. Salt will destroy leather shoes and boots; winter visitors will be wise to bring a cheap pair. In the summer, loose-fitting, casual clothing will see you through both day and evening events. Women should pack a sweater or shawl for summer evenings, which can get cool, and for restaurants that run their air conditioners full blast. Men will need a jacket and tie for the better restaurants and many of the night spots. Jeans are as popular in Toronto as they are elsewhere and are perfectly acceptable for sightseeing and informal dining. Toronto has an extremely low crime rate and is a wonderful place for wandering on foot, so bring comfortable walking shoes. Consider packing a bathing suit for your hotel pool.

The electrical current is the same as in the United States: 110 volts, 60 cycles.

Taking Money Abroad

Traveler's checks and major U.S. credit cards are accepted in Toronto. You'll need cash for some of the small restaurants and shops. Many establishments accept U.S. dollars. Although you pay more for Canadian dollars in the U.S., it's wise to buy some before you leave home to avoid long lines at airport currency exchange booths. If your local bank can't exchange your money into Canadian dollars, Deak International will. To find the office nearest you, contact them at 630 Fifth Ave., New York, NY 10011, tel. 212/635–0515.

The most recognized traveler's checks are American Express, Barclay's, Thomas Cook, and those issued through major commercial banks such as Citibank and Bank of America. Some banks will issue the checks free to established customers, but most charge a 1% commission fee. Buy part of the traveler's checks in small denominations to cash toward the end of your trip. This will save you from having to cash a large check and ending up with more foreign money than you need. You can also buy traveler's checks in Canadian dollars, a good idea if the U.S. dollar is falling and you want to lock in the current rate. Remember to take the addresses of offices where you can get refunds for lost or stolen traveler's checks.

Banks and bank-operated currency-exchange kiosks in airports, railway stations, and bus terminals are the best places to change money. Hotels and privately run exchange firms will give you a significantly lower rate of exchange.

Like the American dollar, the Canadian one floats (and often sinks) on the world's money markets, but it will probably remain in the United States 80¢–85¢ range over the next few years. Since 1987, the $1 bill has slowly been phased out in Canada and replaced with a funny-looking coin that has been nicknamed "The Loonie," due to the drawing of the Canadian loon on one side. But these bills (as well as the far more useful $5, $10, and $20 bills—and, yes, the always welcome $2 Canadian denomination) should remain in circulation into the 1990s.

U.S. currency is eagerly accepted at most good-size stores and restaurants, and with good reason: owners are always happy to give far less exchange than the daily rate. So it is financially wise for all visitors to go to a Canadian bank or exchange firm within a few hours of arrival. The sooner you exchange your money for the worth-less (if not yet worthless) Canadian dollar, the more money you'll save. When you use your credit cards, you can be assured that your expenditures will automatically go through as Canadian funds, and you will get the proper exchange rate.

There are more bank branches in this country than there are pubs, which tells you something, does it not? But the banks have rather abbreviated hours—usually Monday to Thursday from 10 to 3, and Fridays 10 to 6. **Deak International Foreign Exchange** has longer hours. There are branches at 10 King St. E, near Yonge St., tel. 416/863–1611; in the Manulife Centre, 55 Bloor St. W at Bay St., tel. 416/961–9822; 60 Bloor St. W, tel. 416/923–6549; the Sheraton Centre hotel lobby, 123 Queen St. W, across from the New City Hall, tel. 416/363–4867;

Yorkdale Pl., tel. 416/789–1827; and the Skyline Hotel lobby, 655 Dixon Rd., near the airport, tel. 416/247–4600.

Getting Money from Home

There are at least three ways to get money from home: (1) Have it sent through a large commercial bank with a branch in Toronto. The only drawback is that you must have an account with the bank; if not, you'll have to go through your own bank and the process will be slower and more expensive. (2) Get it through American Express. If you are a cardholder, you can cash a personal check or a counter check at an American Express office for up to $1,000; $200 will be in cash and $800 in traveler's checks. There is a 1% commission on the traveler's checks. You can also receive money through American Express MoneyGram. With this service, you can receive up to $5,000 cash. It works this way: You call home and ask someone to go to an American Express office or an American Express MoneyGram agent located in a retail outlet, and fill out an American Express MoneyGram. It can be paid for with cash or any major credit card. The person making the payment is given a reference number and telephones you with that number. The American Express MoneyGram agent calls an 800 number and authorizes the transfer of funds to an American Express office or participating agency in Toronto. In most cases, the money is available immediately. You pick it up by showing identification and giving the reference number. Fees vary according to the amount of money sent. For sending $300, the fee is $22; for $5,000, $150. For the American Express MoneyGram location nearest your home, call 800/543–4080. You do not have to be a cardholder to use this service. (3) Have it sent through Western Union (tel. 800/988–4726). If you have MasterCard or Visa, you can have money sent for any amount up to your credit limit. If not, have someone take cash or a certified cashier's check to a Western Union office. The money will be delivered to a bank in Toronto within 24 hours. Fees vary with the amount of money sent. For sending $500, the fee is $35; for $1,000, $45.

Canadian Currency

The units of currency in Canada are the Canadian dollar (C$) and the cent, in the same denominations as U.S. currency. There are also a $2 bill and a $1 coin, nicknamed "the Loonie." At press time, the exchange rate was fluctuating at around C$1.20 to U.S. $1 and C$2.22 to £1.

What It Will Cost

Note: Throughout this guide, unless otherwise stated, prices are quoted in Canadian dollars.

It's true that the U.S. dollar is worth some 15%–20% more than the Canadian dollar, but this translates into upwards of a 15% savings only when goods in both countries are sold at the same price. The fact is that goods and services are priced slightly higher in Canada than in the United States, so the actual savings is closer to 10%. In Toronto, a can of Coke costs about 75¢; a taxi, as soon as the meter is turned on, $2; a movie, about $6.50; and a glass of beer in a bar, $3.

The airport departure tax is 10% of a fare, plus $4, to a maximum of $50. In other words, if you are flying to Toronto and back from Los Angeles, and the flight costs an even U.S. $400, you will end up paying U.S. $444. You will rarely be aware of this obnoxious little tax; it will be written into the total ticket cost at the time of purchase.

Passports and Visas

Because there is so much border traffic between Canada and the United States (for example, many people live in Windsor, [Ontario], and work in Detroit), entry requirements are fairly simple. Citizens and legal residents of the United States do not require a passport or a visa to enter Canada, but proof of citizenship (a birth certificate) may be requested. If you return to the United States by air, possession of a passport can save a long wait on line. Resident aliens should be in possession of their U.S. Alien Registration or "green" card.

British citizens should consult Tips for British Travelers.

Customs and Duties

On Arrival Clothing and personal items may be brought in without charge or restriction. American and British visitors may bring in the following items duty-free: 200 cigarettes, 50 cigars, and two pounds of tobacco; personal cars (for less than 6 months); boats or canoes; rifles and shotguns (but no handguns or automatic weapons); 200 rounds of ammunition; cameras, radios, sports equipment, and typewriters. A deposit is sometimes required for trailers and household equipment (refunded upon return). If you are driving a rented car, be sure to keep the contract with you. Cats may enter freely, but dogs must have proof of a veterinary inspection to ensure that they are free of communicable diseases. Plant material must be declared and inspected.

On Departure Passengers flying from Toronto to the United States will clear U.S. Customs in Toronto, so allow extra time before your flight. If you have brought any foreign-made equipment from home, such as cameras, it's wise to carry the original receipt with you or to register it with U.S. Customs before you leave home (Form 4457). Otherwise, you may end up having to pay duty on your return. U.S. residents visiting Canada for at least 48 hours may bring home up to $400 in foreign goods duty-free. Each member of the family is entitled to the same exemption, regardless of age, and exemptions may be pooled. For the next $1,000 worth of goods, a flat 10% rate is assessed; above $1,400, duties vary with the merchandise. Travelers 21 or older may bring home one liter of alcohol, 100 cigars (non-Cuban), and 200 cigarettes. Only one bottle of perfume trademarked in the United States may be brought in. There is no duty on antiques or art over 100 years old. Anything exceeding these limits will be taxed at the port of entry, and may be taxed additionally in the traveler's home state. Gifts valued at under $50 may be mailed to friends or relatives at home duty-free, but not more than one package per day to any one addressee, and not including perfumes costing more than $5, tobacco, or liquor.

Since the passage of the so-called Free Trade Agreement between the United States and Canada in late 1988, many people have come to think that all duties were being dropped overnight. Au contraire, mon frère: On the vast majority of goods, these duties are being eliminated gradually, many not before Jan. 1, 1998. It is recommended that you pick up the brochure, Free Trade and the Traveller, published by the government, outlining how the FTA will affect goods brought into Canada from the United States. It's available at Customs offices, airport departure lounges, and border crossing points.

Tips for British Travelers

Passports and Visas You will need a valid passport (cost: £15). Visas and vaccinations are not required.

Customs Returning to Britain you may bring home: (1) 200 cigarettes or 100 cigarillos or 50 cigars or 250 grams of tobacco; (2) two liters of table wine and, in addition, (a) one liter of alcohol over 22% by volume (most spirits), (b) two liters of alcohol under 22% by volume (fortified or sparkling wine), or (c) two more liters of table wine; (3) 50 grams of perfume and ¼ liter of toilet water; and (4) other goods up to a value of £32.

Insurance To cover health and motoring mishaps, insure yourself through **Europ Assistance** (252 High St., Croydon, Surrey CR0 1NF, tel. 01/680–1234).

It is also wise to take out insurance to cover lost luggage (though make sure this isn't already covered in your existing homeowner's policy). Trip-cancellation insurance is another wise buy. The **Association of British Insurers** (Aldermary House, Queen St., London EC4N 1TT, tel. 01/248–4477) will give comprehensive advice on all aspects of vacation insurance.

Tour Operators **American Connection** (242 High St., Slough, Berkshire SL1 1NB, tel. 0753/69252) offers "land only" tours (airfares not included). Their three-day minibreak to Toronto and Niagara Falls costs from £99. They also offer fly-drive vacations to Toronto with prices from £317 per week. Many companies offer hotel accommodations on a voucher system. You can book your hotel rooms before you leave and pay with your vouchers, or buy open hotel vouchers, one voucher for each night required. All taxes are included. Vouchers cost from £18 per night per person sharing a twin-bedded room. Many packages include car rentals at reasonable rates. **National Holidays Ltd.** (George House, George St., Wakefield, West Yorkshire WF1 1LY, tel. 0924/383888) will put together a complete package to Canada, with flights, from £289, or a week's car rental alone, from £88. Similar plans are offered by **Hickie Borman Holidays** (73 High St., Ewell, Surrey KT17 1RX, tel. 01/393–0127) and **American Airplan** (Box 267, Walton-on-Thames, Surrey KT12 2TS, tel. 0932/246166).

Airfares Round-trip APEX fares to Toronto cost about £298. Major airlines serving Toronto are **Air Canada** (tel. 01/759–2636), **British Airways** (tel. 01/897–4000), **Northwest Airlines** (tel. 01/629–5353), and **Wardair** (tel. 0345/222333). Travel agents can book charter flights through Regent Tours; the carrier is Worldways. If you can afford to be flexible about when you travel, look for last-minute flight bargains, which are advertised in the Sunday newspapers; such round-trip fares as we went to press were about £160.

Traveling with Film

If your camera is new, shoot and develop a few rolls before leaving home. Pack some lens tissue and an extra battery for your built-in light meter. Invest about $10 in a skylight filter and screw it onto the front of your lens. It will protect the lens and also reduce haze.

Film doesn't like hot weather. If you're driving in summer, don't store film in the glove compartment or on the shelf under the rear window. Put it behind the front seat on the floor, on the side opposite the exhaust pipe.

On a plane trip, never pack unprocessed film in check-in luggage; if your bags get X-rayed, say goodbye to your pictures. Always carry undeveloped film with you through security and ask to have it inspected by hand. (It helps to isolate your film in a plastic bag, ready for quick inspection.) Inspectors at American airports are required by law to honor requests for hand inspection; abroad, you'll have to depend on the kindness of strangers.

The old airport scanning machines—still in use in some Third World countries—use heavy doses of radiation that can turn a family portrait into an early morning fog. The newer models—used in all U.S. and Canadian airports—are safe for anything from five to 500 scans, depending on the speed of your film. The effects are cumulative; you can put the same roll of film through several scans without worry. After five scans, though, you're asking for trouble.

If your film gets fogged and you want an explanation, send it to the National Association of Photographic Manufacturers (600 Mamaroneck Ave., Harrison, NY 10528). They will try to determine what went wrong. The service is free.

Language

It amuses Canadians to see how many visitors assume (in fear) that "everyone will speak French to me." Canada is, indeed, a bilingual country, in that it has two official languages, French and English. And visitors are charmed, even fascinated, to see the cereal boxes and road signs in both languages. But Toronto is the Anglophone center of Canada, which means that 99% of the people living here will speak to you in English.

Staying Healthy

Shots and Medications There are no health risks associated with travel to Canada. No inoculations are needed. If you have a health problem that might require purchasing prescription drugs while in Canada, have your doctor write a prescription using the drug's generic name. Brand names vary widely from country to country.

Doctors The **International Association for Medical Assistance to Travelers** (IAMAT) is a worldwide association offering a list of approved doctors whose training meets very high standards. For a list of Canadian physicians and clinics that are part of this network, contact IAMAT, 736 Center St., Lewiston, NY 14092, tel. 716/754-4883. In Canada: 188 Nicklin Rd., Guelph,

Ont. NIH 7L5. In Europe: Gotthardstrasse 17, 6300 Zug, Switzerland. Membership is free.

Insurance

Travelers may seek insurance coverage in three areas: health and accident, loss of luggage, and trip cancellation. Your first step is to review your existing health and homeowner policies; some health insurance plans cover health expenses incurred while traveling, some major medical plans cover emergency transportation, and some homeowner policies cover the theft of luggage.

Health and Accident Several companies offer coverage designed to supplement existing health insurance for travelers:

Carefree Travel Insurance (Box 310, 120 Mineola Blvd., Mineola, NY 11501, tel. 516/294–0220 or 800/645–2424) provides coverage for medical evacuation. It also offers 24-hour medical phone advice.

Health Care Abroad, International Underwriters Group (243 Church St. W, Vienna, VA 22180, tel. 703/281–9500 or 800/237–6615), offers comprehensive medical coverage, including emergency evacuation, for trips of 10–90 days.

International SOS Insurance (Box 11568, Philadelphia, PA 19116, tel. 215/244–1500 or 800/523–8930) does not offer medical insurance but provides medical evacuation services to its clients, including many international corporations.

Travel Guard International (1100 Centerpoint Dr., Stevens Point, WI 54481, tel. 715/345–0505 or 800/782–5151), underwritten by Cygna, offers medical insurance, with coverage for emergency evacuation when Travel Guard's representatives in the United States say it is necessary.

Loss of Luggage Luggage loss is usually covered as part of a comprehensive travel insurance package that includes personal accident, trip cancellation, and sometimes default and bankruptcy insurance. Several companies offer comprehensive policies:

Access America Inc. (Box 807, New York, NY 10163, tel. 800/851–2800), a subsidiary of Blue Cross/Blue Shield.

Near, Inc. (1900 N. MacArthur Blvd., Suite 210, Oklahoma City, OK 73127, tel. 800/654–6700).

Travel Guard International (*see* Health and Accident).

Trip Cancellation Flight insurance is often included in the price of a ticket when paid for with American Express, Visa, and other major credit cards. It is usually included in combination travel insurance packages available from most tour operators, travel agents, and insurance agents.

Renting Cars

If you're flying into Toronto and planning to spend some time there before exploring the rest of Ontario, save money by arranging to pick up your car in the city and then head off into the province. You'll have to weigh the added expense of renting a car from a major company with an airport office against the savings on a car from a budget company with offices in town.

You could waste precious hours trying to locate the budget company in return for only a small financial savings. If you're arriving and departing from different airports, look for a one-way car rental with no return fees. Rental rates vary widely, depending on size and model, number of days you use the car, insurance coverage, and whether drop-off fees are imposed. In most cases, rates quoted include unlimited free mileage and standard liability protection. Not included are the Collision Damage Waiver (CDW), which eliminates your deductible payment should you have an accident; personal accident insurance; gasoline; and a 7% sales tax.

Driver's licenses issued in the United States are valid in Canada. Although you can legally drive a car at age 16 in Toronto, you must be at least 21 to rent a car.

It's best to arrange a car rental before you leave home. You won't save money by waiting until you arrive in Toronto, and you may find that the type of car you want is not available at the last minute. Rental companies usually charge according to the exchange rate of the U.S. dollar at the time the car is returned or when the credit card payment is processed. Rental companies that serve Toronto include **Avis** (tel. 416/964–2051 or 800/331–1212), **Budget Rent-a-Car** (tel. 416/673–3322 or 800/527–0700), **Hertz** (tel. 416/961–3320, 800/223–6472 or in NY, 800/522–5568), and **National** (tel. 416/488–2400 or 800/CAR-RENT).

Student and Youth Travel

Discount Cards

The **International Student Identity Card** entitles students to youth rail passes, special fares on local transportation, and discounts at museums, theaters, sports events, and many other attractions. If the card is purchased in the United States, the $10 cost also includes $2,000 in emergency medical insurance plus hospital coverage of $100 a day for up to 60 days. Apply to the Council on International Educational Exchange (CIEE), 205 E. 42d St., New York, NY 10017, tel. 212/661–1414. In Canada, the ISIC is available for C$10 from the Association of Student Councils, 187 College St., Toronto, Ont. M5T 1P7.

The **Youth International Educational Exchange Card** (YIEE) provides similar services to nonstudents under the age of 26. In the United States, the card costs $10 and is available from CIEE (address above) or from ISE, Europa House, 802 W. Oregon St., Urbana, IL 61801, tel. 217/344–5863. In Canada, the YIEE is available from the Canadian Hostelling Association (CHA), 333 River Rd., Vanier, Ottawa, Ont. K1L 8H9, tel. 613/476–3844.

Accommodations

An **International Youth Hostel Federation** (IYHF) membership card is the key to inexpensive dormitory-style accommodations at thousands of youth hostels around the world. Hostels provide separate sleeping quarters for men and women, at rates ranging from $7 to $15 a night per person, in a variety of facilities, including converted farmhouses, villas, and restored castles, as well as specially constructed modern buildings. IYHF membership costs $20 a year and is available in the United States through American Youth Hostels, Box 37613,

Washington, DC 20013, tel. 202/783–6161. AYH also publishes an extensive directory of youth hostels around the world.

In addition to the **Toronto International Hostel** (223 Church St., tel. 416/368–0207), inexpensive accommodations are available at the **Central YMCA** (20 Grosvenor St., tel. 416/921–5171) and the **YWCA Woodlawn Residence** (80 Woodlawn Ave. E, tel. 416/923–8454). In the summer, university residences offer inexpensive accommodations to the public, often at special student rates. Contact the **University of Toronto** (Administrative Services, tel. 416/978–8735), **York University** (Main Campus, tel. 416/667–3394), or **Glendon College** (tel. 416/487–6204). For longer stays, try the **Campus Co-op Residence** (tel. 416/979–2161), which operates about 20 houses near the University of Toronto campus.

Tours Economical **bicycle tours** for small groups of adventurous, energetic students are another popular AYH student travel service. For information, contact the address above.

Council Travel, a CIEE subsidiary, is the foremost U.S. student travel agency, specializing in low-cost charters and serving as the exclusive U.S. agent for many student airfare bargains and student tours. CIEE's 80-page *Student Travel Catalog* and "Council Charter" brochure are available free from any Council Travel office in the United States (enclose $1 postage if ordering by mail). There are Council Travel offices in Berkeley, La Jolla, Long Beach, Los Angeles, San Diego, San Francisco, Chicago, Amherst (MA), Boston, Cambridge, Portland (OR), Providence, Austin, Dallas, Seattle, and Washington, DC.

The **Educational Travel Center,** another student travel specialist worth contacting for information on student tours, bargain fares, and bookings, may be reached at 438 N. Frances St., Madison, WI 53703, tel. 608/256–5551.

Further Information CIEE publishes many books of interest to the student traveler, including *Work, Study, Travel Abroad: The whole world handbook* ($8.95 plus $1 postage); *Work Your Way Around the World* ($10.95 plus $1 postage); and *Volunteer! The Comprehensive Guide to Voluntary Service in the U.S. and Abroad* ($5.50 plus $1 postage).

The Information Center at the **Institute of International Education** (809 U.N. Plaza, New York, NY 10017, tel. 212/984–5413) has reference books, foreign university catalogues, study-abroad brochures, and other materials, which may be consulted by students and nonstudents alike, free of charge. It is open weekdays 10–4; Wednesdays until 7.

Traveling with Children

Publications *Family Travel Times*, an 8- to 12-page newsletter published 10 times a year by TWYCH (Travel with Your Children, 80 8th Ave., New York, NY 10011, tel. 212/206–0688). Subscription includes access to back issues and twice-weekly opportunities to call in for specific advice. *Toronto Loves Kids*, by M. Weisman (The Can-Do Publishing Co., Inc., Toronto; $6.95), is filled with activities, sights, resources. Another resource is *Kid-Bits: Dini Petty's Guide to Toronto for Children*, by Merike Weiler and Dini Petty (Methuen; $9.95). *Kids Toronto* (Kids Canada Publishing, 540 Mt. Pleasant Rd., Suite 202, Toronto, Ont. M4S 2M6, tel. 416/481–5696) is a newspaper for parents, with complete listings of activities, resources, etc. It's free at libraries, bookstores, supermarkets, and nursery schools. It also publishes *Kids Toronto Directory*, which is available at Toronto bookstores.

Hotels **The Delta Chelsea Inn** (33 Gerrard St., Toronto, Ont. M5G 1Z4, tel. 800/268–1133) maintains a supervised Children's Creative Center and allows children under 18 to stay free with their parents. **The Inn on the Park,** a Four Seasons hotel (1100 Eglinton Ave. E, North York, Ont. M3C 1H8, tel. 416/444–2561), has a supervised children's program. The friendly **Town Inn Hotel** (620 Church St., Toronto, Ont. M4Y 262, tel. 416/964–3311) offers reliable baby-sitting services.

Home Exchange See *Home Exchanging: A Complete Sourcebook for Travelers at Home or Abroad* by James Dearing (Globe Pequot Press, Box Q, Chester, CT 06412, tel. 800/243–0495, in CT 800/962–0973).

Getting There On international flights, children under 2 not occupying a seat pay 10% of adult fare. Various discounts apply to children 2–12. Reserve a seat behind the bulkhead of the plane, which offers more leg room and can usually fit a bassinet (supplied by the airline). At the same time, inquire about special children's meals or snacks, offered by most airlines. (See "TWYCH's Airline Guide," in the February 1988 issue of *Family Travel Times*, for a rundown on the services offered by 46 airlines.) Ask the airline in advance if you can bring aboard your child's car seat. For the booklet "Child/Infant Safety Seats Acceptable for Use in Aircraft," write Community and Consumer Liaison Division (APA-400 Federal Aviation Administration, Washington, DC 20591, tel. 202/267–3479).

Baby-sitting Services **Active Home Services** (110 St. Clair Ave. W, tel. 416/962–0296) has been around for two decades, providing sitters as far west as Jane Street, a few miles east of the airport. There's a five-hour minimum by day and a four-hour minimum at night.

Christopher Robin Services (5 Whitecap Blvd., Scarborough, tel. 416/265–2212) covers all of Metro Toronto. Service is also based on a five-hour daily and a four-hour nightly minimum.

Kingsway Household Services (tel. 416/233–9983) has been offering trustworthy sitters for more than three decades. There's a four-hour minimum plus a transportation charge.

Also check *Kids Toronto (see* Publications) for local agencies, or make child-care arrangements through your hotel concierge (*see* Town Inn Hotel in Hotels, above).

Hints for Disabled Travelers

Guide to Ontario Government Programs & Services for Disabled Persons is a superb new—and free—72-page booklet available from the Office for Disabled Persons, 3rd Floor, 700 Bay St., Toronto, Ont. M5G 1Z6, tel. 416/965–3165 (voice/TDD for the hearing-impaired) or 800/387–4456 (voice/TDD). To obtain the booklet in French, call 800/387–4456 (*voix*/ATS).

Toronto with Ease is a free booklet available from the Metropolitan Toronto Convention and Visitors Association (*see* Government Tourist Offices).

The **Toronto Transit Commission** (TTC) offers a bus service, called Wheel-Trans, for disabled people (and friends) who are unable to use regular public vehicles. For advance reservations, phone 416/393–4222; for same-day requests, 416/393–4333; TTD number 416/393–4555.

At press time, two possibilities of handicapped-accessible transport to and from Pearson International Airport are in the works. Wheel-Trans is considering an airport route (for further information, call 416/393–4111). Also, wheelchair-accessible vans are being planned for operation by limousine companies at the airport; by prearrangement, a disabled person can be picked up or dropped off at points at both terminals (for information, call the manager of airport ground transportation at 416/676–3493).

For information on governmental services for the hearing impaired, the TTY-TDD numbers are 416/392–8069 and 416/392–7354. For general information on what's available for the disabled in Toronto, call 416/392–7339 weekdays 9:30–4:30.

Freedom in Traveling (tel. 416/234–8511) is a liaison between the disabled and the travel industry, providing accessibility information. Many travel agents across North America are affiliated with it.

The **Community Information Centre** (tel. 416/863–0505) provides information on various facilities, as well as social and health services for the disabled.

The **Advocacy Resource Centre for the Handicapped** (tel. 416/482–8255 or TTY number 416/482–1254) is a responsible and responsive legal center that defends the rights of the mentally and physically disabled.

The Information Center for Individuals with Disabilities (20 Park Plaza, Rm. 330, Boston, MA 02116, tel. 617/727–5540) offers useful problem-solving assistance, including lists of travel agents that specialize in tours for the disabled.

Moss Rehabilitation Hospital Travel Information Service (12th St. and Taber Rd., Philadelphia, PA 19141, tel. 215/329–5715) provides information on tourist sights, transportation, and accommodations in destinations around the world. The fee is $5 for each destination. Allow one month for delivery.

Mobility International (Box 3551, Eugene, OR 97403, tel. 503/343–1284) has information on accommodations, organized study, etc., around the world.

The Society for the Advancement of Travel for the Handicapped (26 Court St., Brooklyn, NY 11242, tel. 718/858–5483) offers access information. Annual membership costs $40, or $25 for senior travelers and students. Send a stamped, self-addressed envelope.

The Itinerary (Box 1084, Bayonne, NJ 07002, tel. 201/858–3400) is a bimonthly travel magazine for the disabled.

Access to the World: A Travel Guide for the Handicapped by Louise Weiss is useful but out of date. Available from Facts on File (460 Park Ave. S, New York, NY 10016, tel. 212/683–2244). ***Frommer's Guide for Disabled Travelers*** is also useful but dated.

Greyhound-Trailways (tel. 800/531–5332) will carry a disabled person and companion for the price of a single fare. **Amtrak** (tel. 800/USA–RAIL) requests 24-hour notice to provide redcap service, special seats, and a 25% discount.

Hints for Older Travelers

The American Association of Retired Persons (AARP, 1909 K St. NW, Washington, DC 20049, tel. 202/662–4850) has two programs for independent travelers: (1) the Purchase Privilege Program, which offers discounts on hotels, airfare, car rentals, and sightseeing; and (2) the AARP Motoring Plan, which offers emergency aid and trip routing information for an annual fee of $29.95 per couple. The AARP also arranges group tours through two companies: **Olson-Travelworld** (5855 Green Valley Circle, Culver City, CA 90230, tel. 800/227–7737) and **RFD, Inc.** (4401 W. 110th St., Overland Park, KS 66211, tel. 800/448–7010). AARP members must be 50 or older. Annual dues are $5 per person or per couple.

When using an AARP or other identification card, ask for a reduced hotel rate at the time you make your reservation, not when you check out. At restaurants, show your card to the maître d' before you're seated, since discounts may be limited to certain set menus, days, or hours. When renting a car, remember that economy cars, priced at promotional rates, may cost less than cars that are available with your ID card.

Travel Industry and Disabled Exchange (TIDE, 5435 Donna Ave., Tarzana, CA 91356, tel. 818/343–6339) is an industry-based organization with a $15-per-person annual membership fee. Members receive a quarterly newsletter and information on travel agencies and tours.

National Council of Senior Citizens (925 15th St. NW, Washington, DC 20005, tel. 202/347–8800) is a nonprofit advocacy group with some 4,000 local clubs across the country. Annual membership is $10 per person or $14 per couple. Members receive a monthly newspaper with travel information and an ID card for reduced-rate hotels and car rentals.

Mature Outlook (Box 1205, Glenview, IL 60025, tel. 800/336–6330), a subsidiary of Sears Roebuck & Co., is a travel club for people over 50, with hotel and motel discounts and a bimonthly newsletter. Annual membership is $7.50 per couple. Instant membership is available at participating Holiday Inns.

Travel Tips for Senior Citizens (U.S. Dept. of State Publication 8970, revised Sept. 1987) is available for $1 from the Superintendent of Documents (U.S. Government Printing Office, Washington, DC 20402).

Golden Age Passport is a free lifetime pass to all parks, monuments, and recreation areas run by the U.S. government. People over 62 should pick them up in person at any national park that charges admission. A driver's license or other proof of age is required.

Further Reading

Don't miss Michael Ondaatje's award-winning *In the Skin of a Lion*, about Toronto in the 1940s and '50s. The best literary and geographic history is *Toronto Remembered* by William Kilbourn. *Toronto Observed,* by William Dendy and William Kilbourn, is an award-winning book on Toronto's 100 most interesting buildings. Eric Arthur's *No Mean City* is a penetrating look at the city's 19th-century architecture.

Robertson Davies wrote a series of novels about the supernatural, set in Toronto. One is *Fifth Business.*

Margaret Millar's *Wall of Eyes* and Hugh Garner's *Death in Don Mills* are mystery/thrillers set in the area.

Austin Clarke's *Nine Men Who Laughed* and *The Storm of Fortune* are novels about immigrants from the West Indies to Toronto. Mordecai Richler's *The Inconquerable Atuk* is about the life of an Inuit (Eskimo) in Toronto; the picture it paints of the city is rather dated.

Harry J. Pollack's *Gabriel: A Novel* is an autobiographical novel about a Toronto man involved in the literary life. Other suggested titles include: Margaret Atwood's *Life Before Men* and *Edible Woman; Hunger Trace* by Adrienne Clarkson; and *A Casual Affair: A Modern Fairytale* by Sylvia Fraser.

Arriving and Departing

From the United States by Plane

The Airlines There are three types of flights to Toronto: nonstop—no changes, no stops; direct—no changes but one or more stops; and connecting—two or more planes, two or more stops.

Toronto is served by **American** (tel. 800/433–7300), **Delta** (tel. 800/843–9378), **Eastern** (tel. 800/327–8376), **Northwest** (tel. 800/225–2525), **United** (tel. 800/241–6522), **Air Canada** (tel. 800/422–6232), and **Canadian Airlines International** (tel. 800/387–2737).

City Express (tel. 416/360–4444 or 800/387–3060) has inexpensive flights every day between Newark, New Jersey and the Toronto Island Airport, which is barely five minutes from the city's downtown area. In contrast, Toronto's major airport, Pearson International, is a half-hour drive from downtown; of course, it's a longer trip during rush hours. The catch? City Express's planes are Dash 7s and 8s, which are wonderfully reliable but still rather small and propeller-driven, with often limited luggage space.

A new American carrier, **Skyking Airlines International,** (tel. 617/436–1216) recently began operating up to seven return flights between Boston and Toronto every weekday, and three round trips on Saturdays and Sundays, using the Toronto Island Airport. Skyking uses the safe Dash 7 aircraft at prices quite a bit lower than those landing at the horrendously crowded Pearson Airport.

Discount Flights The major airlines offer a range of tickets that can increase the price of any given seat by more than 300%, depending on the day of purchase. As a rule, the further in advance you buy the ticket, the less expensive it is and the greater the penalty (up to 100%) for canceling. Check with airlines for details.

It's important to distinguish between companies that sell seats on charter flights and companies that sell one of a block of tickets on scheduled airlines. Charter flights are the least expensive and the least reliable—with chronically late departures and not infrequent cancellations. They also tend to depart less frequently (usually once a week) than regularly scheduled flights. A wise alternative to a charter is a ticket on a scheduled flight purchased from a wholesaler or ticket broker. It's an unbeatable deal: a scheduled flight at up to 50% off the APEX fare. Tickets can usually be purchased up to three days before departure (but in high season expect to wait in line an hour or so).

The following brokers specialize in discount sales; all charge an annual fee of about $35–$50: **Discount Travel International** (114 Forrest Ave., Narberth, PA 19072, tel. 800/458–0503), **Moment's Notice** (40 E. 49th St., New York, NY 10017, tel. 212/486–0503), **Stand-Buys Ltd.** (311 W. Superior, Suite 414, Chicago, IL 60610, tel. 800/255–0200), and **Worldwide Discount Travel Club** (1674 Meridian Ave., Miami Beach, FL 33139, tel. 305/534–2082).

Flying Time

Flying time from New York is about 1 hour; from Chicago, about 1½ hours; from Miami, 3 hours; from Los Angeles or San Francisco, 5 hours. One should know that Toronto's Pearson airport, in deference to the tens of thousands of nearby residents who must suffer the regular roar of jets, has an evening curfew, and one cannot expect to land there much after 11 PM or before 8 AM. Travelers who are arriving from the west coast will therefore not be able to get flights after 2 or 3 PM. A handful of airlines offer the infamous "red-eye" service, which leaves western cities after midnight, local time, and arrives in Toronto about 8 or 9 AM, sometimes via Chicago.

Luggage Regulations

Checked Luggage

U.S. airlines allow passengers to check in two suitcases whose total dimensions (length + width + height) do not exceed 60″. There are no weight restrictions on these bags.

Rules governing foreign airlines vary from airline to airline, so check with your travel agent or the airline itself before you go. All the airlines allow passengers to check in two bags. In general, expect the weight restriction on the two bags to be not more than 70 pounds each, and the size restriction to be 62″ total dimensions on the first bag, 55″ on the second.

Carry-on Luggage

Under rules in effect since January 1988, passengers are limited to two carry-on bags. For a bag you wish to store under the seat, the maximum dimensions are 9″ × 14″ × 22″, a total of 45″. For bags that can be hung in a closet or on a luggage rack, the maximum dimensions are 4″ × 23″ × 45″, a total of 72″. For bags you wish to store in an overhead bin, the maximum dimensions are 10″ × 14″ × 36″, a total of 60″. Each carry-on must fit one of these sets of dimensions, and any item that exceeds them may be rejected as a carryon and handled as checked baggage. Keep in mind that an airline may adapt these rules to circumstances, so on an especially crowded flight don't be surprised if you are allowed only one carry-on bag.

In addition to the two carry-ons, passengers may also bring aboard: a handbag (pocketbook or purse); an overcoat or wrap; an umbrella; a camera; a reasonable amount of reading material; an infant bag; crutches; cane; braces; or other prosthetic device upon which the passenger is dependent; and an infant/child safety seat.

These regulations are for U.S. airlines only; foreign airlines generally allow one piece of carry-on luggage in tourist class, plus bags filled with duty-free goods. Passengers in first and business class may also bring aboard a garment bag. It is best to check with your airline ahead of time to find out what their exact rules are regarding carry-on luggage.

Luggage Insurance Airlines are responsible for lost or damaged property only up to $1,250 per passenger on domestic flights, $9.07 per pound for checked baggage on international flights, and up to $400 per passenger for unchecked baggage on international flights. If you're carrying valuables, either take them with you on the airplane or purchase additional insurance for lost luggage. Some airlines will issue additional luggage insurance when you check in, but many do not. One that does is American Airlines. Its additional insurance is only for domestic flights or flights to Canada. Rates are $1 for every $100 valuation, with a maximum of $400 valuation per passenger. Hand luggage is not included.

Insurance for lost, damaged, or stolen luggage is available through travel agents or directly through various insurance companies. Two that issue luggage insurance are **Tele-Trip** (tel. 800/228–9792), a subsidiary of Mutual of Omaha, and **The Travelers Insurance Co.** (Ticket and Travel Dept., 1 Tower Sq., Hartford, CT 06183). Tele-Trip operates sales booths at airports and also issues insurance through travel agents. It will insure checked luggage for up to 180 days and for $500 to $3,000 valuation. For 1–3 days, the rate for a $500 valuation is $8.25; for 180 days, $100. The Travelers Insurance Co. will insure checked or hand luggage for $500 to $2,000 valuation per person, and also for a maximum of 180 days. The rate for 1–5 days for $500 valuation is $10; for 180 days, $85. Both companies offer the same rates on domestic and international flights. Check the travel pages of your Sunday newspaper for the names of other companies that insure luggage. Before you go, itemize the contents of each bag in case you need to file an insurance claim. Be certain to put your home address on each piece of luggage, including carry-on bags. If your luggage is stolen and later recovered, the airline must deliver the luggage to your home free of charge.

Toronto's airport, unlike in the States, does not have a person checking each passenger's luggage against his tag as he leaves the baggage claim area. So someone *could* walk off with your luggage. (Of course, it would probably not be a Canadian!) So go directly from the plane to the baggage claim area, and catch your luggage as it sails around the room on the conveyor belt.

Enjoying the Flight Drinking lots of nonalcoholic liquids can help one survive the usually dry air on planes; booze usually adds to jet lag. Since feet swell at high altitudes, it can be more comfortable to remove your shoes (but be prepared to struggle to get them back on). If you are the wandering type, be sure to ask for an aisle seat; if you like to sleep—and not be disturbed by those crazy wanderers—then book a window seat.

Bulkhead seats have more legroom, but they also have no place in front to store bags or briefcases, and trays do not fold down from the seats in front. Furthermore, in some planes the last row in the first-class section is for smokers, and the residue of their pleasure tends to drift straight back to those nonsmokers who sit in the bulkhead.

Dietary Needs It's always good to remember that all airlines offer a wide variety of food services. Vegetarians, lacto-vegetarians, diabetics, and Jews and Muslims with special dietary needs all should remember to ask for their own particular foods at the time they book their flights. Be sure to call again two or three days before the flight, to make sure this request was properly entered in the master computer.

Smoking If smoking bothers you, ask for a seat *far away from* the smoking section. If a U.S. airline tells you there are no nonsmoking seats, insist on one: FAA regulations require U.S. airlines to find seats for all nonsmokers. As of late 1989, nearly all Canadian airlines have eliminated smoking on *all* flights, and a growing number of U.S. companies have done the same—at least on flights of less than two hours.

The Airports With a handful of exceptions—such as planes from Montreal, Ottawa, Buffalo, and Newark that land at Toronto's tiny **Island Airport**—flights into Toronto land at the **Lester B. Pearson International Airport,** so named in 1984 to honor Canada's Nobel Peace Prize–winning prime minister of a quarter-century ago. It's commonly called "the Toronto airport" or "Malton" (after the once-small town where it was built, just northwest of the city), but it's just as often called "impossible," since its two terminals—which will increase to three soon—are inadequate for the number of travelers who use it. Waits for bags are often lengthy—although the free carts are a human touch—and Pearson can be dreadfully overcrowded, both coming and going. The sorely needed Terminal 3 is scheduled to open in June, 1990. Terminal 1, which opened in 1964 to handle 3 million passengers, handled over *10 million* in 1989. And, to the horror of many who need a last, frantic puff before boarding, Terminal 3 will be the **only** one on earth which will allow ***no smoking whatsoever*** in the building (with the rare exception, such as in pubs).

From the Airport to Center City Although Pearson is not far from the downtown area (about 32 kilometers, or 18 miles), the drive can take well over an hour during Toronto's weekday rush hours (7–9 AM and 3:30–6:30 PM). Taxis and limos to a hotel or attraction near the lake can cost $30 or more. Many airport and downtown hotels offer free buses to their locations from each of Toronto's two terminals. Travelers on a budget should consider the express coaches offered by **Grey Coach** (tel. 416/979–3511), which link the airport to three subway stops in the southwest and north-central areas of the city. Buses depart several times each hour, from 8 AM to 11:30 PM. Fares average $5.

Should you be renting a car at the airport, be sure to ask for a street map of the city. Highway 409 runs south, some 3.6 miles to the lakeshore. Here you pick up the Queen Elizabeth Way (QEW) east to the Gardiner Expressway, which runs east into the heart of downtown. If you take the QEW *west*, you'll find yourself swinging around Lake Ontario, toward Hamilton, Niagara-on-the-Lake, and Niagara Falls.

From the United States by Train or Bus

Amtrak (tel. 800/872–7245) runs a daily train to Toronto from Chicago (a 10-hour trip), and another from New York City (11 hours). From Union Station you can walk underground to many hotels—a real boon in inclement weather.

Greyhound-Trailways (no 800 number; check with local information) and **Grey Coach** (tel. 416/979–3511) both have regular bus service into Toronto from all over the United States. From Detroit, the trip takes five hours; from Buffalo, two to three hours; from Chicago and New York City, 11 hours. Buses arrive at 610 Bay Street, just above Dundas Street.

From the United States by Car

Drivers should have proper owner registration and proof of insurance coverage. There is no need for an international driver's license; any valid one will do.

Drivers may be asked several questions at the border crossing, none of them terribly personal or offensive: your place of birth; your citizenship; your expected length of stay. Beyond that, border guards will rarely go. Expect a slight wait at major border crossings. Every fourth or fifth car may be searched, and this can increase the wait at peak visiting times to 30 minutes.

The wonderfully wide Highway 401—it reaches up to 16 lanes as it slashes across Metro Toronto from the airport on the west almost as far as the zoo on the east—is the major link between Windsor, Ontario (and Detroit), and Montreal, Quebec. It's also known as the Macdonald-Cartier Freeway but is really never called anything other than "401." There are no tolls anywhere along it, but you should be warned: Between 7:30 and 9 each weekday morning and from 3:30 to 6:30 each afternoon, the 401 can become dreadfully crowded, even stop-and-go. Plan your trips to avoid these rush hours.

Those who are driving from Buffalo, New York, or Niagara Falls should take the Queen Elizabeth Way (fondly called the QEW or Queen E), which curves up along the western shore of Lake Ontario and eventually turns into the Gardiner Expressway, which flows right into the downtown core.

Yonge Street, which divides the west side of Toronto from the east (much like Manhattan's Fifth Avenue and Detroit's Woodward), begins at the Lakefront. Yonge Street is called Highway 11 once you get north of Toronto, and continues all the way to the Ontario-Minnesota border, at Rainy River. At 1,896.2 km (1,178.3 mi), it is the longest street in the world (as noted in the *Guinness Book of World Records).*

From New York City 851 km (532 mi); from Washington, DC, 899 km (562 mi); from Miami 2,741 km (1,713 mi); from Montreal 558 km (349 mi); from Detroit 378 km (236 mi); from Chicago 854 km (534 mi); from St. Louis 1,310 km (1,023 mi); from Denver 2,485 km (1,553 mi); from Los Angeles 4,384 km (2,740 mi).

From the United Kingdom by Plane

Toronto is served by several airlines that fly daily from London's Heathrow and Gatwick airports. **British Airways, Air Canada,** and **Wardair** have regularly scheduled flights out of Heathrow. Air Canada has the most flights daily—three—two of them direct, and a third that stops at Montreal's Mirabel airport. **KLM** and **Air France** also fly between London and Toronto, the former stopping in Amsterdam on the way, the latter in Paris. Gatwick is the home of many charters, often at heavily discounted prices.

The flying time from London to Toronto is approximately seven hours and 45 minutes, to which one must add (or subtract) the five-hour time difference between the Mother Country and Her Former Colony.

Staying in Toronto

Important Addresses and Numbers

Tourist Offices The **Metropolitan Toronto Convention & Visitors Association** has its office at Queen's Quay Terminal (207 Queen's Quay W, Suite 509, M5J LA7, tel. 416/~~368–9821~~). Booths providing brochures and pamphlets about the city and its attractions, as well as accommodations, are set up in the summer outside the Eaton Centre, on Yonge Street just below Dundas Street, and outside the Royal Ontario Museum.

416-203-2500

The **Traveller's Aid Society** is not just for the down-and-out. This is a nonprofit group whose 130 volunteers can recommend restaurants and hotels, and distribute subway maps, tourist publications, and Ontario sales tax rebate forms. *In Union Station, the society is located in Room B23, on the basement level; tel. 416/366–7788. Open daily 9* AM*–9* PM*. In Terminal I at Toronto's Pearson International Airport, the society has its booth on the Arrivals Level, directly across from the exit, just past Customs, near Area B; tel. 416/676–2868. Open daily 9* AM *–10* PM*. In Terminal II, the booth is located between International and Domestic Arrivals, on the Arrivals Level; tel. 416/676–2860. Open daily 9* AM*–10* PM.

Embassies The **Consulate General of the United States** (360 University Ave., just north of Queen St., M56 1S4, tel. 416/595–1700).

The **Consulate General of Britain** (777 Bay St., at the corner of College St., M56 2G2, tel. 416/593–1267).

For all other consulates—there are dozens of countries represented in Toronto—look up "Consulate Generals" in the white pages of the phone book.

Emergencies Dial 911 for **police** and **ambulance.**

Doctors and Dentists. Check the Yellow Pages or ask at your hotel desk. Also, call *Dial-a-Doctor* (tel. 416/492–4713), or the *Dental Emergency Service* (tel. 416/924–8041).

24-Hour Pharmacies. *Boots Drug Store* (Church St. and Wellesley Ave., about a mile from New City Hall, tel. 416/266–8724). *Shoppers Drug Mart* (2500 Hurontario St., Mississauga, near the airport, tel. 416/277–3665).

24-Hour Pet Emergency Service. *Veterinary Emergency Clinic*, 201 Sheppard Ave. E, about a half-mile east of Yonge St., and a few blocks north of Highway 401, tel. 416/226–3663.

Road Emergencies. The *CAA* (the Canadian version of AAA) has 24-hour road service (tel. 416/966–3000).

24-Hour Gas Stations and Auto Repairs. *Texaco Stations*, at 153 Dundas St. W, behind New City Hall, near Bay St.; 333 Davenport, just south of Casa Loma; and 601 Eglington Ave. E, west of the Ontario Science Center. *Cross Town Service Center*, 1467 Bathurst St., at the corner of St. Clair Ave. W, is well-known and respected for both gas and repairs. *Jim McCormack Esso*, 2901 Sheppard Ave. E, in the Scarborough area, heading toward the Metro Zoo. *Guido's Esso*, 1104 Albion Rd., not far from the airport.

Poison Information Center. *The Hospital for Sick Children* (tel. 416/598–5900) or for the hearing-impaired (tel. 416/597–0215).

Other Numbers

Black Traveler's Information Hotline. In early 1988, a Torontonian set up a hotline for black visitors, with the aim of helping them get to know Toronto (tel. 416/255–2072).

Concert Line. For a list of upcoming musical events, primarily rock and pop, tel. 416/870–9119.

Road Report. Phone the CAA at tel. 416/966–3000.

Ski Information and Weather. Tel. 416/362–4151.

Weather Information. For a taped three-day forecast, phone 416/676–3066, 24 hours a day. If you want to hear a human voice, try 416/676–4567.

Camera Repairs. Queen Street Camera Exchange (tel. 416/862–0300).

24-Hour Restaurants. Golden Griddle (Jarvis St. and Front St.), Fran's Restaurant (20 College St., just a few steps west of Yonge St.).

Staying in Touch

Telephones

Phones work as they do in the United States. Drop 25¢ in the slot (the machine eagerly accepts American change, unlike U.S. phones, which spit out Canadian money), and dial the number. There are no problems dialing direct to the United States; U.S. telephone credit cards are accepted. For directory assistance, dial 411.

Mail

The Canadian mail service leaves a great deal to be desired. Indeed, many in Canada like to say that "Postal Service" is an oxymoron—a contradiction in terms. Within Canada, postcards and letters up to 30 grams cost 38¢. (There seems little doubt that this will rise to 39¢ in 1990.) From 30 to 50 grams, the cost increases to 59¢. Letters and postcards to the United States cost 44¢ for up to 30 grams; 64¢ for 30–100 grams. These prices may well increase by a penny or two in early 1990.

International mail and postcards run 76¢ for up to 20 grams; $1.14 for 20–50.

Mail may be sent to you care of General Delivery, Toronto Adelaide Post Office, 36 Adelaide St. E, Toronto, Ont. M5C 1J0. American Express clients—cardholders and those who purchase traveler's checks or travel services—may pick up mail without charge at American Express, 12 Richmond St. E, Toronto, Ont. M5C 1M5.

Getting Around Toronto

Most of Toronto is laid out on a grid pattern. The key street to remember is Yonge Street (pronounced "young"), which is the main north–south artery. Most major cross streets are numbered east and west of Yonge Street. In other words, if you are looking for 180 St. Clair Avenue West, you want a building a few blocks *west* of Yonge Street; 75 Queen Street East is a block or so *east* of Yonge Street.

At press time, the fare for buses, streetcars, and trolleys is $1.05. However, one can purchase eight adult tickets/tokens for $7.50, which lowers the price per journey a bit. All fares will undoubtedly rise at least a nickel during the first week of 1990; they invariably do, every January. Two-fare tickets are available for $2. Visitors who plan to stay in Toronto for more than a month should consider the **Metropass,** a photo-identity card that costs $49. (And probably a few dollars more than that, as of January 1990.)

Families should take advantage of the savings on the **Sunday** (or **Holiday**) **Pass.** It costs $4 and is good for unlimited travel on any Sunday or holiday (except Labor Day) on every route in Metro Toronto. It is good for up to five persons, with a maximum of two adults. Phone 416/393–INFO from 7 **AM** to 11:30 **PM** for information on how to take public transit to any street or attraction in the city.

A very useful **Ride Guide** is published by the Toronto Transit Commission each year. It shows nearly every major place of interest in the city and how to reach it by public transit. These guides are available in most subways and many other places around the city.

The subways stop running by 2 **AM**, but the Toronto Transit Commission runs an all-night bus service along Bloor Street and Yonge Street.

By Subway There is little argument that the Toronto Transit Commission runs one of the safest, cleanest, most trustworthy systems of its kind anywhere. (It keeps winning international awards, which must mean something.) There are two major subway lines, with 60 stations along the way: the **Bloor/Danforth Line,** which crosses Toronto about three miles north of the Lakefront, from east to west, and the **Yonge/University/Spadina Line,** which loops north and south, like a giant "U," with the bottom of the "U" at Union Station. Tokens and tickets are sold in each subway station and at hundreds of convenience stores along the many routes of the TTC. Get your transfers just after you pay your fare and enter the subway; you'll find them in machines on your way down to the trains.

By Bus All buses and streetcars accept exact change, tickets, or tokens. Paper transfers are free; pick one up at the time that you pay your fare.

By Taxi The meter begins at $2, and the rate per 0.305 kilometers is 25¢. This means that one can take a cab across downtown Toronto for little more than $5. These rates may go up slightly during 1990, but probably not more than 10%–15%. The largest companies are **Co-op** (tel. 416/364–8161), **Diamond** (416/366–6868), and **Metro** (416/363–5611).

By Car Seatbelt use is mandatory in the province of Ontario; unlike the response in the United States, where this is often seen as an infringement on one's right to die, the vast majority of Canadians welcomed this governmental move some years ago. The law applies to everyone in the car, and hefty fines have been known to be given. And that means infants as well; holding one upon the lap is as illegal as it is risky. Canada went metric some years ago, so gas is sold by the liter, and signs are in kilometers. The "100 km" signs on various highways are not an invitation to accelerate but, rather, a warning not to go more than 60 miles per hour.

Pedestrian crosswalks are sprinkled throughout the city; they are marked clearly by overhead signs and very large painted Xs. All a pedestrian has to do is stick out a hand, and cars screech to a halt in both directions. And they must do it, too. Naturally, if you happen to be the pedestrian, don't be foolish; wait until the traffic acknowledges you, and begins to stop, before venturing into the crosswalk. You'll be amazed at your power.

Right turns on red lights are nearly always permitted, except where otherwise posted. You must come to a complete stop before making the turn.

Opening and Closing Times

Most retail stores are open Monday–Saturday 10–6. Downtown stores are usually open until 9 PM. Some shops are open Friday evenings, too. Shopping malls tend to be open 9:30 AM to 9 or 9:30 PM.

The Lord's Day Act—which is being challenged in court as we go to press—keeps much of the city closed on Sunday. However, in February 1989, the provincial government passed a new Sunday shopping law, which dumps the choice of to open or not to open on the various municipalities of Ontario. This means that all of Toronto could be swinging on Sundays, as of 1990. In the meantime, the only tourist areas that are in full swing on Sunday are Markham Village (near Bathurst and Bloor Sts.), Chinatown (in the Spadina Ave./Dundas St. area) and Queen's Quay, down at Harbourfront, on Lake Ontario. Casa Loma, the CN Tower, and the Metro Zoo, among other places, are open on Sunday, too.

Banks are open Monday to Thursday 10–3 and Friday 10–6. Some banks and trust companies open as early as 8:30 AM and on Saturdays as well.

The main civic and national holidays observed in Toronto are: New Year's Day; Good Friday, Easter Sunday, and Easter Monday; Victoria Day—the fourth Monday in May; the country's birthday—Canada Day, or Dominion Day—on July 1; Simcoe Day—the first Monday in August; Labor Day—the first Monday in September; Thanksgiving—the second Monday in October (note that this is more than five weeks earlier than the U.S. Thanksgiving; the harvest and the frost arrive much earlier in Canada); Remembrance Day on November 11; Christmas Day; and since the old Blue Laws prevent shopping until *the day after* Boxing Day, this means that December 27 is the big sale day.

Guided Tours

Orientation Tours

Toronto Harbour and Islands Boat Tours are provided by **Gray Line** (tel. 416/364–2412) on attractive, sleek, Amsterdam-style touring boats, with competent tour guides. The hourly tour visits the Toronto Islands, with lovely views of the Toronto cityscape. Boats leave from the Queen's Quay Terminal daily from late April through mid-October 10:15–6:15. Tours leave as late as 8:15 PM over the summer. Other boats depart from the Harbour Castle Westin. Prices are $7.95 adults, $6.95 senior citizens, $4.95 children ages 4–12.

Toronto Tours (tel. 416/869–1372 or 868–0400) also provides one-hour boat tours of the Toronto harborfront for similar prices from mid-May through October. They also run an informative 90-minute tour aboard a restored 1920s trolley car; it goes by both city halls, and through the financial district and the historic St. Lawrence area. The cost is $13.95 for adults, $8 for children 12 and under. For tours to Niagara Falls and Niagara-on-the-Lake, visitors are picked up at their hotel by an air-conditioned bus. Lunch is included in the fee, which is $54.95 per person; $35 for children 12 and under.

Insight Planners (tel. 416/868–6565) has been providing creative and reliable tours, particularly to art galleries, since 1974.

Reception Ontario (tel. 416/636–0082) provides complete tour-planning services, including sightseeing tours, entertainment packages, hotel accommodations, and even guides in various languages.

Happy Day Tours (tel. 416/593–6220) runs half-day tours of Toronto for about $30 per person, which include admission to Black Creek Pioneer Village and visits to the mansions of Forest Hills, Casa Loma, Chinatown, Queen's Park, Yorkville, and Harbourfront. Book ahead.

Gray Line Sightseeing Bus Tours (tel. 416/979–3511) leave from the Bus Terminal (Bay and Dundas Sts.) and spend 2½ hours visiting such places as Eaton Centre, both city halls, Queen's Park, the University of Toronto, Yorkville, Ontario Place, and Casa Loma—the latter, for a full hour. Costs run about $16 for adults, $11 for children under 12.

Special-Interest Tours

Antours (tel. 416/481–2862) provides several tours of Niagara-on-the-Lake, which include lunch and major performances at the Shaw Festival.

Art Tours of Toronto (tel. 416/845–4044) offers a series of fall and spring gallery and walking tours. Most tours include lunch, and range from $40 to $50 per person.

The **Toronto Stock Exchange** (tel. 416/947–4676) has tours of its exciting new facilities weekdays at 2 PM.

The **Bruce Trail Association** (tel. 416/690–4453) arranges day and overnight hikes around Toronto and environs.

Mysteriously Yours . . . should be of special interest to murder-mystery buffs. On Friday and Saturday evenings, a "despicable crime" is perpetrated at the Royal York Hotel. The mystery begins to unravel over cocktails at 6:30 and is solved after dinner, by 10. The complete dinner and mystery costs about $45 per person, including tax and tip. Call Brian Caws at 416/767–8687 or 800/387–8716. Caws also handles complete tour packages, including hotel, theaters, meals, and sightseeing.

Tipping

Restaurants. Fifteen percent of the total bill is what most waiters and waitresses expect.

Taxis. We have always found the taxi and airport limousine drivers in Toronto to be a decent, polite lot, so a tip of 10% to 15% is usually in order.

Porters and doormen. Around 50¢ a bag; $1 or more in luxury hotels.

Room service. In moderate hotels, $1 per day; in luxury hotels, $2.

American money is always welcome (a U.S. $1 tip is worth about C$1.15–$1.20), so don't worry if you run out of Canadian money.

Mass Media

One of the best ways to become acclimated to a new city is to check out its newspapers, magazines, and electronic media. But which to buy, read, and listen to? The following descriptive listing should be of help, whether you're arriving by car (radio) or settling down in your room (newspaper and magazine).

Radio

AM Stations

CKEY (590) brings you oldies of the '50s and '60s—solid, solid gold, although more representative of those years than CHUM.

CFGM (640) is where you can find traditional country music.

CFTR (680) is an old-style top-40 music station, with heavy repetition—one hit after another after another. "Commercial-free Sundays" have been a welcome gimmick.

CBL (740)—the Canadian Broadcasting Corporation's Toronto affiliate—is where one can get the truest sense of Toronto and all of Canada.

CHAM (820), out of Hamilton, is the best country station in southwestern Ontario. Top-40 country hits.

CJBC (860) is broadcast entirely in French.

CHUM (1050), the number one rock station for years, went to the soft side in the mid-'80s, with sounds of the '60s, '70s, and '80s. "When in doubt, play the Beatles." Rarely hard rock, and few commercials, with songs strung together in clusters of five, seven, even 10.

CHIN (1640) is the ethnic station, with the Greek hour, the Italian hour, the Jewish hour, and so on. This is the place to hear your particular culture or news, presented in your language.

FM Stations

CJRT (91.1) is a private, nonprofit station that struggles along on government grants and listeners' donations. Educational classes, classical music, and some of the best jazz heard on Canadian radio, all commercial-free.

CBC STEREO (94.1) is one of two stations for classical music and serious talk. It has some of the most thought-provoking discussions you'll ever hear, plus excellent news and weather at the top of each hour.

CFMX (96.3) is the only commercial classical station in the country. Its programing is described as "tending towards the top 40 of classical music," and away from vocal music and modern works.

CJEZ (97.3) is easy listening, new age music, and instrumentals. Montevani still lives.

CHFI (98.1) is soft AC, or adult contemporary.

CFNY (102.1) is "modern rock" or new wave music, of Talking Heads or British-oriented variety.

CHUM (104.5) is *The Big Chill* station: rock for aging baby boomers, the upwardly mobile, and youthful lawyers.

CILQ (107), known as Q-107, is medium to hard rock, although softer than a decade ago. Its emphasis is on contemporary rock for young adults.

Newspapers ***The Toronto Star*** has the largest circulation in Canada, although it is primarily read across Metro Toronto and the province of Ontario. It has not totally renounced its left-wing, socialist origins, though it has grown slightly more conservative as it has aged. Its entertainment section is remarkably thorough—especially its Friday edition, with its massive "What's On" section.

The Globe and Mail calls itself "Canada's national newspaper," and in the sense that it is sent by satellite every night and printed in other provinces across the country, it really is. Its columnists are the best in the North, from Jay Scott and Rick Groen on film to Joanne Kates on restaurants; some of the political commentators are top-notch, too. Its business section is a must for all Canadians. There's no Sunday edition, so Saturday's is the issue of choice.

The Toronto Sun is this city's smart-alecky tabloid: too-brief stories, sexist photos of scantily clothed women (and, yes, men), and what seems like thousands of advertisements. Its political hue is to the right of Attila the Hun, but for all its shrillness and vulgarity, it's really fun to read. The movie, TV, and cultural reviews are mainly pap, but if you want to get a true sense of what hoi polloi are thinking, this is the place to find out.

Magazines ***Toronto Life*** is one of Canada's great magazines: glossy, handsome, filled with valuable reviews and listings of what's happening in Toronto, as well as superior articles.

Now is a real charmer. A weekly freebie, found in hundreds of stores, hotels, and buildings across the city, it overflows with arts reviews and listings.

Smoking

Nonsmokers may be pleased to learn that Toronto's stringent "no smoking" regulations apply to all public areas, sections of most restaurants, and even in all taxis.

2 Portrait of Toronto

The Changing of the Guard

by William Kilbourn

A historian, former city councillor, and past president of the Toronto Arts Council, William Kilbourn is also the author of several books, including Toronto in Words and Pictures, Toronto Remembered: An Anthology of Essays and Poems, *and* Toronto Observed: Its Architecture, Patrons, and History. *This article was reprinted from the Toronto* Globe and Mail's *monthly magazine,* Toronto *(March 1988).*

Back in the year that hurricane Hazel blew and the first subway trains rolled down Yonge Street and Marilyn Bell conquered Lake Ontario, the mayor of Toronto was a former Salvation Army bandmaster named Leslie H. Saunders, deputy grand master of the Grand Orange Lodge of Canada and soon to be world head of the Orange Order. Tall and handsome, he had a war veteran's erect carriage and a face like a stone carving. His cornet solo of "The Holy City" was famous far beyond the local citadels of the Salvationists. Defender of the British race, the Protestant church, the royal family, abstinence from alcohol, the closed Sunday, high public virtue, and low civic budgets, he seemed the very embodiment of Toronto the Good.

Like his predecessors for more than four generations, Mayor Saunders participated in the grand parade through the city streets on the 12th of July, ancient anniversary of Britain's Protestant monarch triumphing over his Roman Catholic foes. Led by the figure of King William on his white charger, the flutes and drums played "Lillibullero"; the gloriously sashed men in dark suits bore Union Jacks, Loyalist banners, and biblical tableaux; and the ladies—they would not have called themselves women—followed in their white hats and white gloves, white dresses and white shoes. At its peak, organizers boasted that the procession of Anglo-Protestant Toronto took four hours to wind its way through the young town.

In the 1980s, the remnants of Toronto's Orangemen still walk proudly on the Glorious Twelfth. But the big summer events nowadays are the West Indian Caribana parade, the multicultural Caravan festival, and huge ethnic picnics in the parks. The mayor of Toronto is a Catholic (the very first we've elected). Not one Orangeman is left on the City Council. And now there's a St. Patrick's Day Parade.

The differences between today's Toronto and that of Leslie Saunders show up in the demographics. In the census figures from 1951 through 1981, the population of the city of Toronto proper remained more or less stable at between six and seven hundred thousand. But the proportion of people with British ancestry dropped from more than two-thirds of the population in 1951 to one-third 30 years later. In the same period the Catholics doubled from 20% to 40%. And since 1981 the process of de-Anglicization has accelerated. "WASPs are becoming an endangered species," says Don Miller, the Jamaican-born president of Multifax Communications Corp., a firm specializing in ethnic polling and market research. In this decade, according to Miller, the WASP proportion of Metropolitan Toronto's population keeps dropping at a steady rate, transforming WASPs into just one of many ethnic groups. "And that," says Miller, "changes the way we communicate, trade, and play the political game."

Of course, WASPs still dominate big business, the rosters of the Toronto and York clubs, and the boards of major hospitals and universities. But politicians know that the new power brokers are to be found in the ethnic clubs and societies—Italian, Chinese, Greek, and the rest.

Does this mean the traditional qualities of sobriety and shrewdness that made this a functional city, as well as a bland and stuffy one, are on their way out? And do citizens even understand where the character of their city came from?

The experience of a young friend of mine at a multicultural school fair a while ago presages one kind of answer. Her class president assigned everybody to some ethnic activity—singing, dancing, cooking, costume-making—except for my friend, the only WASP in class, who was clearly a puzzle. "I guess you people don't have a culture," she concluded thoughtfully, "so how about you handle the cloakroom?"

As they shrink to the size of just another ethnic group, Toronto's Anglo-Celts are freer now to celebrate their own very distinctive culture. Certainly, it's hard to imagine the shape of our city without them.

The beginnings of Toronto the Good can be dated precisely enough. When the city was incorporated in 1834, it numbered about 9,000 souls. A half-century later, the population had so swollen—to more than 100,000—that poor drinking water and sewage disposal were a danger to public health. Its hundreds of taverns and grogshops (one for every three dozen adult males) dispensing dirt-cheap raw spirits, accompanied by much public drunkenness and prostitution, were an offense to bourgeois Victorian sensibilities. At City Hall, the incumbent mayor was a developer and beer magnate and most of the aldermen were in league with the tavern owners. Nobody wanted to disturb the prosperous, easy-going status quo by strictly enforcing bylaws or raising taxes for public works. It was, in some ways, Toronto the Bad.

Then, in 1885, "Toronto the Good" became the mayoralty campaign theme of a young moral and social reformer named William Howland, son of Ontario's second lieutenant-governor. His evangelical Anglican zeal led him to concern for not only the souls but the living conditions and education of Toronto's poor. In a crusade to make Toronto virtuous by means of law and order, he was solidly supported by the Protestant clergy, newly enfranchised widows and spinsters, and enough middle-class and working-class males to beat out the superior experience and organization of his opponents. Howland improved city administration, cut liquor licenses, and appointed a police inspector who was the scourge of the York Street taverns and brothels.

Howland died young, at age 49, but his idealism proved long-lasting. That mix of temperance and the impulse to social reform, forces that were then exciting cities across North America, fell on particularly fertile ground among the Protestant, work-oriented inhabitants of Toronto. Within a generation, our first medical officer of health, William Canniff, and his successors had dramatically reduced the death rate from water pollution and aroused enough public concern to begin attacking slum conditions. Other reform politicians brought in a board of control to counterbalance the local concerns of aldermanic ward heelers, reduced patronage drastically, and began to professionalize the public service.

Still, the crusaders left a mixed legacy. The battle against dirt, disease, and disorder had a prim moralist underpinning that, over time, caused Toronto to become narrow, prudish, and intolerant—increasingly frowning on booze, foreigners, and violation of the Sabbath. Though Sabbatarian forces finally lost on the issue of whether streetcars should be allowed to operate on Sunday—a major civic issue in the 1890s—they did manage to have children arrested for playing on the streets on Sundays, and in 1912 they put a stop to Sunday tobogganing in High Park. Today's debate over Sunday shopping has deep roots.

As for booze, Howland's program of mere temperance turned after 1916 into something close to provincewide Prohibition. My father could recall inspectors boarding the Montreal train in search of illicit bottles from Quebec, and white-coated doctors stationed in provincial liquor outlets to issue $1 medical permits—because the law permitted the consumption of alcohol primarily "for medicinal purposes."

The two faces of Toronto found perfect expression in Ontario's Orange Lodges. Almost all of the city's mayors between 1845 and 1972 were Orangemen. As fraternal, benevolent societies in a pioneer land, the lodges protected the individual from adversity and provided him with ceremony and fellowship, a focus for his British loyalties and a means of political action. But even as the lodges emerged as a political force, they remained a major inspiration for suspicion and hatred of all things French Canadian and "foreign." They whipped up support for hanging Louis Riel and for stopping publicly funded Catholic schools in Manitoba (though they couldn't eliminate them in Ontario) and campaigned for British-only immigration during the 1920s.

Orangeism at its most virulent was not so much the essence of Toronto the Good as its shadow side.

From the mid-19th century on, Orange power seemed total and ordained forever, like Toronto's solid support of the federal Conservative party. Yet it was during Leslie Saunders's 40-year span in civic office (he was first elected as a member of the Toronto Board of Education in 1939) that noticeable cracks began to appear in the armor of WASP Toronto's respectability. In 1947 Premier George Drew permitted cocktail lounges in Ontario. In 1950 came Sunday sports, voted in by a narrow majority in the face of a vigorous campaign by the newspapers, churches, and middle-class leaders. Sunday movies and the Yonge Street strip were to follow. And the cracks widened with the flood of hundreds of thousands of immigrants pouring in from the ruins of postwar Europe to seek a better life in Canada's richest city.

In 1955, Saunders was defeated for the mayor's job in a close three-way race by Nathan Phillips. The victory of "Nate," Toronto's first Jewish chief magistrate and self-styled "mayor of *all* the people," proved richly symbolic of the city's multicultural future. So did the new city hall and civic square. Deliberately designed for public pleasure, celebration, and even mass protest, they were eventually to be chief symbols of an exciting metropolis, the opposite of the "sanctimonious icebox" that used to appall visitors and produce those jokes about Toronto's dullness.

And contrary to the fears of many Hogtown WASPs, Toronto's new rainbow-colored majority soon proved that it would reinforce, rather than erode, the most essential elements of Toronto the Good. Today, the streets and squares and parks may be busier, and better-used on Sundays, but they are still clean. The violent-crime rate—one-tenth that of Detroit—remains stable. The Protestant work ethic is more than rivaled by that of Koreans manning convenience stores seven days a week, and old-fashioned WASP Puritanism has met its match among the strict practices of Muslim and Hindu parents.

Some now claim we have the best of both worlds. But what about the structures of class and power? It is all very well to have Sri Lankan cuisine in our restaurants and tofu in our refrigerators. But isn't Toronto still a vertical mosaic with the WASPs on top? True enough in the world of big business, but in the domain of other key public authority figures, major changes are coming. Visible minorities (mainly blacks and Asians) in management positions at city hall have moved from a minuscule proportion in the early 1980s to 10% today. At the board of education the number of public school principals and vice-principals from these groups has more than doubled in just five years. Even on the police force, their proportion has crept up a bit, from next to nothing to 3.5%.

The future threat to Toronto's virtue lies elsewhere—in the consequences of the city's rapid expansion. Back in the 1970s, a group of reformers, like Mayor Howland and his successors a century ago, captured city hall and wrestled with the city's problems. Some of their solutions—saving older communities and buildings and canceling the proposed inner-city expressway network—are still in place, but they are now threatened by headlong commercial development.

As for the issues of Toronto the Good, old-style WASP, I thought I would see what Leslie Saunders had to say. After all, he was not only our strongest Orangeman but one of our best budget chiefs. I asked Saunders what he thought of the city's having a St. Patrick's Day Parade this month. Now a hale 88, he replied after a pause: "Well, I guess they can do that. We fought for those freedoms. This is a British city after all." Once, of course, it was. My own childhood was pure British colonial—from *Boy's Own Annual* at Christmas to Canada's national war song, "There'll Always Be an England." But I know I couldn't stand living in that kind of Toronto now. Instead, I think of my two Italian grandsons and my Chilean granddaughter, and of this city as a welcoming and exciting place for them, and I celebrate my non-WASP home.

3 Exploring Toronto

Orientation

Well, now you're in Toronto, and probably in the downtown area. It's rather confusing, isn't it? We're not talking Avenue A, B, and C here, or 33rd, 34th, and 35th streets, either, so already we're on somewhat shaky ground.

But once you establish that Lake Ontario runs along the south of the city, and that the fabulous Harbourfront complex is there, as well as the ferry to the lovely Toronto Islands, you are well on your way to orienting yourself.

It's a shame to turn your back on our now-blossoming waterfront, but when you do, you meet the striking, often magnificent high-rise buildings that give Toronto so much of its skyline. Banks, banks, and banks: Yes, the church may have stood the highest and proudest in most Western towns since medieval times, but today it is the god Mammon who towers over what was once called (both mockingly and with reverence) Toronto the Good. (May we remind you that there were no movies shown on Sundays until the late 1950s and no Sunday newspapers until the late 1970s.)

Every one of the major banks of Canada, which are far wealthier and more powerful than most of their U.S. counterparts, has its headquarters in downtown Toronto, between University Avenue and Yonge Street.

This edifice complex first expressed itself in the black 54-story tower of the **Toronto-Dominion Bank** (T-D Centre), designed by the justly admired German-American architect Mies van der Rohe. There are four towers there now, eclipsed by I.M. Pei's silver and mirrorlike **Bank of Commerce** building, right across the street.

Only a few years later—and only a few feet away—came the **Bank of Montreal**'s tower, covered with handsome marble and now holder of the title "Tallest Building in the Whole British Commonwealth." In the end, Toronto's most stunning bank building would be not the tallest but the most extraordinary: the **Royal Bank Building,** designed by the very gifted Torontonian Boris Zerafa. Born in Cairo to parents of Italian and English descent—which is late 20th-century Toronto in a nutshell—Zerafa is also the designer of Toronto's Richmond-Adelaide Centre and the **Bank of Nova Scotia,** which opened in 1989.

The new **Scotiabank Tower** looks like another winner, but it would be hard to beat the Royal Bank for sheer beauty. Its golden exterior, coated with fully 2,500 ounces of real gold (purchased when it was only $100 an ounce) in order to keep the heat in and the cold out (or vice versa, depending on the season), truly defines the skyline of Toronto. It's "a palette of color and texture as well as mass," in Zerafa's own words; "it has a cathedral feeling, due to natural light." It is certainly worth a visit.

After seeing all the bank buildings, the next best place to get a sense of orientation would be, without doubt, the **CN Tower.** One local wag suggested that the 180-story, 130,000-ton structure was built to teach Canadian men humility. Perhaps. But for all its basic ugliness, the CN Tower is the ideal place to get a

Toronto Exploring *(Boxes Refer to Detail Maps)*

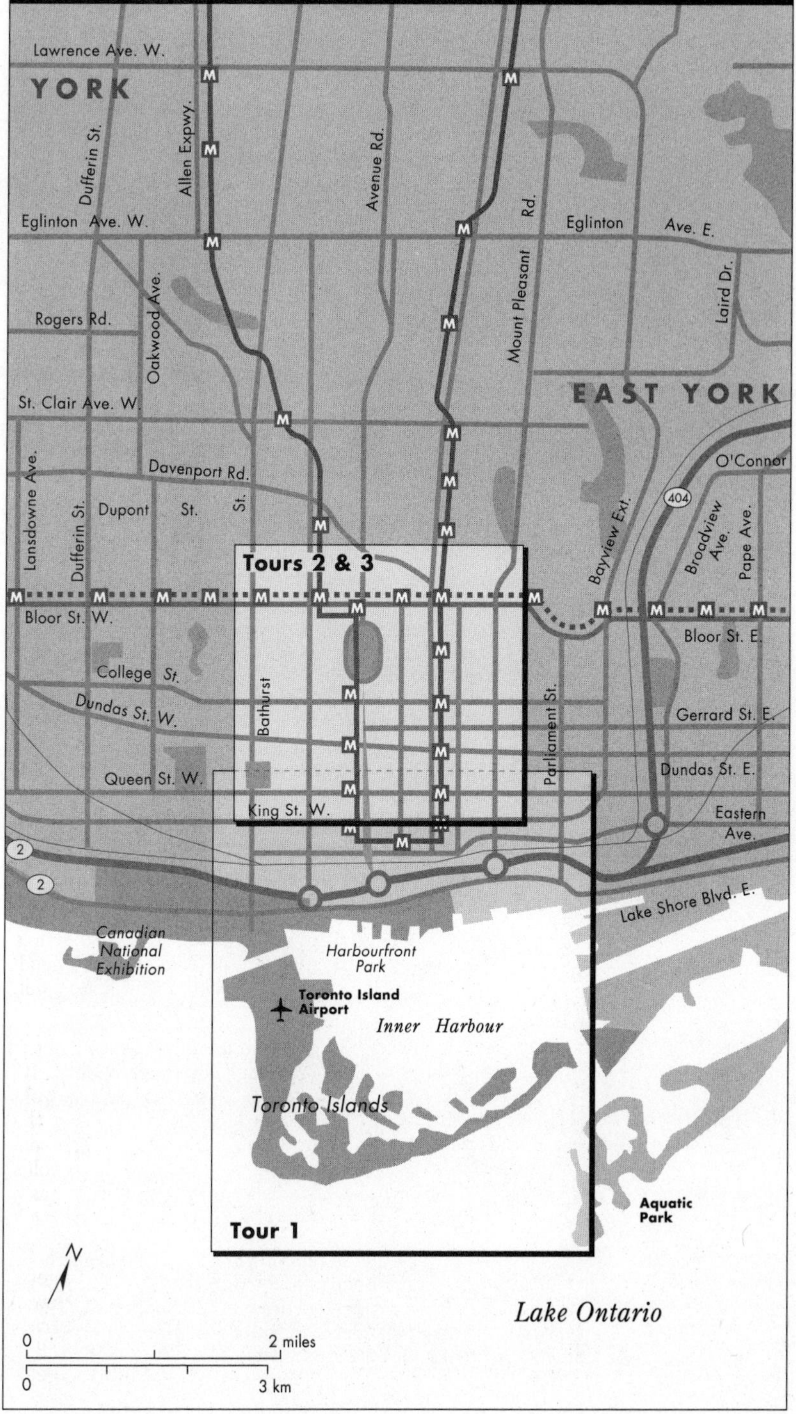
Lawrence Ave. W.
YORK
Dufferin St.
Allen Expwy.
Avenue Rd.
Eglinton Ave. W.
Rd.
Eglinton Ave. E.
Laird Dr.
Mount Pleasant
Oakwood Ave.
Rogers Rd.
EAST YORK
St. Clair Ave. W.
Davenport Rd.
O'Connor
404
Lansdowne Ave.
Dufferin St.
Dupont St.
St.
Bayview Ext.
Broadview Ave.
Pape Ave.
Tours 2 & 3
Bloor St. W.
Bloor St. E.
College St.
Bathurst
Parliament St.
Dundas St. W.
Gerrard St. E.
Queen St. W.
Dundas St. E.
King St. W.
Eastern Ave.
2
2
Lake Shore Blvd. E.
Canadian National Exhibition
Harbourfront Park
Toronto Island Airport
Inner Harbour
Toronto Islands
Aquatic Park
Tour 1
N
Lake Ontario
0
2 miles
0
3 km

sense of the layout of Toronto. The food here is terrible, but those of you who enjoy an overpriced drink now and then should make a reservation and head up the tower any clear day between noon and five.

Back on terra firma, imagine the downtown area of Toronto as a large rectangle. The southern part is, as you already know, Lake Ontario. The western part, shooting north to Bloor Street and beyond, is Spadina Road, near the foot of which stands the CN Tower, Harbourfront, and the spectacular new SkyDome Stadium. On the east, running from the lakefront north for hundreds of miles (believe it or not), is Yonge Street, which divides the city in half. University Avenue, a major road that parallels Yonge Street, for some reason changes its name to Avenue Road at the corner of Bloor Street, next to the Royal Ontario Museum. A further note: College Street, legitimately named since many of the University of Toronto's buildings run along it, becomes Carlton Street where it intersects Yonge Street, then heads east.

Tour 1: Waterfront, St. Lawrence, the Financial District, and the Underground City

Numbers in the margin correspond with points of interest on the Tour 1 map.

Since, as we noted, Toronto has a waterfront as its southernmost border, it seems logical that we begin there. And it shouldn't be too hard to get there, since it's just south of Union Station, which is the terminus of both the University Avenue/ Spadina Avenue and Yonge Street subways. Unfortunately, only a handful of the city's major north–south streets—Bay, Jarvis, and York streets—go right to Lake Ontario from the city center. A new streetcar line between Union Station and the lakefront will not be in operation until late 1989, at the earliest. But the very fact that it *is* being built underlines civic awareness of the growing importance of the central waterfront, both residentially and recreationally.

It was not always thus. Indeed, until quite recently, Toronto was notoriously negligent about its waterfront. The Gardiner Expressway, Lakeshore Boulevard, and a network of rusty rail yards stood as hideous barriers to the natural beauty of Lake Ontario. The city wished it could drop the expressway underground, but an estimated cost of several billion dollars put a rapid halt to that discussion.

Just over a decade ago, thank heaven, the various levels of government—city, Metro, provincial (Ontario) and federal (Ottawa)—began a struggle to change this unfortunate situation. By that time, most of the area just south of the Gardiner Expressway and Lakeshore Boulevard was overflowing with grain silos, various warehouses, and most unattractive (and unsweet-smelling) towers of malt, used by local breweries.

Part of the answer was the building of a very handsome hotel, the Harbour Castle Westin (which, until the fall of 1987, was a Hilton hotel), and an attractive tower of condominiums. The hotel has an exterior, glassed-in elevator that offers guests a view of the waterfront and the Toronto Islands.

Toronto Islands ❶

Just behind the giant Harbour Castle Westin is the debarkation point for ferries to the **Toronto Islands,** surely one of the highlights of any trip to the city—especially from May to October. It takes only eight minutes for the quaint little ferries to chug across the tiny bay. The islands make up one of the world's great parks.

The four thin, curved, tree-lined islands—Centre, Ward's, Algonquin, and Hanlan's Point—have been attracting visitors since 1833, four years before Victoria became queen and just a year before the town of York changed its name to Toronto. And the more than 550 acres of parkland are irresistible, especially during the hot summer months, when downtown Toronto seems to be melting as rapidly as the ice-cream cones sold everywhere on the islands.

Be warned: The crowds always head to Centre Island, since that's where most of the amusements are located. It gets so crowded, in fact, that no bicycles are allowed on the ferry to that island during summer weekends. Take one of the equally frequent ferries to Ward's or Hanlan's, both of which are quiet, delightful places to picnic, sunbathe, read under a tree, or simply escape the city. You'll enjoy spectacular views of Toronto's majestic skyline, especially as the setting sun turns the Royal Bank Tower and other downtown skyscrapers to gold, silver, and bronze.

The beaches on Ward's tend to be the least crowded. They're also the cleanest, although there have been problems with the cleanliness of Lake Ontario's water over the past decade. Except for the hottest days in August, the Great Lake tends to be uncomfortably chilly, so bring appropriate clothing. You'll be wise to rent a bike for an hour or more and work your way across the interconnected islands. (Students of the petty politics of the petit bourgeois might enjoy hearing about the endless controversy over the hundred or so homes on Ward's and neighboring Algonquin Island that many city politicians have been fighting to tear down for years. Some argue that having people living in a much-used park makes it safer to visit; others insist that the "squatters" are using up precious parkland. Whoever is "right," it appears that the homes on the Islands are safe for the next decade, at least.)

If you are traveling with children, Centre Island is certainly the one to check out first. Signs everywhere read Please Walk on the Grass, which should charm visitors to pieces, even before they begin to explore. A few hundred yards from the ferry docks lies **Centreville,** an amusement park that's supposed to be a turn-of-the-century children's village. The concept works wondrously well: True, the pizza, fries, and hot dogs are barely edible—pack a lunch!!—but on the little Main Street there are charming shops, a town hall, a little railroad station, and over a dozen rides, including a restored 1890s merry-go-round with over four dozen hand-carved animals. And there's no entrance fee to the modest, 14-acre amusement park, although you'll have to pay a nominal charge for each ride. Perhaps most enjoyable for children is the free **Far Enough Farm,** which is near enough to walk to. It has all kinds of animals to pet and feed, ranging from piglets to geese, cows to birds. *Tel. 416/363–1112. Centreville is open weekends only Apr. 30–May 15; daily Vic-*

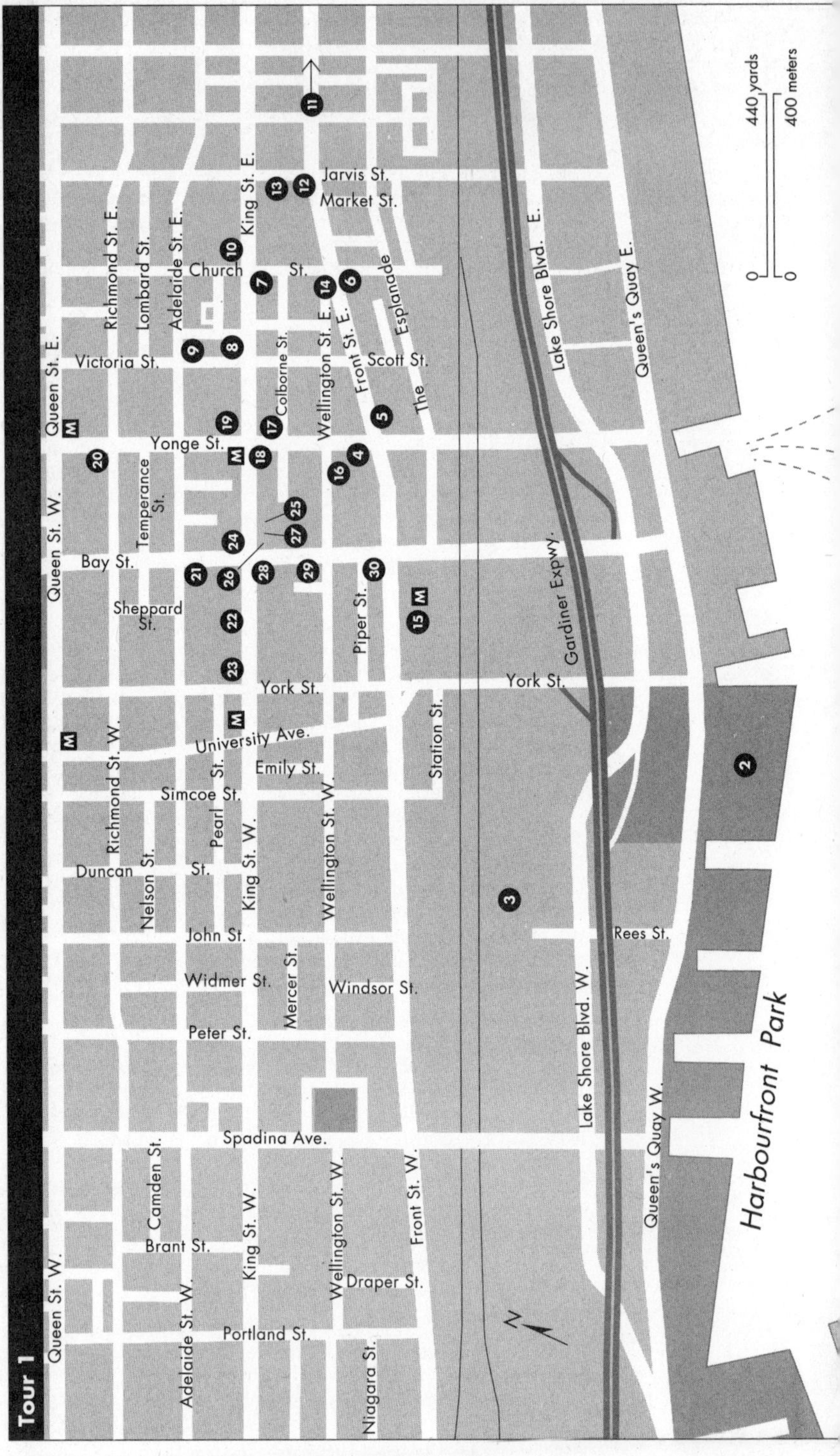
Tour 1
Queen St. W.
Queen St. E.
Richmond St. E.
Richmond St. W.
Lombard St.
Adelaide St. E.
Adelaide St. W.
King St. E.
King St. W.
Colborne St.
Wellington St. E.
Wellington St. W.
Front St. E.
Front St. W.
The Esplanade
Jarvis St.
Market St.
Church St.
Victoria St.
Scott St.
Yonge St.
Temperance St.
Bay St.
Sheppard St.
Piper St.
York St.
University Ave.
Pearl St.
Emily St.
Simcoe St.
Station St.
Duncan St.
Nelson St.
John St.
Widmer St.
Mercer St.
Windsor St.
Peter St.
Spadina Ave.
Camden St.
Brant St.
Draper St.
Portland St.
Niagara St.
Lake Shore Blvd. E.
Lake Shore Blvd. W.
Gardiner Expwy.
Queen's Quay E.
Queen's Quay W.
Rees St.
Harbourfront Park
M
N
0 440 yards
0 400 meters
2
3
4
5
6
7
8
9
10
11
12
13
14
15
16
17
18
19
20
21
22
23
24
25
26
27
28
29
30

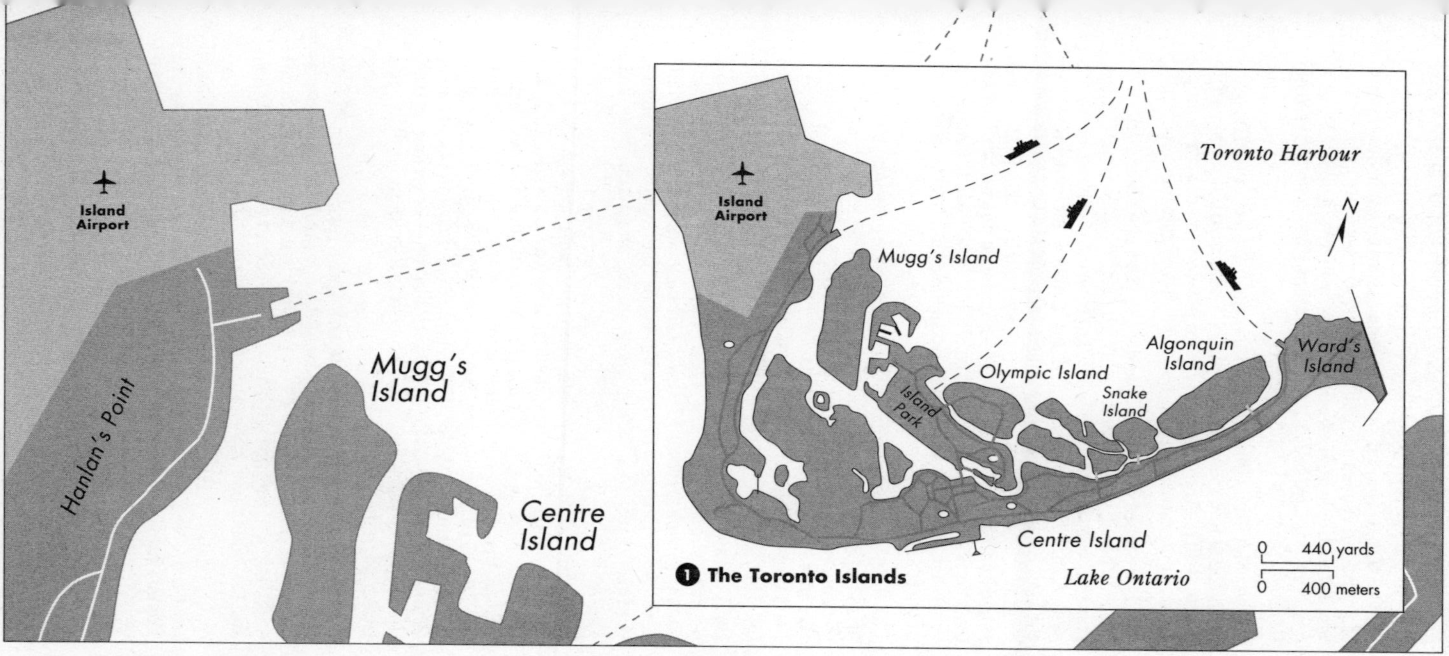

❶ **The Toronto Islands**

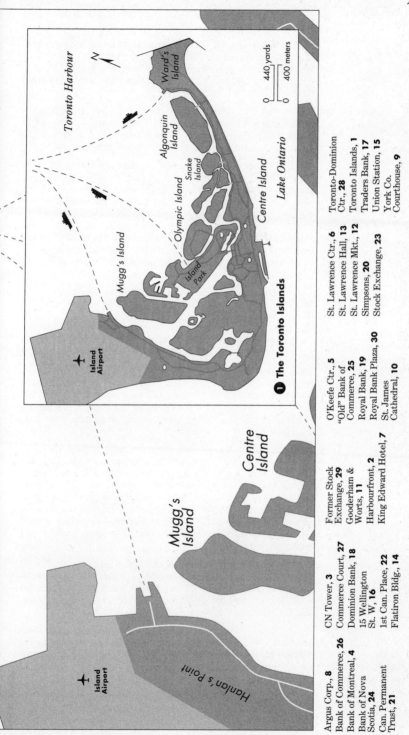

Argus Corp., **8**
Bank of Commerce, **26**
Bank of Montreal, **4**
Bank of Nova Scotia, **24**
Can. Permanent Trust, **21**
CN Tower, **3**
Commerce Court, **27**
Dominion Bank, **18**
15 Wellington St. W, **16**
1st Can. Place, **22**
Flatiron Bldg., **14**
Former Stock Exchange, **29**
Gooderham & Worts, **11**
Harbourfront, **2**
King Edward Hotel, **7**
O'Keefe Ctr., **5**
"Old" Bank of Commerce, **25**
Royal Bank, **19**
Royal Bank Plaza, **30**
St. James Cathedral, **10**
St. Lawrence Ctr., **6**
St. Lawrence Hall, **13**
St. Lawrence Mkt., **12**
Simpsons, **20**
Stock Exchange, **23**
Toronto-Dominion Ctr., **28**
Toronto Islands, **1**
Traders Bank, **17**
Union Station, **15**
York Co. Courthouse, **9**

toria Day (mid-May)–Labor Day; weekends again Sept. 10–25.

All transportation on these islands comes to you compliments of your feet: No cars are allowed anywhere. Your nostrils will wonder at the lack of exhaust fumes, while your feet will wonder why you walked all the way along the boardwalk from Centre to Ward's Island (1.5 mi).

There you'll find **Gibraltar Lighthouse,** built back in 1808, making it the oldest monument in the city that is still standing on its original site. Right next to it is a pond stocked with rainbow trout, and a concession for buying bait and renting rods.

Sandy beaches circle the islands, the best ones being those on the southeast tip of Ward's, the southernmost edge of Centre, and the west side of Hanlan's. There are free changing rooms near each of these areas, but no facilities for checking your clothes. Swimming in the various lagoons and channels is prohibited. The winter can be bitter cold on the island, but snowshoeing and cross-country skiing with downtown Toronto over your shoulder will be irresistible to many. In the summer, there are rowboat and canoe rentals, tennis courts, gardens, playgrounds, and a wildlife sanctuary.

The ferries run irregularly during the winter: every half-hour or so until 10 or 11 AM, and then every few hours thereafter. In the summer, the ferries leave three times an hour at the foot of Bay Street. The cost is $2 adults, 75¢ senior citizens, 35¢ children. For a recording giving the schedule and prices, call 416/392–8193; for other information, call 416/392–8186.

Harbourfront
❷

Back at the ferry docks on the mainland, your next move should be to **Harbourfront.** This is a trip that is well worth planning ahead—check *Now* and *Toronto Life* magazines, as well as daily newspaper listings, to see what concerts, dances, art shows, festivals, etc., are taking place there, and build your visit around them.

For many years, as we said, Toronto had good reason to be ashamed of its God-given, man-taken-away waterfront. Today Harbourfront has become a 100-acre culture-and-recreation center, drawing over three million visitors each year. Stretching from just west of the Harbour Castle Westin for nearly a mile to Bathurst Street, the complex has become the scene of fabulous entertainment, exquisite buildings, glorious attractions—a true match for San Francisco's Pier 39 and Baltimore's Inner Harbor.

Highlights are many. The **Queen's Quay** (pronounced "key") **Terminal** is a must: The 57-year-old food warehouse was transformed in 1983, at a cost of over $60 million, into a magnificent eight-story structure with delightful specialty shops, eateries, and the handsome 450-seat Premiere Dance Theatre.

Contemporary art exhibits of painting and sculpture, architecture and video, photography and design, now take place at the **Power Plant,** just west of Queen's Quay. (The building started in 1927 as a power station for an ice-making plant; you can spot it by the tall red smokestack.)

York Quay Centre has concerts, live theater, readings, even skilled artisans at work in open craft studios. A shallow pond at the south end is used for canoe lessons in warmer months, and as the largest artificial ice-skating rink in North America in more wintry times. The Nautical Centre nearby has many private firms offering lessons in sailing and canoeing, and vessels for rent.

On **Maple Leaf Quay,** the very popular **Antique Market** takes place every day but Monday. The 70 dealers triple in number each Sunday.

Here are some of the seasonal highlights: *Late January:* an Ice Canoe Race. *February:* two weekends of Winterfest. *April:* an Easter program. *May:* the Milk International Childrens' Festival and the Canoe Festival. *June:* a Jazz Festival. *July:* Canada Day celebrations and a Parade of Lights. *August:* the Zingy Dingy Boat Race and Teddy Bears Fair. *September:* a youth-oriented Labor Day weekend. *October:* the world-acclaimed Authors' Festival, a Harvest Festival, and Francophone Week. *November:* the Swedish Christmas Fair. *December:* Festive Trees, the Cavalcade of Lights, and a New Year's Eve Party.

Harbourfront is within walking distance of Union Station. Drivers should head for the foot of Bay Street or Spadina Avenue, and park in one of the many lots. For information, call 416/364–5665.

3 From Harbourfront, it's a short walk to the **CN Tower,** an attraction second only to Eaton Centre.

The CN Tower, the tallest free-standing structure in the world, is tall with a cause: So many high buildings had been built over the past few decades that shorter radio and TV transmission towers were having trouble broadcasting over them.

And so the Tower stands, rather arrogantly, on Front Street near Spadina Avenue, not far from the waterfront. It's fully 1,815 feet, 5 inches high and it really is worth a visit, *if the weather is clear.* And it's in the *Guinness Book of World Records.*

Four elevators zoom up the outside of the $57-million tower, which weighs 130,000 tons and contains enough concrete to build a curb along Highway 401 from Toronto to Kingston, some 163 miles to the west. The ride takes but a minute, going at 20 feet a second, a rate of ascent similar to that of a jet-plane takeoff. But each elevator has only one floor-to-ceiling glass wall, preventing vertigo.

The **Skypod,** about two-thirds up the tower, is seven stories high, and it has two observation decks, a nightclub, and a revolving restaurant. It also has oodles of microwave equipment that is not open to the public but is its true *raison d'être.*

Level 2 is the **outdoor observation deck,** with an enclosed promenade, and an outdoor balcony for looking straight down at the ground. Level 3 of the Skypod, the **indoor observation deck,** has not only conventional telescopes, but high-powered peritelescopes that almost simulate flight. Also here is a unique Tour Wand System, which provides an audio tour of the City of Toronto. Over the summer months, an award-winning film, *To the Top,* (cost: $1), shows how the edifice was constructed.

The **Space Deck,** which is 33 stories higher, costs another dollar; at an elevation of 1,465 feet, it is the world's highest public observation gallery. But even from the Skypod below, you can often see Lake Simcoe to the north, and the mist rising from

Niagara Falls to the south. All the decks provide spectacular panoramic views of Toronto, Lake Ontario, and the Toronto Islands.

CN Tower, 301 Front St. W, tel. 416/360–8500. Observation deck $8 adults; $5 senior citizens and youths (13–17); $3.50 for children 12 and under. This will increase by some 5% during 1990. The Audio Tour Wand is included in the price. Peak visiting hours: between 11 AM and 4 PM, especially on weekends. Open summers, 9 AM–midnight; the rest of the year, weekdays 10–10, weekends 9:30 AM–11 PM.

A charming one-hour experience is **Tour of the Universe,** located at the base of the CN Tower. It's a simulated space shuttle journey to Jupiter in the year 2019, with everything from a 64-screen Multivision Wall that briefs you on your upcoming flight, laser "inoculation," an InterPlanetary Passport souvenir, and a too-brief ride in a flight simulator that provides physical motion to match the spectacular special-effects film. Although not cheap, it's very well done and a pleasant break before or after the CN Tower visit. *Admission $11.95 adults, $4 children 12 and under, $7.95 seniors. This will also increase by some 5% during 1990. Summer hours, 10–10; phone 416/363–TOUR for hours in other seasons.*

St. Lawrence

From Harbourfront and the CN Tower, you may wish to experience the area of **St. Lawrence,** where the 19th century meets the 21st, before you head back into the 20th century of the financial district. Back when the city fathers divided up the city, in 1834, they gave each district a saint's name. The area that lay farthest to the south, extending from the lake up to King Street and from Yonge Street east to Parliament, they christened St. Lawrence.

Much like the waterfront before Harbourfront, it was for years a depressing, tacky section of old, dirty buildings, factories, and railway tracks. But like so many parts of this city, it has been born again, as any area with a saint's name should be capable of doing.

During any walk through the St. Lawrence area, you will jog between the centuries: from strikingly beautiful, centuries-old buildings to the new St. Lawrence project, just south of The Esplanade, designed to house close to 10,000 people. It's part of Toronto's genius, this peaceful coexistence of classy condominiums and low-cost (alias subsidized) housing. No, downtowns do not necessarily have to be dead, dirty, and dangerous.

This area is where Toronto began, as the village of York, back in
1793, which is before our time. Start at the northwest corner of
4 Yonge and Front streets at the **Bank of Montreal building,** an
early example of ostentatious bank architecture. Built in the mid-1880s by the architects Darling & Curry, it is a significant city landmark—and a huge new project on this spot has promised to save it for posterity. Note the richly carved Ohio stone, and don't miss the Hermes figure supporting the chimney near the back of the building. It's a beauty.

On the southeast corner of Yonge and Front streets is one of the
major showcases for live theater, opera, and ballet in the city:
5 the gigantic **O'Keefe Centre.** Another block east, at the corner
6 of Church Street, is the two-theater complex of the **St. Law-**

rence Centre, which has a number of repertory companies and many concerts year-round (*see* The Arts).

Walk up to King Street and admire the very attractive (and
7 ritzy) **King Edward Hotel,** built in 1903 and recently refurbished in grand fashion. Note the details both inside and out; the architect was none other than E.J. Lennox, who also designed Old City Hall, Massey Hall, and Casa Loma.

Looking north from King Street, on the west side of Toronto
8 Street, is the very understated head office of **Argus Corporation,** one of Canada's major conglomerates. It was originally built in 1853 as a post office. Still farther to the north is the
9 **York County Magistrate's Courthouse,** built in 1852 and restored in 1982.

10 At the corner of Church and King streets stands **St. James Cathedral** (Anglican), with its noble, gothic spires. The steeple is the tallest in Canada—even if the bank towers dwarf it now—and its illuminated spire clock once guided ships into the harbor. (Which was once far closer; everything south of Front Street is land fill!) This is the fourth St. James Cathedral on this site; the third one burned down in the Great Fire of 1849.

Continue east to Trinity Street and walk south. The first dis-
11 tillery in Canada—**Gooderham and Worts**—celebrated its 185th birthday in 1987. The massive limestone building is still used today to make rum spirits from molasses. The brothers-in-law began their company as a flour mill but soon began making alcohol out of the surplus grain.

Return along Front Street to the corner of Jarvis Street. There
12 it is—the **St. Lawrence Market.** Built in 1844 as Toronto's first city hall (what other city has four extant?), it now has an exhibition hall upstairs where the original council chambers stood. It continues to serve the citizens of the city, although in a more delicious fashion—as a food market. It grew up around the city hall at the turn of the century. (Who says governments never produce anything?)

Renovated in 1978, the market is renowned for its wide range of foods—from kiwi fruit to Ontario cheddar, from homemade bread to conch meat. Its four dozen stalls are open each Tuesday through Saturday, and are an ideal place to create lunches for the Metro Zoo, Canada's Wonderland, or the nearby Toronto Islands—three places where the excellence of the attractions in no way guarantees excellence in cuisine.

The plain brick building just across Front Street, on the north side, is another superb farmer's market, but it is only open on Saturdays. As early as 4 AM, the finest produce from farms just north of Toronto pours into this cornucopia.

Walk just behind the market, one block north, and you'll find, on the south side of King Street, another treasure: the second city
13 hall of Toronto, today called **St. Lawrence Hall.** This is Victorian architecture at its finest (built in 1850). Erected originally for musical performances and balls, this is where Jenny Lind sang and where P.T. Barnum first presented his midget Tom Thumb. For the last several years, it has been the home of the National Ballet of Canada. Take time to admire its interior and its exterior; it is an architectural gem.

Back on Front Street, heading west toward Yonge Street and the heart of downtown, you'll encounter a building that has relatives in pie-shaped lots all over North America—the **Flatiron Building.** There it stands, on the little triangle of Wellington, Church, and Front streets. It was erected in 1892 as the head office of the Gooderham and Worts distilling company, and it is now a prestigious office building. You may wish to take a ride in its original elevator.

14

One more treat before we head into Toronto's Financial District: As you walk west along the sweet little park that sits behind the Flatiron Building, look back at the witty mural by Derek Besant (on the west side of the Flatiron Building). It's a giant painting of a painting of windows, drawn around the real windows of the structure; it looks as though it's been tacked up on the wall and is peeling off. It plays tricks with your eyes, makes children and adults giggle, and is a pleasant way to end your walk through St. Lawrence.

Financial District

15

One doesn't always recommend visits to a train station, but **Union Station** is special. On the south side of Front Street, between Bay and York streets (and across from the handsome Royal York Hotel), Union Station is a most historic building, though it is of this century. It was designed back in 1907, when trains were still as exciting as space shuttles are today, and it was opened in 1927 by the Prince of Wales. As the popular historian Pierre Berton has written, its planning recalls "the love lavished on medieval churches." Of course, the latter used to take centuries to build; this shrine to Our Lady of the Train was put up in less than two decades.

Put up? More like erect. Establish. Create. Try to imagine the awe of the immigrants who poured into Toronto between the wars by the tens of thousands, staring up at the towering ceiling of Italian tile or leaning against one of the 22 pillars, each one 40 feet tall and weighing 75 tons. Walk along the lengthy concourse and study the mellow reflection in its walls. Get a sense of the beauty of the light flooding through the high, arched windows at each end of the mammoth hall.

When you look up, you almost expect to see a rose window; instead, you can read the names of the towns and cities of Canada that were served by the two railroads that used Union Station when it first opened. Many of those places are no longer served by trains, which take too long in a world that now seems to travel at the speed of light. That the remarkable structure still remains, its trains (and, more recently, hundreds of very modern subway cars) still chugging back and forth several levels below its glorious canopy, is no thanks to the many local politicians of the 1970s who wanted it torn down. But once again, Torontonians rallied, petitioned, and won the day.

As you come out of Union Station, walk back to Yonge Street and the beautiful **Bank of Montreal** building, at the northwest corner of Front Street. Just steps north of it is a shabby row of shops, which are among the oldest surviving commercial buildings in the city. Many of the original Georgian facades have been drastically altered, but the one- and two-story buildings give you a sense of the scale of buildings from the 1850s and are the last remnants of the early business community of the then-brand-new city of Toronto.

Make a left turn at the first intersection, which is Wellington
16 Street West. **Number 15** is the oldest building on this walk, an elegant stone bank designed in the Greek Revival style. It's one of the earliest (1845!) projects of William Thomas, the talented architect who also designed the St. Lawrence Hall, which we recently visited.

Head back a few steps to Yonge Street and go north again, away from Front Street. On the northeast corner of Yonge and
17 Melinda streets, at 67 Yonge Street, is **Traders Bank,** the first "skyscraper" of the city when it went up in 1905–06, complete with an observation deck. It's fun to see what was considered the CN Tower of the turn of the century. The next building to the north (69 Yonge St.) was built in 1913, and it helped turn the intersection into a grouping of the tallest buildings in North America, outside of Manhattan. After over 75 years, it is still owned by **Canadian Pacific,** the largest private employer in Canada (planes, trains, hotels, and more).

Just across the street, at the southwest corner of King and
18 Yonge streets, is the **Dominion Bank building** (1 King St. W), erected in 1913 by the same architects who designed the voluptuous Bank of Montreal building we saw at Yonge and Front streets. It's a classic Chicago-style skyscraper and is well worth a visit inside. Climb the marble-and-bronze stairway to the opulent banking hall on the second floor, and enjoy the marble floor, marble walls, and the ornate plaster ceiling, which features the coats of arms of the then nine Canadian provinces. (Newfoundland did not join the Confederation until 1949). No, they most certainly do not build places like this anymore.

On the northeast corner of Yonge and King streets (2 King St.
19 E) is the original **Royal Bank building,** also put up in 1913. Note the distinctive cornice, the overhanging roof, the decorative pattern of sculpted ox skulls above the ground-floor windows, and the classically detailed leaves at the top of the Corinthian columns. Greek culture lives!

Walking several blocks farther north along Yonge Street, you
20 reach the original **Simpsons department store,** on the northwest corner of Richmond Street West and Yonge Street (176 Yonge St.). Built in 1895, it was one of the city's first buildings with a steel-frame construction. There are attractive terra-cotta decorations in the section closest to Yonge Street, which went up in 1908; the part along Richmond Street, near Bay Street, added in 1928, is a fine example of the Art Deco style, popular between the two world wars.

Continue a few steps west to Bay Street, a name synonymous with finance and power in Canada, as Wall Street is in the United States. Head south (left), back toward the lakefront. Just south of Adelaide Street, on the west side of Bay Street, is
21 the **Canada Permanent Trust Building** (320 Bay St.). Built in the very year of the stock market crash (and we don't mean the 1987 one), it's a skyscraper in the New York wedding-cake style. Look up at the ornate stone carvings both on the lower stories and on the top, where carved, stylized faces peer down to the street below. Walk through the imposing vaulted entrance with its polished brass doors, and note that even the elevator doors in the foyer are embossed brass. The spacious banking hall has a vaulted ceiling, marble walls and pillars, and

a marble floor with mosaic borders. Those were the days—or so they thought.

Turn right (west) along King Street, and you arrive at the first of the towering bank buildings that have defined Toronto's sky-
22 line over the past two decades. This is **First Canadian Place** (100 King St. W), built in the early 1970s by the firm of Bregman and Hamann, Architects, with consultation from Edward Durrell Stone. Also called the Bank of Montreal tower, its 72 stories were deliberately faced with white marble to contrast with the black of the Toronto-Dominion Centre, to the south, and with the silver of the Commerce Court Tower. The second phase of
23 the project, opened in 1983, houses the ultramodern **Toronto Stock Exchange (TSE).**

The Exchange Tower (2 First Canadian Pl.) has a Visitors' Center that should be visited by anyone interested in the world of high finance. Enter the Exchange Tower and proceed to the TSE reception area on the ground floor. The nearby escalator and circular staircase lead to the Visitors' Center and observation gallery.

This is the pulse of the Canadian economy, where papers fly, traders scoot about, tickers tick away, phones ring off the hooks, and fortunes are made or lost. Here, visitors can learn about the securities industry through colorful displays, or even join in daily presentations. The attractions are many: a 100-foot public gallery. A 140-seat auditorium. Recorded tours. A mini slide show of the TSE 300 Composite Index (an echo of the Dow Jones Average). *Tel. 416/947–4670. Admission free. Open weekdays 10–4. Public tour daily at 2 PM.*

On the northeast corner of King and Bay streets (44 King St.
24 W) is the **Bank of Nova Scotia.** Built between 1949 and 1951, and partially replaced by the recently completed Scotia Tower just to the east, it has sculptural panels inspired by Greek mythology above the large, exterior windows. In the lobby, there are reliefs symbolizing four regions of Canada and a brightly colored gilded plaster ceiling. The original stainless steel and glass stairway with marine motifs is attractive, as are the marble counters and floors. The north wall relief depicts some of the industries and enterprises financed by the bank.

25 On the southeast corner of King and Bay streets is the **"Old" Bank of Commerce Tower,** which for a third of a century was the tallest building in the British Commonwealth. Its base has bas-relief carvings, and marvelous animal and floral ornamentation around the vaulted entrance. Because the top is set back, you must look up to see the huge, carved human heads on all four sides of the building. These are "the wise old men of commerce," who are supposed to be looking out over the city.

26 The **Bank of Commerce building** (25 King St. W) was built in the two years following the stock market crash of 1929, but the hard times didn't prevent the creation of a stunning interior of marble floors, limestone walls, and bronze vestibule doors decorated with masks, owls, and animals. In the alcoves on either side of the entrance are murals that trace the history of transportation. The bronze elevator doors are richly decorated, the vaulted banking hall is lit by period chandeliers, and each desk has its own lamp. What a difference from the often cold, brittle skyscrapers of today!

27 Just south of the "old tower," at 243 Bay Street, is **Commerce Court,** the bank's 57-story stainless-steel sister. And due west, just across Bay Street, also on the south side of King Street,
28 are the two black towers of the **Toronto-Dominion Centre,** the first International Style skyscrapers built in Toronto, thanks to the "less is more" man, Mies van der Rohe. The two towers went up in the mid-1960s, and they are starkly plain and stripped of ornament. The only decoration consists of geometric repetition and the only extravagance is the use of rich materials, such as marble counters and leather-covered furniture.

Immediately south of the T-D Centre towers, at 232 Bay
29 Street, is the **former Toronto Stock Exchange building,** which, for close to half a century, was the financial hub of Toronto. Built in 1937 of polished pink granite and smooth buff limestone, it's a delightful example of Art Deco design. The stainless steel doors are a wonder, as is the wise and witty stone frieze carved above them. Don't miss the hilarious social commentary up there—the banker with the top hat marching behind the laborer, his hand sneaking into the worker's pocket. Only in Canada, where socialism has always been a strong political force, would you find such an artistic statement on the side of a stock exchange!

Walk south another block, still heading toward Lake Ontario, to the northwest corner of Bay and Front streets: There, in all
30 its golden glory, is the **Royal Bank Plaza,** built only in 1976 but already a classic of its kind. Be sure to go into the 120-foot-high banking hall and admire the lovely hanging sculpture by Jesus Raphael Soto.

And there you have our tour of the waterfront, St. Lawrence, and the Financial District, which could take anywhere from several hours to one or two days, depending on whether or not you head off to the Toronto Islands, spend several hours shopping at Harbourfront, or catch some theater and meals along the way. But in all three portions of this walk, you have encountered what makes Toronto so admirable: the coexistence of the city's oldest and newest buildings, often side by side. The fact that many of the older properties have been included on the city's Inventory of Buildings of Architectural and Historical Importance proves just how determined Toronto is not to destroy its history. Only two cheers, though. There was massive destruction of great 19th-century buildings throughout the first quarter of this century; many of their still-striking facades, porticos, and columns can be seen on the grounds of the Guild Inn, in Scarborough, about a half-hour's drive to the northeast of downtown Toronto (*see* Off the Beaten Track in Lodging for more information about that forlorn and often moving collection of architectural artifacts).

And now, if you cross Front Street to its south side and return to Union Station, you can begin another rather fascinating walk—and a very welcome one, should the weather be windy, cold, snowy, slushy, or even too hot: Toronto's Underground City.

Underground City

The origins of Toronto's **Underground City**—purportedly the largest pedestrian walkway in the world, and over four times the size of Montreal's, the world's second largest—go back over a generation, and it somehow all came about with very little assistance from the powers that be. As each major new building went up, the respective developers kept agreeing to interconnect their underground shopping areas, until it finally all came together. One can walk—and shop, eat, browse, etc.—without ever seeing the light of day, from beneath Union Station to the Royal York Hotel, the Toronto-Dominion Centre, First Canadian Place, the Sheraton Centre, Simpsons, the Eaton Centre, and the Atrium. Altogether, it extends through nearly three miles of tunnels and seven subway stops! But these are not the depressing, even dangerous subway tunnels that one encounters in Paris, London, and New York; they are sparklingly clean, and the underground is wall-to-wall with over 300 eateries, shops, banks, even dental offices and theaters.

One can respond with civic pride ("The world's only weatherproof city!" "The ultimate in climate control!") or with cynicism, echoing King Lear's lament over Cordelia: "Why should cars and animals have fresh air while we are forced to live, breathe, and shop underground?" But one is *not* forced, which is part of the Underground City's charm. Shop along the main streets of Toronto as you wish—but isn't it nice to know that there's a subterranean complex, running for dozens of blocks, just a few feet below you? And with Toronto's weather—so often inclement—it's kind of an insurance policy against sudden or insistent storms, or merely the exhaust fumes of cars.

The Underground City has been called a must-see for visitors, but that's debatable; Toronto is so overflowing with attractions and first-class shopping that it's hard to recommend that one rush "downstairs." And, indeed, there are numerous other, but far smaller, underground retail passageways: beneath Bloor Street, running east of Yonge Street; and along College Street, between Yonge and Bay streets. And there are offshoots of the Underground City reaching all the way to the New City Hall and beyond. Enter the subterranean community from anywhere between Dundas Street on the north and Union Station on the south, and you'll encounter everything from art exhibitions to buskers (the city actually auditions young musicians and licenses the best to perform throughout its subway system and elsewhere) to walkways, fountains, and trees growing as much as two stories high. Because up to 50% of the complex lies underneath Toronto's multibillion-dollar Financial District, you will keep bumping into men and women in business suits, browsing or on lunch breaks.

So don't see this so much as a walking tour but rather as a very pleasant option to escape sun, rain, snow, or heat. It's just another example of Toronto's architectural ingenuity—making a city that occasionally lacks a livable climate more livable.

Tour 2: From Eaton Centre to the City Halls and the Far and Middle East

Numbers in the margin correspond with points of interest on the Tours 2 and 3 map.

From the corners of Yonge and Queen streets, one can begin a tour that will include several of this city's most popular attractions, as well as some of its most interesting neighborhoods. Alas, one of these, Eaton Centre, is closed on Sunday, as of this writing, while others thrive on what is still considered the

Lord's Day in the province of Ontario. Still, the following walking/driving tour should make for a very pleasant day in the central and western portions of Toronto's downtown.

Eaton Centre and City Hall

1 **Eaton Centre,** a three-million-square-foot building that extends along the west side of Yonge Street all the way from Queen Street up to Dundas Street (with subway stops at each end), has quickly become the number-one tourist attraction of Toronto. Even people who rank shopping with the flu will still be charmed, even dazzled, for this is a very beautiful environment indeed.

The handsome collection of over 300 stores and services, just a few blocks from Toronto's New City Hall, was quite controversial in the late 1970s, when some Torontonians attacked it as "a sterile and artificial environment." Yet others, like Jane Jacobs, author of *Death and Life of Great American Cities,* wrote that "people like the environment of the Galleria. Its popularity has lessons for Yonge Street."

And lessons for most cities of the world, as well. From its graceful glass roof, arching 127 feet above the lowest of the mall levels, to Michael Snow's exquisite flock of fiberglass Canada geese floating poetically in the open space of the Galleria, to the glass-enclosed elevators, porthole windows, and nearly two dozen long and graceful escalators, there are plenty of good reasons for visiting Eaton Centre.

Such a wide selection of shops and eateries can be confusing, however, so here's a simple rule: Galleria Level 1 contains two food courts; popularly priced fashions; photo, electronics and record stores; and much "convenience" merchandise. Level 2 is directed to the middle-income shopper, while Level 3, suitably, has the highest elevation, fashion, and prices. **Eaton's,** one of Canada's classic department-store chains, has a nine-floor branch here. At the southern end of Level 3 is a skywalk that connects the Centre to the seven-floor **Simpsons** department store, across Queen Street.

Dozens of restaurants, from snack to full-service, can be found here. A 17-theater cinema complex—the initial unit of the now worldwide Cineplex chain—is located at the Dundas Street entrance. (Tuesdays are close-to-half-price days for movie tickets, and it's a cheap 90-minute break from shopping.)

There are safe, well-lighted parking garages sprinkled around the centre, with spaces for some 1,800 cars. *Admission free. Open weekdays 10–9,* Sat. 9:30–6.

Exit the Eaton Centre at Queen Street and walk just one long block west to Toronto's city halls. Yes, the plural is correct.

2 **Old City Hall** is the very beautiful building at the northeast corner of Queen and Bay streets, sweetly coexisting with the
3 futuristic **New City Hall,** just across the street, on the west side.

The creator of the old one, which opened in 1899, was none other than E.J. Lennox, who would later design Casa Loma. It was considered one of North America's most impressive municipal halls in its heyday, and since the opening of its younger sister, it has been the site for the provincial courts, county offices, and thousands of low-cost marriages. Do note the hideous gargoyles above the front steps, which were apparently the ar-

Tour 2
Anshei Minsk, **13**
Art Gallery of Ont., **11**
Chinese Cath. Church, **7**
Chinese Home for the Aged, **8**
Eaton Centre, **1**
52nd Div. Police Sta., **6**
Kensington Mkt., **12**
Kiever Synagogue, **14**
Mirvish Village, **15**
Mon Kuo, **5**
New City Hall, **3**
Old City Hall, **2**
Ont. College of Art, **9**
Shing Wah Daily News, **4**
Village by the Grange, **10**

Tour 3
A&A Records, **39**
Bloor & Yorkville, **32**
Campbell House, **16**
College Park, **37**
Colonnade, **33**
Fisher Library, **23**
Gardiner Mus., **29**
Hart House, **18**
Hazelton Lanes, **35**
Knox College, **20**
McLaughlin Planetarium, **30**
Med. Sci. Bldg., **21**
Metro Toronto Lib., **34**
Ont. Legisl. Bldg., **26**
Parliament Bldg., **27**
Public Relats Ofc., **24**
Queen's Park, **25**
Robarts Library, **22**
Royal Ont. Mus., **28**
Sam the Record Man, **38**
Sigmund Samuel Can. College, **31**
Univ. College, **19**
Univ. Toronto, **17**
Yorkville, **36**

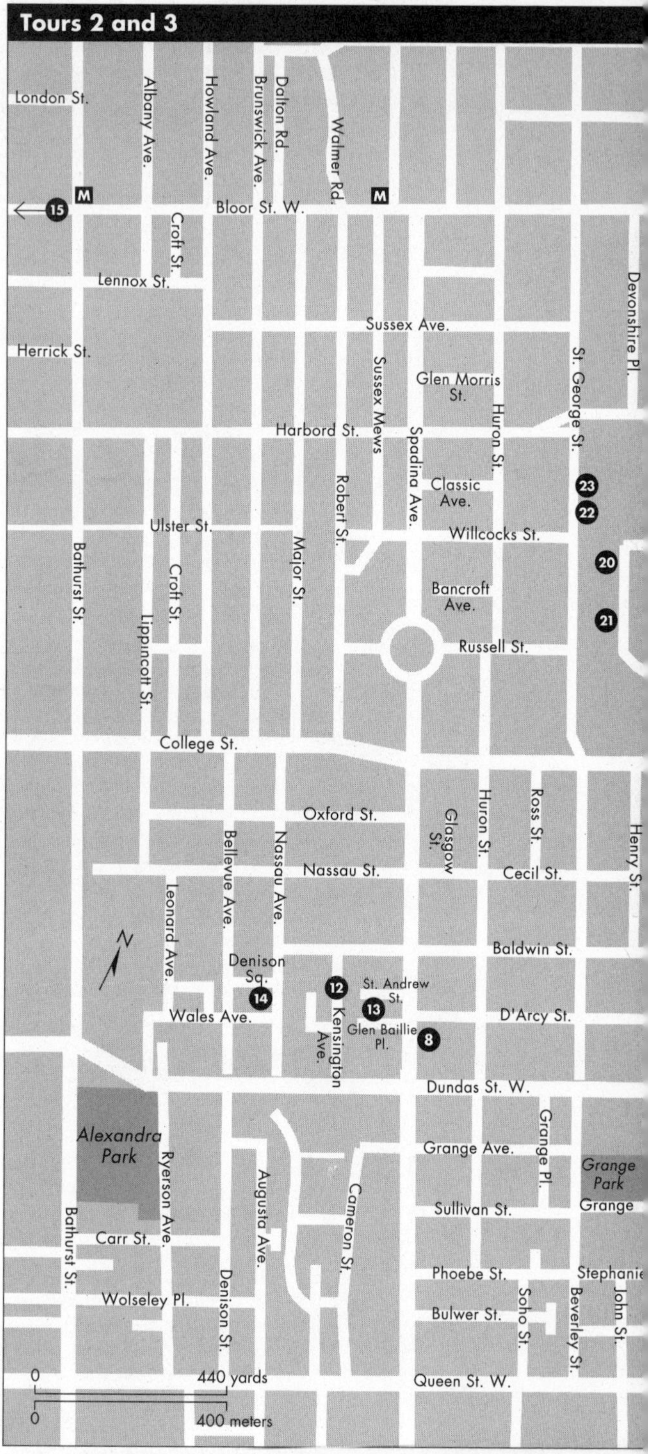

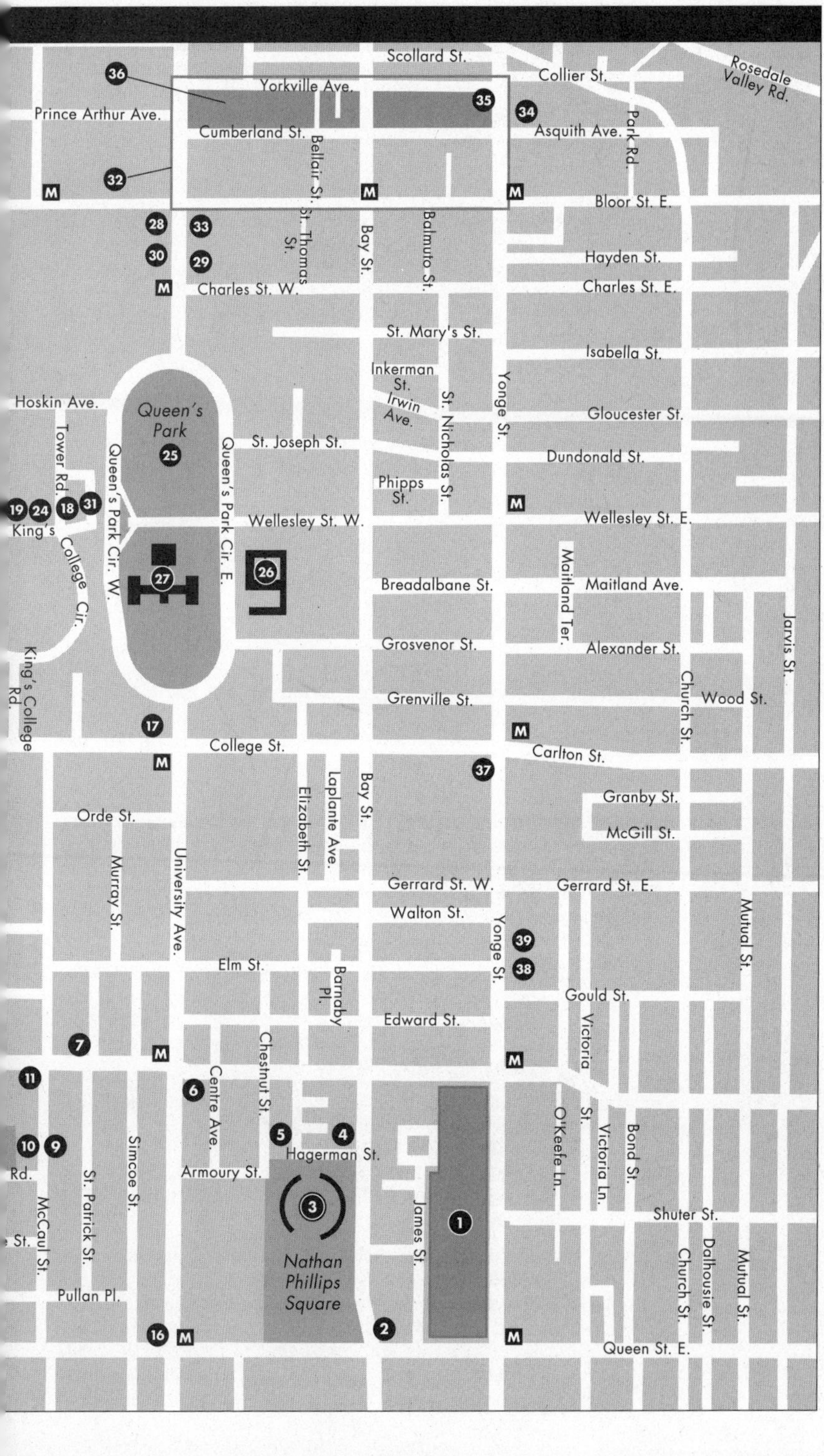
Scollard St.
Collier St.
Rosedale Valley Rd.
Yorkville Ave.
Prince Arthur Ave.
Cumberland St.
Asquith Ave.
Park Rd.
Bellair St.
Bloor St. E.
St. Thomas St.
Bay St.
Balmuto St.
Hayden St.
Charles St. W.
Charles St. E.
St. Mary's St.
Isabella St.
Inkerman St.
Irwin Ave.
St. Nicholas St.
Yonge St.
Hoskin Ave.
Queen's Park
Gloucester St.
Tower Rd.
Queen's Park Cir. W.
St. Joseph St.
Queen's Park Cir. E.
Dundonald St.
Phipps St.
Wellesley St. W.
Wellesley St. E.
King's College Cir.
Breadalbane St.
Maitland Ter.
Maitland Ave.
Grosvenor St.
Alexander St.
Jarvis St.
King's College Rd.
Grenville St.
Church St.
Wood St.
College St.
Carlton St.
Laplante Ave.
Elizabeth St.
Granby St.
Orde St.
McGill St.
Murray St.
University Ave.
Gerrard St. W.
Gerrard St. E.
Walton St.
Mutual St.
Elm St.
Barnaby Pl.
Gould St.
Edward St.
Victoria St.
Chestnut St.
Centre Ave.
O'Keefe Ln.
Victoria Ln.
Bond St.
Simcoe St.
Hagerman St.
Armoury St.
St. Patrick St.
McCaul St.
Shuter St.
James St.
Nathan Phillips Square
Dalhousie St.
Pullan Pl.
Queen St. E.
Rd.
St.
M
1
2
3
4
5
6
7
9
10
11
16
17
18
19
24
25
26
27
28
29
30
31
32
33
34
35
36
37
38
39

chitect's witty way of mocking certain politicians of the time. The designer also carved his name under the eaves on all four faces of the building—a cry for recognition from nearly a century ago. The great stained-glass window as you enter is attractive, and the handsome old structure stands in delightful contrast to its daring and unique sibling.

The New City Hall—humorously described by many as "a urinal for the Jolly Green Giant"—was the result of a massive international competition in 1958, to which some 520 architects from 42 countries submitted designs. The winning presentation by Finnish architect Viljo Revell was very controversial: two towers of differing height, and curved, yet! But there was and is a logic to it all: An aerial view of the New City Hall shows a circular council chamber sitting like an eye between the two tower "eyelids."

Within months of its opening in 1965, the New City Hall became a symbol of a thriving city, with a silhouette as recognizable as, say, the Eiffel Tower. How sad that architect Revell died before his masterwork was opened to the public.

The entire area is a living, breathing environment, with Nathan Phillips Square (named after the mayor who initiated the project) spreading across a nine-acre plaza in front of the building. It has become a true gathering place for the community, whether for royal visits, protest rallies, picnic lunches, or concerts. The reflecting pool is a delight in the summer, and even more so in the winter, when office workers come down and skate during lunch. There is a Peace Garden for quiet meditation, a striking bronze sculpture by famed British sculptor Henry Moore (*The Archer*), and a remarkable mural within the main entrance of the New City Hall, *Metropolis*, put together by sculptor David Partridge from 100,000 common nails.

Annual events at the New City Hall include the Spring Flower Show in late March; the Toronto Outdoor Art Exhibition early each July (the 29th annual one will be in the summer of 1990), and the Cavalcade of Lights from late November through Christmas each year, when over 100,000 sparkling lights are illuminated across both city halls.

Tel. 416/392–7341 for details; for information on facilities for the disabled, 416/392–7732. Underground garage for 2,400 cars. Open to the public weekdays 8:30–4:30. Free 30-minute guided tours on weekdays. Cafeteria in the basement of the New City Hall open daily 7:30–4.

Chinatown and the Museums

Just north of the New City Hall begins Toronto's main **Chinatown,** which is the largest in all of North America—and that includes San Francisco. There are over 100,000 Chinese living in the city, which is not bad, considering that just over a century ago there was only one—Sam Ching, who ran a hand laundry on Adelaide Street.

Today Chinatown covers much of the area of Spadina Avenue from Queen Street to College Street, running along Dundas Street nearly as far east as Bay Street. The old Chinatown used to be stuck behind the Old City Hall, but it was uprooted by the building of the New City Hall, and began to spread to the west. This was helped by the huge influx of Chinese immigrants, which began some two decades ago and still continues. Most come from Hong Kong, bringing money, skills, and intelligence to the already burgeoning community that had been here before.

One of the best times to explore Chinatown is on a Sunday, when, up and down Spadina Avenue and along Dundas Street, Chinese music blasts from storefronts, cash registers ring, abacuses clack, and bakeries, markets, herbalists, and restaurants do their best business of the week.

But whatever day you wander through Toronto's impressive Chinatown—we recommend that you start on Elizabeth Street, just north of the New City Hall, and walk north to Dundas Street, east toward Bay Street, and west to Spadina Avenue. You will be thrilled by the diversity, the excitement, the liveliness—the sheer foreignness of it all! (Remember the cliché: If the United States is a melting pot, Canada is a mosaic —with each piece maintaining its individuality and differences.)

4 The **Shing Wah Daily News** on Hagerman Street, near Bay Street, due north of the New City Hall (tel. 416/977–3745) will show you some of the 10,000 Chinese characters being typeset and printed, plus samples of Blondie and Dagwood speaking
5 Cantonese. **Mon Kuo Trading Co. Ltd.** (120 Elizabeth St., also just north of New City Hall) cultivates tens of thousands of bean sprouts under a sprinkler system in the basement, on their one-week growth to maturity.

On Dundas Street, you'll pass shops selling reasonably priced silk blouses and antique porcelain; silk kimonos for less than half the price elsewhere; lovely saki sets; and ladies' suits made
6 from silk. Huge Chinese characters hang over the **52nd Division police station,** a large building on the west side of University Avenue, on the south side of Dundas Street. Many of the banks still have abacuses, to help those who prefer to use 4,000-year-old "hand-held calculators" over the modern ones.

7 Just to the north, on St. Patrick Street, is the **Chinese Catholic**
8 **Church.** Over on D'Arcy Street is the modern **Chinese home for the aged,** with charming crafts rooms, hydroponic gardens, and lots of goldfish, because an Eastern tradition has it that every time a goldfish dies, a human being is guaranteed long life.

9 Just to the south of Dundas Street is the **Ontario College of Art** (100 McCaul St.), one of the major colleges of animation, design, advertising art, tapestry, glassblowing, sculpture, and
10 painting in Canada. Directly across the street is **Village by the Grange** (89 McCaul St.), an apartment-and-shopping complex that contains more than a hundred shops selling everything from ethnic fast food to serious art. It's a perfect example of what more cities need in their downtown areas: a wise, careful blending of the commercial and the residential.

11 Return to Dundas Street, and head west to the **Art Gallery of Ontario,** which has been slowly but steadily evolving into one of the better art museums in North America. From extremely modest beginnings in 1900, the AGO is now in the big leagues in terms of exhibits and support. Its membership of over 25,000 is one of the largest among the continent's museums, and recent international exhibits of King Tut, van Gogh, Turner, Judy Chicago, William Blake, and Picasso will give you an idea of the gallery's importance, image, and profile.

In 1988, the AGO began its "Stage 3 expansion," costing $28 million, to be completed in 1991. This will increase its exhibition space by nearly 50% and will include new galleries for contemporary art, Inuit art, and an indoor sculpture court. But this in no way denies the excellence of its over 10,000 art treasures of today.

The **Henry Moore Sculpture Centre** on the second floor has the largest public collection of Moore's sculpture in the world. (Do not miss Moore's large *Two Forms*, which stands outside the AGO, at the southwest corner of McCaul Street. Adults as well as children love to climb in and around it.)

Also on the second floor is the **Samuel and Ayala Zacks Wing**, with its fine collection of 20th-century sculpture. The **Canadian Wing** includes major works by such northern lights as Emily Carr, Cornelius Krieghoff, David Milne, and Homer Watson, plus a broad selection from the Group of Seven, which is no rock group—although they *did* paint rocks. On the lower level is a "hands on" room where kids are invited to paint, make slides, and otherwise creatively muck about (open Sundays, summers, and holidays).

The Art Gallery of Ontario also has a growing collection of Rembrandt, Hals, Van Dyck, Hogarth, Reynolds, Chardin, Renoir, de Kooning, Rothko, Oldenburg, Picasso, Rodin, Degas, Matisse, and many others. And it also has **The Grange**, a historic house located just behind the AGO, in a large park. (Its joys are described in Historic Buildings and Sites, and its admission is included with that of the AGO.) In early 1989, the AGO unveiled a new, computerized reinstallation of paintings and sketches by Tom Thomson and the Group of Seven. Installed near some of the oil sketches, there are computers and telephones that give simple messages about the paintings and related topics as well as explanatory material.

The AGO, 317 Dundas St. W, 3 blocks west of the St. Patrick station of the University subway line; tel. 416/977–0414. Admission: $4.50 adults, $2.50 children 12–18 and senior citizens, $9 families. These prices may rise slightly during 1990. Free Wed. after 5:30 PM; free Fri. for senior citizens. Open Tues.–Sun. 11–5:30, Wed. until 9. Closed Christmas, Dec. 26, New Year's Day, Jan. 2.

Across from the AGO and The Grange is Village by the Grange, as noted above. It is a perfect place to browse, either before or after a visit to the art gallery.

Check out some of the commercial art galleries on the north side of Dundas Street, across from the AGO, many of which display classical and contemporary Chinese paintings. Then head west, back through Chinatown. **Champion House** (478 Dundas St. W, near Spadina) is a good bet for lunch.

Spadina and the Marketplaces

Toronto's widest street, **Spadina Avenue**, has been pronounced "Spa-*dye*-nah" for a century and a half, and we are too polite to point out that it really should be called "Spa-*dee*-na." To explain why it's 48 meters (149 feet) wide, double the width of almost every other vintage street in town, we have to go back to 1802, when a 27-year-old Irish physician named William Warren Baldwin came to Muddy York. He soon married a very rich young woman, built a pleasant home where Casa Loma now sits, and decided to cut a giant swath through the forest from

Bloor Street down to Queen Street so they could look down—literally and socially—on Lake Ontario. Alas, their view disappeared in 1874, when a thankless granddaughter sold the land at the crescent just above College Street for the site of Knox College, which moved to the University of Toronto campus several decades later. Now covered with vines, the Victorian college building still sits in the crescent, a number of the chestnut trees planted by Dr. Baldwin still stand on the west side of the crescent. Little else remains of Dr. Baldwin's Spadina, except for a handful of Victorian mansions.

Spadina, running from Queen Street north to College Street, has never been fashionable, or even worth a visit by most tourists. Way back, it was just a collection of inexpensive stores, factories that sold to you wholesale if you had connections, ethnic food and fruit stores, and eateries that gave you your 2¢ worth, usually plain.

And so it remains, with the exception of some often first-class, if modest-looking, Chinese restaurants sprinkled throughout the area. Each new wave of immigrants—Jewish, Chinese, Portuguese, East and West Indian, South American—added its own flavor to the mix, but Spadina-Kensington's basic bill of fare is still "bargains galore." Here you'll find gourmet cheeses at gourmet prices, fresh (no, not fresh-frozen) ocean fish, fine European kitchenware at half the price of stores in the Yorkville area, yards of remnants piled high in bins, designer clothes minus the labels, and the occasional rock-and-roll night spot and interesting greasy spoon.

For any visitor who plans to be in Toronto for over four or five days, a few hours exploring the ins and outs of the garment district could bring great pleasure—and even greater bargains. Park your car at the lot just west of Spadina Avenue on St. Andrew's Street (a long block north of Dundas St.), or take the College or Queen streetcar to Spadina Avenue. Be warned: This area can be extraordinarily crowded on weekends, when smart suburbanites head here for top-quality luggage and handbags at unbelievably low prices; wholesale dry-goods stores overflowing with brand-name socks, underwear, and towels; designer jeans and jackets; women's evening wear, coats, sportswear, and dresses; new and used furs; and more.

We cannot resist mentioning a few of our favorites. **Slack's Wholesale** (323 Spadina Ave., tel. 416/977–3619), just north of Dundas Street, could be the best and lowest priced children's clothing shop in the city. **Fortune Housewares** (388 Spadina Ave., tel. 416/593–6999), is possibly the best kitchenware shop in Toronto. There's a good selection of cookbooks, too, and the staff is both knowledgeable and helpful. Also recommended is the new **Dragon City Food Court** (tel. 416/977–2368), located on the southwest corner of Dundas and Spadina, where 11 independent outlets offer a kaleidoscope of exotic Asian foods. It is open daily 10 AM–midnight.

12 And then there's **Kensington Market**, a delightful side tour off Spadina Avenue. Here, the bargains are of the more edible kind. All your senses will be titillated by this old, steamy, smelly, raucous, colorful, European-style marketplace. Come and explore, especially during warmer weather, when the goods pour out into the narrow streets: Russian rye breads, barrels of dill pickles, fresh fish on ice, mountains of cheese,

bushels of ripe fruit, and crates of chickens and rabbits that will have your children both giggling and horrified.

Kensington Market sprang up just after the turn of the century, when Russian, Polish, and Jewish inhabitants set up stalls in front of their houses. Since then, the market—named after the area's major street, just west of Spadina Avenue—has become a United Nations of stores. Unlike the UN, however, these people get along fabulously with one another. Jewish and Eastern European stores sit side by side with Portuguese, Caribbean, Latin American, and East Indian stores—with Vietnamese, Japanese, and Chinese establishments sprinkled throughout. Most shops are open every day except Sunday, from as early as 6 AM.

Lovers of religious architecture may wish to visit the two hauntingly attractive old synagogues in the market area:
13 **Anshei Minsk** (10 St. Andrew's St., just west of Spadina Ave.)
14 and, just a few short blocks away, the **Kiever Synagogue** (corner of Denison Sq. and Bellevue Ave.).

Afterward, you can rest in **Bellevue Square** (corner of Denison Sq. and Augusta Pl.), a lovely little park with shady trees, benches, and a wading pool and playground for kids.

15 **Mirvish** (or **Markham**) **Village** is a small, delightful tourist area —ut no tourist trap!—one block west of Bathurst Street, running south from Bloor Street. It is open on Sundays.

The history is interesting: Ed Mirvish is an inspired capitalist who has run a big, ugly, barnlike bargain-basement store called **Honest Ed's** for the past four decades. The place is nothing special; Americans have its equivalent in every city (although his sheer vulgarity is disarming; the world's largest neon sign on his store screams out such sayings as "Honest Ed's no midwife . . . but the bargains he delivers are real babies"). As if to make up for the crudeness of his selling techniques (which include daily "door crashers," such as five pounds of white flour for 79¢), Mirvish saved the magnificent Royal Alexandra Theatre from destruction, and he even decided to purchase the venerable Old Vic, in London, England. When Mirvish tried to tear down all the houses on the block behind his store to build a parking lot, he was prevented by zoning bylaws. No problem: He thought up the brilliant alternative of Mirvish, or Markham, Village. By officially being declared a tourist attraction, the village could legally be open on Sundays; and so, though it is in the unfashionable Bloor/Bathurst area, it can be a lifesaver for weekend visitors with time to kill. Most stores are open daily 10–6 (*see* Shopping).

Ed's Ice Cream Parlour (corner of Bloor and Markham Sts.) has cappuccino and, of course, the cold stuff. **The Children's Book Store** calls itself the largest children's bookstore in the world, and carries books from all *over* the world. Folksingers, artists, and writers often make personal appearances to sing, show off, or read from their works, usually on Sundays. This place is a beauty—the Louvre of kiddie lit. The irresistible **Memory Lane** sells vintage movie posters and old comic books and magazines. **David Mirvish Books on Art,** run by Ed's son, has many remaindered books at shockingly low prices, as well as a fine collection of new volumes.

Before you turn back to Bloor Street, note the wonderful house at the corner of Markham and Lennox streets: the hexagonal corner tower, the fine leaded-glass butterfly window to one side of its front door, and the stunning oval window on the other. This is old Toronto architecture at its most attractive.

Tour 3: Academia, Culture, Commercialism, Crassness

Numbers in the margin correspond with points of interest on the Tours 2 and 3 map.

University Avenue, running from Front Street for about three miles north to Bloor Street, where it changes its name to Avenue Road and continues north, is one of Toronto's few mistakes. It's horribly boring, with hospital after office building after insurance company after office building. Yet it is still an interesting start for a healthy walk, because it does have lovely flowerbeds and fountains in a well-maintained strip along its middle. Still, you may wish to drive this part of the tour.

16 One highlight is **Campbell House** (northwest corner of Queen St. and University Ave.), the stately Georgian mansion of Sir William Campbell, the sixth chief justice of Upper Canada. Built in 1822 and tastefully restored with elegant 18th- and early 19th-century furniture, it is one of Toronto's most charming "living museums." Costumed hostesses will tell you about the social life of the upper class. Note the model of the town of York as it was in the 1820s, and the original, restored kitchen sans Cuisinart! *Tel. 416/597–0227. Admission: $1.50 adults; 75¢ students and senior citizens. Guided tours available. Open Oct.–mid May, weekdays 9:30 AM–12:30 PM, and 2:30–4:30 PM; summers, weekdays 9:30 AM–12:30 PM and 2–4:30, weekends noon–4:30.*

17 College Street is the southern boundary of the **University of Toronto.** A city the size of Toronto is too large to be labeled a college town, but with a staff and student population of over 50,000, and over 225 buildings on three campuses, the university is almost a city in itself.

It goes back to 1827, when King George IV signed a charter for a "King's College in the Town of York, Capital of Upper Canada." The Church of England had control then, but by 1850 the college was proclaimed nondenominational, renamed the University of Toronto, and put under the control of the province. And then, in a spirit of good Christian competition, the Anglicans started Trinity College, the Methodists began Victoria, and the Roman Catholics begat St. Michael's; by the time the Presbyterians founded Knox College, the whole thing was almost out of hand.

But not really: The 17 schools and faculties are now united, and they welcome anyone who can pass its entrance exams and afford the tuition, which, thanks to generous government funding, is still only about $1,500 a year.

The architecture is interesting, if uneven—yours would be, too, if you'd been built in bits and pieces over 150 years. We recommend a walking tour. Enter the campus just behind the Parliament buildings, where Wellesley Street ends. Go under the bridge, past the guardhouse (whose keeper will not let you pass if you are encased in an automobile), and turn right, around King's College Circle.

18 At the top of the circle is **Hart House,** a Gothic-style student center built during the teens of this century by the Masseys—the folks who brought us Massey-Ferguson farm equipment, Massey Hall, Vincent Massey (a governor-general of Canada), and Raymond Massey, the actor. It was once an all-male enclave, today anyone may visit the Great Hall and the library, both self-conscious imitations of Oxford and Cambridge. Check out the dining hall for its amazing stained-glass windows as well as its food, which is cheap and rather good.

As you continue around King's College Circle, you'll see on
19 your right the Romanesque **University College,** built in 1859.
20 Next is **Knox College,** whose Scottish origins are evident in the bagpipe music that escapes from the building at odd hours. It's been training ministers since 1844, although the building went up only yesterday—1915.

21 You may well wish to tip your hat to the **Medical Sciences Building,** which is no beauty but is where, in 1921, Drs. Banting, Best, and others discovered the insulin that has saved the lives of tens of millions of diabetics around the world.

Just a few hundred yards west is St. George Street and the
22 23 **Robarts Research Library,** and **Thomas Fisher Rare Books Library,** (*see* Libraries and Special Collections in Sites and Attractions).

There is lots more to see and do around the main campus of the
24 University of Toronto. Visit the **Public and Community Relations Office** (Room 133S, 27 King's College Circle, tel. 416/978–2021), across the field from Hart House, and pick up free maps of the school grounds. Guided one-hour walking tours are held on summer weekdays, setting out from the map room of Hart House at 10:30, 12:30, and 2:30 (tel. 416/978–5000).

Back at College Street and University Avenue, you can see the Victorian structure of the Parliament buildings to the north, with Queen's Park just north of them.

Queen's Park

There are a number of meanings to **Queen's Park,** for the native
25 Torontonian as well as the visitor. The term can refer to a charming circular park just a few hundred yards southeast of the Royal Ontario Museum (on University Ave., just below Bloor St.). This is a grand place to rest your feet after a long day of shopping or visiting the Royal Ontario Museum. But
26 Queen's Park also refers to the **Ontario Legislative Building,** which is nothing less than what Albany is to New York State or Lansing is to Michigan: the home of the provincial parliament. The mammoth building was opened back in 1893, a century ago, and is really quite extraordinary, with its rectangular towers, triangled roofs, and circular and oval glass. Like the New City Hall, it was the product of an international contest among architects; it was won, naturally, by a young Briton who was residing in Buffalo, New York.

27 The **Parliament Building** itself looks grotesque to some, with its pink exterior and heavy, almost Romanesque quality. But a close look will show the beautifully complex detail carved in its stone, and on the inside there are huge, lovely halls that echo

half a millennium of English architecture. (The pink color does not necessarily reflect the politics of the men and women within, by the way; that's the color of Ontario's sandstone.)

Do go inside; the long hallways are hung with hundreds of oils by Canadian artists, most of which capture scenes of the province's natural beauty. Should you choose to take one of the frequent (and free) tours, you will see the chamber where the 130 elected representatives from across Ontario, called MPPs (Members of Provincial Parliament), meet on a regular basis. There are two heritage rooms—one each for the parliamentary histories of Britain and Ontario—filled with old newspapers, periodicals, and pictures. And the lobby holds a fine collection of minerals and rocks of the province.

On the lawn in front of the Parliament buildings, facing College Street, are many statues, including one of Queen Victoria and one of Canada's first prime minister, Sir John A. Macdonald.

Tel. 416/965–4028. Guided tours from mid-May to Labor Day, daily on the hour 9–4; frequent tours the rest of the year; also at 6:45 PM *when evening sessions are held. Queen's Park can be reached via the University Ave. subway; get off at College St. and walk north 1 block. If you drive, there are parking lots in the area, and meters around Queen's Park Circle.*

28 Just to the northwest of Queen's Park is the world-class **Royal Ontario Museum.** Its supporters pointed out that "ROM wasn't built in a day" during a major fund-raising effort earlier this decade. How true. Although once labeled "Canada's single greatest cultural asset" by the Canada Council, the museum floundered throughout much of its existence, which began in 1912 (the same day the *Titanic* sank). It never stopped collecting—always with brilliance—reaching over six million items altogether. But by the 1970s, the monstrous building had had leaky roofs, no climate control, and had little space to display its glorious treasures.

What a difference just $80 million can make! Today, at last, the museum has the space it needs, and when expansion is completed sometime in the 1990s, the ROM will be the second-largest museum in North America, after New York's Metropolitan Museum of Art.

What makes the ROM so unique is the fact that science, art, and archaeology exhibits are all under one roof. The **Dinosaur Collection** will stun children and adults alike. The **Evolution Gallery** has an ongoing audiovisual program on Darwin's theories of evolution. The **Roman Gallery** has the most extensive collection of Roman artifacts in Canada. The **Textile Collection** has been ranked fifth in the world in size and scope. The collection of **Chinese art and antiquities** is one of the finest this side of Beijing. And the **European Musical Instruments Gallery** has a revolutionary audio system and over 1,200 instruments dating back to the late 16th century.

The **Discovery Gallery** allows children (over age 6) to handle objects from the ROM's collections and to study them, using microscopes, ultraviolet light, and magnifying glasses.

The new **Bat Cave,** opened in early 1988, contains 4,000 freeze-dried and artificial bats in a lifelike presentation. Piped-in narration directs visitors on a 15-minute walk through a dimly lit replica of an eight-foot-high limestone tunnel in Jamaica, filled with sounds of dripping water and bat squeaks. Yes, the dinosaurs and mummies have a new rival in popularity.

From a massive Ming tomb to an Islamic home, from Egyptian mummies to a Buddhist temple, from a towering totem pole to suits of armor, the Royal Ontario Museum is simply fabulous. The **Mankind Discovering Gallery** tells about the museum itself and helps one choose what to see.

ROM (tel. 416/586–5549) open daily 10–6 (Tues. and Thurs. until 8). Closed New Year's Day. Admission: $5 adults, $2.50 children, students, and senior citizens; $10 maximum for a family. These prices could well increase slightly during 1990. Free Tues. for senior citizens, after 4:30 Tues. for the general public. Discovery Gallery open Sept.–June weekdays noon–4, weekends and holidays 1–5; July–Aug. weekdays 11 AM. *To get there, take the University subway to the Museum stop; parking is expensive.*

29 The **George R. Gardiner Museum of Ceramic Art** has now merged with the ROM, meaning that it costs not a penny more to visit a magnificent $25-million collection of rare European ceramics. The collection features 17th-century English delftware and 18th-century yellow European porcelain. Most popular is the second-floor display of Italian commedia del l'arte figures, especially Harlequin. *Located across the street from the ROM, on the east side of University Ave., just south of Bloor St. Same hours as the ROM.*

30 Next door to the ROM, to its south, is the **McLaughlin Planetarium,** which attracts some 250,000 visitors a year. There are four new 45-minute star shows each year. Open since 1986 is the **Astrocentre,** which has hands-on exhibits, computer terminals designed for both adults and children, and an animated model of the star system. *The planetarium (tel. 416/586–5536) has the same hours as the ROM, plus evening hours for the star shows. Admission: $4 adults; $2.50 children, students, and senior citizens. Senior citizens free on Tues. A combined admission ticket is available to ROM and planetarium, should you plan to visit both on the same day. Tel. 416/586–5751 for a taped description of the current night sky.*

A five-minute walk due south of the planetarium will bring you
31 to the **Sigmund Samuel Canadiana Collection,** which is also part of the ROM and may be seen at no extra charge. Here is where you can view early Canadian furnishings, glassware, silver, and six settings of furniture displayed in typical 18th- and 19th-century homes. *14 Queen's Park Crescent W, on the northwest corner of University Ave. and College St. Open Mon.–Sat. 10–5, Sun., 1–5.*

After so much culture, you may wish to enjoy one of the most
32 dynamic and expensive areas of Toronto—**Bloor and Yorkville.** A recent article in one of Toronto's newspapers began, "If Imelda Marcos came to Toronto, she would shop on Bloor St. W. This is the home of the $1,300 loafers, the $110,000 fur coat, the $350 belt, and the $14,000 travel trunk, a chic zone where style is everything and cost is no object."

Not every store on these half-dozen-plus blocks between University Avenue and Yonge Street—and the two blocks running north and parallel to them—is so costly, but when monthly rents go above $100 per square foot, one can't sell discount, can one?

When Joseph Bloor made his brewery fortune and built his family home on this street over a century ago, how was he to know that his name would become synonymous with success and high fashion? Had he known, he would never have sold an inch of his property, that's for sure.

Some call it Toronto's Rodeo Drive; others call it Toronto's Fifth Avenue. (Smug Torontonians have been known to call Fifth Avenue New York's Bloor Street, but that may be pushing it.) One thing is certain: These blocks are packed with high-price stores specializing in designer clothes, furs, jewels, specialty shops, ritzy restaurants, and more.

33 **The Colonnade,** on the south side of Bloor Street, a few doors east of University Avenue, has recently undergone a $10-million face-lift. In addition to several levels of luxury residential apartments and private offices, it also has more than two floors of stores selling quality leather goods, perfumes, jewelry, and European apparel.

Along the south side of Bloor Street are such stores as **Zoe,** with haute couture designs; **Creed's,** for over seven decades the place for the latest fashions in furs, accessories, sportswear, lingerie, and shoes; **Sportables** (in the handsome Manulife Centre, at the southeast corner of Bloor and Bay Sts.), which has sophisticated sportswear for men and women; **The Bay** (at the northeast corner of Bloor and Yonge Sts.), a department store with elegant, high-fashion designer clothes for men and women; **Holt Renfrew,** possibly the most stunning store in Toronto, with marble, chrome, glass, and glittering fashions for both sexes; **Eddie Bauer,** selling sturdily made and cleverly designed clothing, equipment, and accessories for all sports; **William Ashley,** which has the finest quality china, crystal, and silver available in Canada, at competitive prices; **David's,** with the finest footwear at the highest prices; and **Bowring,** which has linens, cookware, woodenware, china, crystal, and interesting accessories. **110 Bloor Street West** (near the northeast corner of Avenue Rd. and Bloor St., almost across from The Colonnade) is a dazzling complex of condos, offices, and retail shops ranging from **Rodier Paris** to **Celine.**

A block north of Bloor and Yonge streets is the magnificent
34 **Metropolitan Toronto Library.** Arranged around a tall and wide interior atrium, the library gives a fabulous sense of open space. It was designed by one of Canada's most admired architects, Raymond Moriyama, who also created the Ontario Science Centre. Among the highlights is a fascinating fabric sculpture, *Lyra*, designed by artist Aiko Suzuki. Overhanging the pool and waterfall in the foyer, it was meant to create a transition from the bustle of Yonge Street to the quiet library. It took eight months to complete—the artist walking over 250 miles back and forth in her studio to create it. Glass-enclosed elevators glide swiftly and silently up and down one side of the atrium, allowing you to admire the beautiful banners that hang from the ceiling, announcing the collections on each floor.

Browsers will appreciate that fully one-third of the more than 1.3 million books—spread across 28 miles of shelves—are open to the public. The many audio carrels have headphones, which you may use to listen to any one of over 10,000 albums.

The **Arthur Conan Doyle Room** will be of special interest to Baker Street regulars. It houses the finest public collection of Holmesiana anywhere, with records, films, photos, books, manuscripts, letters, and even cartoon books starring *Sesame Street's* Sherlock Hemlock. *789 Yonge St., just steps north of Bloor St., tel. 416/393–7000. Open weekdays 10–9, Sat. 10–6, Sun. (Oct.–Apr.) 1:30–5. To get an answer to any question, on any subject, tel. 416/393–7131.*

Back on the east side of Avenue Road, two blocks north of Bloor Street and two blocks west of the Metro Library, is a real don't-miss shopping area—**Hazelton Lanes** (416/968–8600). Offering everything from Swiss chocolates to Hermès silks and Giorgio Armani's latest fashions, this is a wonderful, magical paean to capitalism. And in 1989 it doubled, in size and glory, with the addition of some 80 new stores.

35

36 And then there is what is still called **Yorkville,** which runs along the street of the same name, between Avenue Road and Yonge Street, but also includes Cumberland, Bellair, Bay, Scollard, and Hazelton streets. This little gathering of low-rise buildings, mostly old Victorian town houses turned into marvelous storefronts, has gone through many changes over the years: from a conservative middle-class residential district, to the gathering place for Ontario's revolutionaries, drug pushers, hippies, runaway kids, and avant-garde artists, to what it is today—a very chic, very expensive shopping district. (A century ago, it was a real village, just north of Toronto, with its own town hall, planked sidewalks, and horse-drawn streetcars linking it to the city's downtown.)

All along these streets—especially Cumberland and Yorkville—you will find many of Toronto's finest commercial art galleries (*see* Art Galleries in Sites and Attractions). Just to the south is the best shopping in the city (with the exception of Bloor St.).

For a sense of what all this costly beauty was like before haute couture moved in, walk along Scollard and Berryman streets, just north of Yorkville Street. The rows of Victorian houses will be a rest for your overworked eyes and pocketbooks. Should you want to experience the seedy side of this rather uptight town, simply head over to Yonge Street and walk slowly south from Bloor Street as far as you desire. It's called The Strip, although it really doesn't strip anymore; there was quite a movement to clean it up back in the 1970s. (This is Toronto, Canada, not the average American city; when one cleans up in a place like this, one starts at a much cleaner level of dirtiness.)

Still, by the time you reach Dundas Street, some two miles to the south, you'll have passed the soft-core-porn bookstores, the movie houses, the pinball arcades, the harmonica-playing vagabonds, the street vendors peddling jewelry, the hustlers and whores, the endless rows of fast-food dives, the occasional future politician, and the ubiquitous patroling cops (who are, in Toronto, there when you need them, though you rarely do).

No, Times Square this isn't. Back in the early 1970s, The Strip did indeed radiate a sense of vulgarity, danger, and despair; today, it has more the air of a tacky carnival. Three million dollars was spent refurbishing streets adjoining Yonge Street, adding trees, benches, outdoor cafés, and Victorian-style lampposts to create a fresher look. And, in the great tradition of keeping the downtown of Toronto healthy, many thousands of people keep moving to within a few blocks of this major street, making it more and more a living community. The massage parlors have long been closed and most heavy drug peddlers are gone. Yonge Street today is a safe area packed with people—both residents and visitors—enjoying the punk rockers, the far-out clothing shops, and the raucous music blaring from many of the storefronts. It's certainly Toronto's *liveliest* street, if also its most vulgar and least "Toronto-like."

37 You really should not miss **College Park,** at the southwest corner of Yonge and College streets. This building, complete with marble walls and brass railings, was a major Eaton's department store from 1930 to the late '70s, when the chain put most of its marbles (and money) into the gigantic Eaton Centre, just a few blocks to the south. But would Toronto *dare* to tear down such an architectural wonder? Not on your life! They simply redid it brilliantly, renamed it College Park, and filled it with dozens of beautiful stores and eateries—one more example of how cities can preserve their pasts while they march proudly into the future.

Just before you reach the Eaton Centre, on the east side of Yonge Street, are two major record stores—among the largest
38 on the North American continent—**Sam the Record Man** (347
39 Yonge St.) and **A & A Records and Tapes** (351 Yonge St.). Both are open late every night but Sunday.

And that's the Yonge Street walk. Do you feel dirty all over? Are you worried that we won't respect you anymore? Not at all. If it will make you feel better, think historic: You have just walked the street where Canada's first streetcar line was inaugurated in 1861; where the first section of road in British North America was macadamized and tested in 1833; and where the first subway line in all of Canada was built, in the early 1950s.

Feel better now?

Tour 4: Toronto's Finest Neighborhoods

Numbers in the margin correspond with points of interest on the Tour 4: The Neighborhoods map.

The major reason for Toronto's success as a city is its inspired preservation of handsome, clean, safe neighborhoods—often just steps from the heart of its vibrant, booming downtown. Many of these neighborhoods are practically little villages in their own right (indeed, many of them began that way). But because they are sprinkled across the city, it is difficult to walk to most of them, even if every single one is well worth walking through.

What we've done is to gather together several of Toronto's most interesting neighborhoods: (1) Rosedale, (2) Forest Hill, (3) the Annex and Casa Loma, (4) the Beaches, (5) Cabbagetown, and (6) others with a distinct ethnic flavor.

Rosedale Morley Callaghan, the Toronto author who used to box with Ernest Hemingway and quarrel with F. Scott Fitzgerald, called the neighborhood "a fine and private place." Others have called it Blueblood Alley or Millionaire Row. But whatever it is called, most of it is exceptionally beautiful and, once again, just blocks from the heart of downtown Toronto.

1 The place is **Rosedale,** the posh residential area of Toronto and still the symbol of old money. For visitors, Rosedale is a lovely place to walk, bike, or drive and admire the handsome, oversize houses. The neighborhood is bounded by Yonge Street on the west, the Don Valley Parkway on the east, St. Clair Avenue to the north, and the Rosedale Ravine (just above Bloor St. E) to the south. It is as if Mother Nature herself planted ravines around the area to keep out the riffraff.

Some years ago, a child of the privileged wrote a pithy article entitled "Rosedale Ain't What It Used to Be," and, in fact, it ain't. Many of the old families have gone, and their mansions have been chopped up into expensive flats. Pseudo-Georgian town houses have sprouted up in side gardens, like so many weeds.

Speaking of gardens, that's where this original Suburb of the Rich and Famous got its name. Rosedale began as the country estate of Sheriff William Jarvis, one of the powers that were, back in the 1820s. He brought his wife, Mary, to settle on the 200-acre estate, and she named her home Rosedale because of the wild roses that blossomed in profusion. Most of the roses are gone now; so are the magnificent elms that once lined Elm Avenue—including the famous Rosedale Elm, planted by Mary Jarvis herself back in 1835. Dutch elm disease hit even the very rich during the last generation.

Yet, there is surely not another metropolis in North America that maintains such an upper-class neighborhood just steps from the city's heart—a jumble of Edwardian, Victorian, Georgian, and Tudor. And massive maple trees cast their heavenly shade upon it all.

The heart of Rosedale is just a few yards north of the Castle Frank subway station on the Bloor Line. Walk up Castle Frank to Hawthorne Gardens. On the northeast corner of the two streets stands the old Seagram (as in booze) mansion, which was converted into five condominiums back in the early 1980s. Two doors north, along Castle Frank, is the impressive home of the Thomson family, the people who brought us *The London Times*, the Hudson's Bay Company, and some three dozen papers across North America, including *The Globe and Mail.* From here, follow your inclination along Elm Avenue, Milkman's Road, Craigleigh Gardens, and South Drive.

Another way to get to Rosedale (other than inheriting several million dollars) is via Roxborough Street or Crescent Road, just eight blocks north of Bloor Street, going east from Yonge Street. It is easy to find, because there is a Rosedale subway stop on the Yonge Line. Just follow the streets down and around all the ravines. Some of our favorites—all blooming with gigantic mansions—are Beaumont Road, a cul-de-sac called Old George Place, and a little park called Craigleigh Gardens. Listen carefully and you may just hear the delicate clicking of teacups as they are set down on their Wedgwood saucers.

Forest Hill

The closest rival to Rosedale in prestige is an area about two miles to the north and west of Yonge and Bloor streets
2 called **Forest Hill.** A sense of this community can be obtained by recalling a Great Controversy back in 1982: Would the former village of Forest Hill continue to have backyard garbage pick-

up, or would the villagers have to (gulp!) drag their rubbish out front like everyone else in Metro Toronto? The City Council finally voted to continue the special service, on the principle that "invisible garbage" was one of the unwritten terms of Forest Hill's amalgamation with Toronto, in 1968.

This golden square of about 940 acres is bounded by Bathurst Street on the west, Avenue Road on the east, Eglinton Avenue on the north, and St. Clair Avenue West on the south. Today Forest Hill is home to approximately 25,000 rather well-heeled people, although it numbered but some 2,100 souls in 1923 when it chose to become a village on its own. Its first reeve passed a bylaw requiring that a tree be planted in front of every house; you can see the shady results of his campaign today. At that time, there were no paved streets. Eglinton Avenue was a wagon trail, and Old Forest Hill Road was part of an old Indian path that meandered from the Humber River to Lake Ontario.

Forest Hill remained its own little village, with its own police and fire departments and school system, until it was incorporated into Toronto. Today, apart from the green street signs and the right to leave the garbage where it properly belongs, it is mainly a state of mind.

You don't need a car to see Forest Hill. Either bike or walk along some of the streets, and you are in for an enjoyable hour or two. It lacks the gorgeous ravines of Rosedale, but you'll see some of this city's grandest homes and gardens. A good place to start is **Forest Hill Road,** just west of Avenue Road and St. Clair Avenue (and only a few blocks northeast of **Casa Loma**). You are now entering the thick of Forest Hill, with its handsome English manors and splendid Georgian homes. Just up the street is **Upper Canada College,** one of the country's most prestigious private schools, which has educated the likes of humorist Stephen Leacock, author Robertson Davies, the Eatons, and numerous bankers, mayors, and prime ministers.

A few blocks west of Upper Canada College is **Bishop Strachan** (rhymes with "yawn") **School.** It is one of the select private girls' schools in the city, and it is much admired, much attended, and much paid for. It's fitting that BSS shares a Forest Hill address with UCC; they both conjure up other initials: M.B.A., MP, MPP, and, in general, VIP.

Admire the homes along Old Forest Hill Road, then head up and down the streets that run north–south: Dunvegan, Warren, and Russell Hill. South of St. Clair Avenue, Russell Hill Road becomes a showpiece of mansions that really should be seen.

The only stores are on Spadina Road (it's Spadina Ave. south of Bloor St.), a few blocks north of St. Clair Avenue. This shopping area, with its fine shops and a superb bakery, still retains the feeling of a small village, which seems proper for the very proper people of Forest Hill.

It's a special part of Toronto, Forest Hill, and like Rosedale, a rare North American example of tranquil beauty and peacefulness, all within a short distance of Bloor and Yonge streets. Come to think of it, a lot of Forest Hill's inhabitants *own* stores at Bloor and Yonge streets. That is why they can afford to live in Forest Hill.

Tour 4: The Neighborhoods

Annex, The, **3**
Beaches, The, **5**
Cabbagetown, **6**
Casa Loma, **4**
East Indian area, **11**
Forest Hill, **2**
German/Ukrainian area, **8**
Greek area, **12**
Italian area, **9**
Polish area, **7**
Rosedale, **1**
West Indian area, **10**

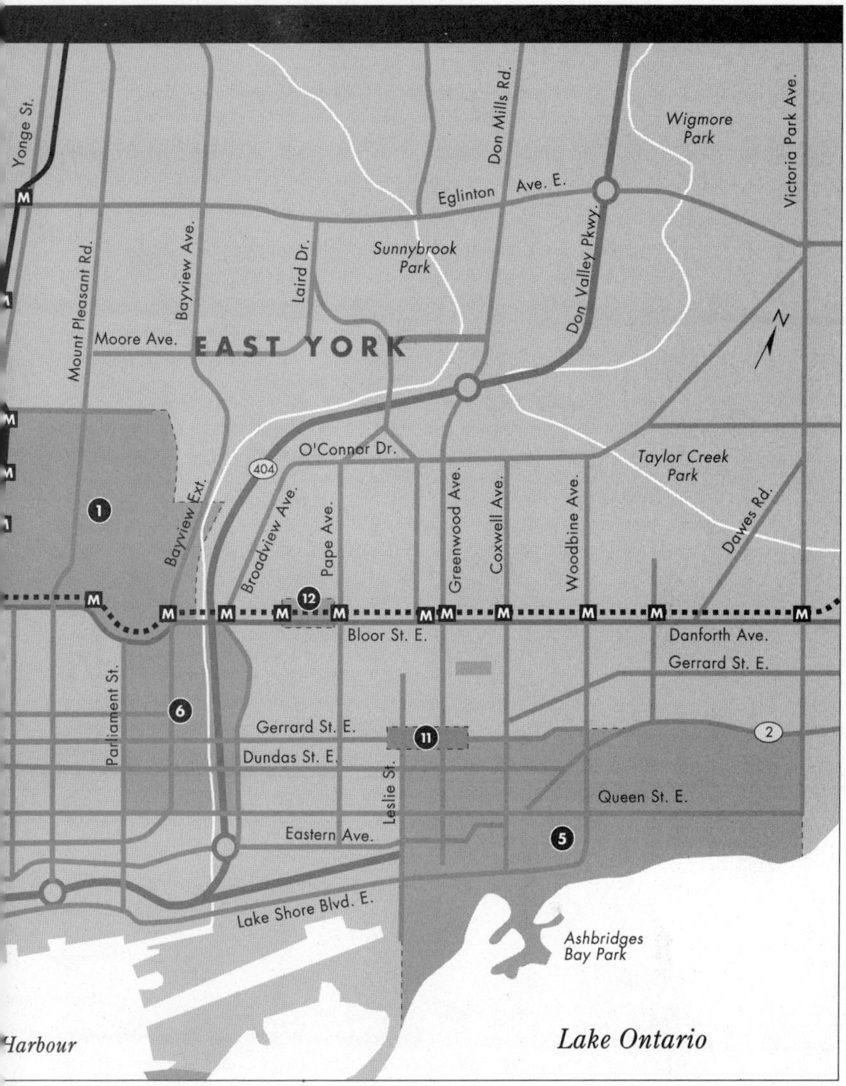

Yonge St.
Mount Pleasant Rd.
Bayview Ave.
Laird Dr.
Don Mills Rd.
Eglinton Ave. E.
Wigmore Park
Victoria Park Ave.
Sunnybrook Park
Don Valley Pkwy.
Moore Ave.
EAST YORK
N
O'Connor Dr.
404
Taylor Creek Park
Bayview Ext.
Broadview Ave.
Pape Ave.
Greenwood Ave.
Coxwell Ave.
Woodbine Ave.
Dawes Rd.
1
12
M
Bloor St. E.
Danforth Ave.
Gerrard St. E.
Parliament St.
6
Gerrard St. E.
11
2
Dundas St. E.
Leslie St.
Queen St. E.
Eastern Ave.
5
Lake Shore Blvd. E.
Ashbridges Bay Park
Harbour
Lake Ontario

The Annex and Casa Loma

3 The origin of **the Annex's** name is hardly the stuff of romance. It was born in 1887, when the burgeoning town of Toronto annexed the area between Bathurst Street and Avenue Road—north from Bloor Street to the Canadian Pacific railway tracks, alias Dupont Street.

The Annex was still country then, so it soon became an enclave for the well-to-do. Timothy Eaton (of department-store fame) and the Gooderham family (of liquor fame) escaped the masses and built north of Bloor Street. Eaton built a handsome structure at 182 Lowther Avenue; the Gooderhams erected a lovely red castle at the corner of St. George Street and Bloor Street, now the home of the exclusive York Club.

As Queen Victoria gave way to King Edward, the old rich gave way to the new rich in the Annex, and the Eatons headed farther north. Ethnic groups came and went, until the arrival of the ultimate neighborhood wrecker—the developer. Now began a war between the 19th and the 20th centuries that continues today. Alas, much of St. George Street has been lost to high rises; and as you near the Spadina subway entrance along Lowther Avenue and Walmer Street, you'll see that many Edwardian mansions have given way to apartment buildings whose architecture will forever remain 1960-ish—and *very* ugly.

Still, the Annex, with its hundreds of attractive old homes, can be cited as a prime example of Toronto's success in preserving lovely, safe streets within blocks of the downtown area. Even today, many examples of late 19th-century architecture can be enjoyed on Admiral Road, Lowther Avenue, and Bloor Street, west of University Avenue. Round turrets, pyramid-shape roofs, and conical and even comical spires are among the pleasures shared by some 20,000 Torontonians who live here—professors, students, writers, lawyers, and all the others who rightly find the area a vibrant place to live.

While the Annex is not number one on any visitor's checklist, it is an important part of the city, and it is lovely to visit. At the western end of the Annex—at Bathurst and Bloor streets—you come to Mirvish (or Markham) Village, described in Tour 2. And at the northern tip is the ultimate version of Your Home as Your Castle: Casa Loma.

4 **Casa Loma** (1 Austin Terr.; on Spadina Rd., just south of St. Clair Ave. W and the St. Clair Ave. subway stop) is truly a stunner: an honest-to-goodness 20th-century castle, with 98 rooms; two towers; secret panels; long, creepy passageways; and some of the best views of Toronto—all just a short distance from the heart of the city.

The medieval-style castle was built shortly before the Great War by Sir Henry Pellatt, a soldier and financier who spent over $3 million to construct his dream (that's 1913 dollars, remember), only to lose it to the taxman just over a decade later. Today it's owned by the city of Toronto and has been operated by the Kiwanis Club of West Toronto since 1937, with profits going to aid its various charities.

Adults and children will be intrigued by the giant pipe organ; the reproduction of Windsor Castle's Peacock Alley; the majestic, 60-foot-high ceiling of the Great Hall; and the mahogany and marble stable—reached by that long, underground passage—with porcelain troughs worthy of Kohler. And architecture lovers will be fascinated by the rooms from English, Spanish, Scottish, and Austrian castles, which Sir Henry picked up during trips across Europe. The architect E.J. Lennox, who also designed Toronto's Old City Hall and King Edward Hotel, has created a remarkable structure; in a world of Disneyland-type plastic models, Toronto's "house on the hill" is a real treat.

There are no more guided tours of Casa Loma—you now get automatic tape recordings. That's all for the best, as you can drift through at your own speed while the children rush off to the stables or towers. You'll walk a good mile by the time you're done, so wear sensible shoes. *Tel. 416/923–1171. Admission: $6 adults, $3 children 5–16 and senior citizens. These rate are expected to increase slightly during 1990. Open daily 10–4; closed Christmas Day and New Year's.*

The Beaches

One of the most charming of all the neighborhoods that make up what we call Metropolitan Toronto is to the east of downtown, reached by the Queen Street streetcar. Called both the Beach
5 and **The Beaches,** the area is bounded by Kingston Road to the north, the Greenwood Raceway to the west, Victoria Park Avenue to the east, and the lake to the south. But The Beaches is really an *attitude,* as much as it is a neighborhood. The chance to live in a small town outside Toronto, with easy access to the city via public transport and even easier access to Lake Ontario, has attracted tens of thousands of residents over the years.

A soldier from London, Joseph Williams, first settled the area back in 1853, having arrived in Toronto with the 2nd Battalion Rifle Brigade five years earlier. His 25-acre grant was named Kew Farms, after London's Kew Gardens, and it was there that he raised vegetables, selling them along with pies and pickles at the St. Lawrence Market on Saturday mornings. (That market is discussed in Tour 1.) When Williams chose to turn his property into a park in 1879, he called it **Kew Gardens.** It was soon flooded by hundreds of hot and sticky Torontonians attracted by the advertisements for "innocent amusements" and the prohibition of "spiritous liquors." Only Canadians would be drawn to such promised innocence!

The youngest son of the *paterfamilias,* suitably named Kew Williams, built a handsome house of stone with a circular staircase and a tower. It stands in Kew Gardens today, The Beaches' own modest version of Casa Loma, serving as home to the park's keeper.

The cottages that once dotted the lakeshore vanished with the waves in 1932, at which time Kew Gardens, Scarborough Beach Park, and Balmy Beach were incorporated into one large park. But on a leisurely walk along the charming streets that run north from the lake to Queen Street, you will still find—and be charmed by—hundreds of New England–style clapboard-and-shingle houses, often standing next door to formal stucco mansions in the Edwardian tradition.

Ride east to the end of the 501 Queen Street streetcar line, to what's called the Neville Park Loop. From here, stroll down to the lake, and walk west toward the city along the delightful, safe, and often crowded (in the summer) boardwalk. Remember, July and August are the only months when one does not risk frostbite when dipping a toe into Lake Ontario. But merely sunbathing can be magical beside The Beaches' boardwalk, which is graced by huge, shady trees. And if you get too warm, there is the free Olympic-size **Somerville Pool** at Woodbine Avenue.

A return walk back up to Queen Street, window shopping along the way, is well worth the time, before grabbing the 501 car westbound and back into the last decade of the 20th century.

Cabbagetown Anyone with less than a week to spend in Toronto may wish to put this way down on their list of must-dos, but anyone with the time and a healthy interest in what makes the city of Toronto so healthy (and interesting), really should take an hour or so to 6 walk through **Cabbagetown**—a cozy neighborhood just east of the downtown area.

We're not talking major historic landmarks here, but it has the charm of street after street of 19th-century houses, giant trees, and the loveliness of its natural boundaries—two fascinating cemeteries and the Don Valley, now slashed through by the parkway of the same name.

Cabbagetown was originally populated by poor Irish immigrants, who gave it its very prosaic name: They used to grow cabbages in their front yards. Today, that name is used with almost wistful irony; the "white painters" eventually descended on the area, brushes and hammers waving, turning houses that sold in the $25,000 range just two decades ago into ones that will fetch $250,000 and more. In other words, Cabbagetown is yet another good example—along with Yorkville (in the Bloor/Avenue/Yonge district) and the St. Lawrence area (near Front/Church/Jarvis)—of the insistent gentrification of Toronto's downtown.

And so, the area that the late Cabbagetown-born-and-bred writer Hugh Garner once described as "the world's largest Anglo-Saxon slum" has Cinderellaed into becoming one of the most popular areas in the city. (Being walking distance from the Eaton Centre, at least in good weather, hasn't hurt.)

The borders of Cabbagetown are not terribly well defined. They extend roughly from Parliament Street on the west (about a mile due east of Yonge St.) to Broadview Avenue on the east, and from Bloor Street (aka The Danforth) on the north to Queen Street East on the south.

Our tour will point out only the highlights, but we think that you might well find the entire neighborhood of interest, especially if you are fond of small-scale domestic Victorian architecture.

The "main street" of Cabbagetown is Parliament, so we'll begin there, at the southeast corner of Carlton Street (alias College St., but on the east side of the city). The street was so named because the first government buildings were built near its foot in the closing years of the 18th century.

Walk south from Carlton and Parliament streets, through the busiest part of the Parliament Street commercial area. Most of the buildings on the west side date from the 1890s, though the fronts of the stores are more recent.

Turn left on Spruce Street, which is the first block you come to. The little brick cottage at **number 35**, set far back from the street, was built in 1860–61 and was once the home of the dean of Trinity College Medical School. Note the fence, as well, which also dates from the last century.

From 1856 to 1914, the entire block to your south was the site of the Toronto General Hospital (which now stands, along with most of the city's other major and modern hospitals, along University Avenue, south of College Street). The building at **41 Spruce Street** was built in 1871, served until 1903 as a medical school, and has now been recycled as part of a residential development. Its history is outlined on the Toronto Historical Board plaque on its front lawn.

Continuing east, to the corner of Spruce and Sumach streets, you'll see **Spruce Court** on the northwest corner. It's one of the earliest and most attractive of Toronto's low-income housing projects. Constructed for the Toronto Housing Company between 1913 and 1926, the individual units not only provided modern conveniences and street access but also opened to a grassy courtyard. Today, it's a residential cooperative, and the humanity of the city continues to flourish.

Around that corner to the right, at **289 Sumach Street,** is the building that once housed the Ontario Women's Medical College, built in 1889 and a forerunner to Women's College Hospital. (Yes, fellow feminists, Toronto was slow to educate female doctors.) The attractiveness of this brick-and-stone building demonstrates well the success with which Victorian architects and builders managed to integrate institutions into streetscapes that were basically residential.

Now, turn around and walk north on Sumach Street. After crossing Spruce Street, look to your right, on the attractive row of small houses at **119–133 Spruce Street.** Erected in 1887, this terrace of workers' cottages is typical of the form of residential architecture built (to every scale) in Toronto between 1875 and 1890. The style, Second Empire, is typified by the high mansard roof punctuated by dormers with marvelous details, such as carved wooden brackets and metal decorative devices.

Continue north on Sumach Street back to Carlton Street, where you'll see some of the area's largest homes. (Note the redbrick surface of the street to the east.) Among the most outstanding is **number 288,** a solid brick house with white stone trim in the Second Empire style built in 1882. The house next door, **number 286,** was built the following year; it has the familiar Toronto-style steep gable and bargeboard trim. Check out the wrought-iron cresting over the round bow window.

The handsome residence at **number 297** is unusual for the area and is more like the stately homes of the Annex area of Toronto. Its interior, fully restored and exquisitely furnished, has been in more magazine pictorials than Elizabeth Taylor. Its neighbor at **295 Carlton Street** is an earlier house of Victorian Gothic design. It was originally the home of an executive of Toronto's first telephone company—be aware that the wondrous machine was invented by Alexander Graham Bell in Brantford, Ontario, just over an hour west of Toronto—and it had one of the first telephones in the entire city. It didn't cost a quarter to make a call back then.

Continue west on Carlton Street to Metcalfe Street, which, thanks to all its trees, fences, and unbroken rows of terraces, is one of the most beautiful streets in Toronto. On the sidewalk, on the east side nearest Carlton Street, is a utility-hole cover from the Victorian era, bearing the date 1889. Happy centenary!

Proceed north to look at 37 **Metcalfe Street,** a house that is unique due to its various additions. The renovations over the years (1891 and 1912) have created an array of beaux-arts classical forms, superimposed on the side of a simple but picturesque Victorian home. It's a fine example of the architectural diversity of the entire area.

Look north again. At the northeast corner of Metcalfe and Winchester streets is the handsome Romanesque **St. Enoch's Presbyterian Church,** erected in 1891. Its scale and style blend nicely with that of the surrounding homes of the same period. Today, it is the home of the Toronto Dance Theatre.

Turn left now, and walk west along Winchester Street, back to Parliament Street. As you dance along, admire the repeated sunburst patterns of carved wood in many of the gables and the very large amount of stained glass, much of it original, some of it recently installed by lovers of Victoriana.

At the southeast corner is the most prominent building in the area, the venerable but (alas) decaying **Winchester Hotel.** The old wing on Winchester bears the plaque "Winchester Hall" and was put up in 1881; the large corner part was built seven years later.

South of the hotel stands an imposing row of large Victorian houses, numbered **502–508 Parliament Street.** Erected in 1879, they are among the largest and most elaborately decorated Second Empire structures still standing in Toronto.

To the north, at the northwest corner of Parliament and Wellesley streets—you can't miss them, sadly—loom the overwhelming apartment towers of **St. James Town,** built in the 1960s and reviled ever since. They wiped out many streets that had been lined with houses like the ones we have been walking by. Yes, Toronto, too, has been occasionally victimized by progress.

On the east side of Parliament Street, just north of Wellesley Street, is **St. James Cemetery,** which is worth a visit. This beautiful final resting place was laid out in the 1840s, making it the eternal home of many of the most prominent early citizens of the then–town of York and the site of some of the most interesting funereal statuary in Toronto. While you are there, observe the small yellow-brick Gothic **Chapel of St. James-the-Less,** built in 1858 and considered to be one of the most beautiful church buildings in the entire country.

Turn right and walk east along Wellesley Street. Be sure to take note of **number 314,** built in 1889–90, with its stonework around the windows and carved stone faces above the door and in the keystones.

Farther east, turn north up the lane marked **Wellesley Cottages.** This row of workers' houses was built in 1886–87 by a carpenter of the time. Much of Toronto's most inexpensive housing of the 19th century was built in this simplified Gothic style, faced with wood lath and stucco. They may look unchanged to you, but some have been extensively modernized.

Back on Wellesley Street, walk north up the lane just east of number 402 to see the **Owl House,** named after the figure on a small terra-cotta plaque under one of its windows. This interesting little house was built in 1893–94.

Wellesley Street comes to an end at **Wellesley Park,** which was, from 1848 to 1888, the site of the area's only major industry, the P.R. Lamb Glue and Blacking Factory, just the thing one wouldn't want next door. Today, it's a small, pleasant neighborhood park and playground, framed by parts of the Don Valley, the Necropolis Cemetery, and the row of houses to the south, for whose occupants the park is a large and lovely front lawn.

Proceed south through Wellesley Park, and turn right along Amelia Street to Sumach Street. Walk south, past Winchester Street, and make a left (east) into **Riverdale Park.** The large stone gateposts on your left were the entrance to the Riverdale Zoo, a public zoo operated by the city from 1894 to 1974, when they finally moved all the animals—and brought in several thousand more—to the magnificent Metro Toronto Zoo, in Scarborough. It will warm your heart to know that this area was laid out on landfill that was dumped by prisoners of the Don Jail, as part of their work program.

It's now **Riverdale Farm,** one of Toronto's most delightful—and free!—attractions, and a very special treat for children. Here is where they can find Herbie and Hughie Clydesdale, Morley and Honey Pony, Jasmine, and Sonny and Cher Goat.

The old birdhouse on the grounds is the last remnant of the old zoo, but the most interesting structure is the original, 19th-century Pennsylvania German–style barn, built in 1858 and moved to the farm in 1975. Inside are various implements, such as a light sleigh from the turn of the century and an exact replica of a Conestoga wagon, the kind used by German-speaking immigrants to this country early in the last century.

Bring along a bathing suit for very young children: There's a wading pond in the lovely park adjacent to the farm.

The Riverdale Farm, 201 Winchester St., near Wellesley and Parliament Sts.; tel. 416/392–6794. Open daily 9 AM*–dusk.*

The **Necropolis** ("city of the dead") **Cemetery** lies just to the north of Riverdale Farm. The nonsectarian burial ground is filled with many of Toronto's early pioneers. Among the most famous (and notorious): Toronto's first mayor, William Lyon Mackenzie, who led a revolt against the city in 1837; Samuel Lount and Peter Matthews, two of Mackenzie's followers, who were hanged for their part in that rebellion; and George Brown, founder of the *Globe* newspaper and one of the fathers of Canada's Confederation.

The beautiful chapel, gate, and gate house of the cemetery, erected in 1872, constitute one of the most picturesque groupings of small Victorian buildings in all of Toronto. The Necropolis is also known for its great variety of trees, flowering shrubs, and rare and exotic plants.

Other Neighborhoods

As we never get tired of pointing out, part of Toronto's magic, and surely one of its major reasons for its success as a "city that works," is its quite extraordinary collection of neighborhoods. Here are a few others worthy of mention.

7 **A Polish community.** The beauty of High Park is described at

length in our Parks and Gardens section (*see* Sites and Attractions); let us merely say that one of North America's loveliest parks is but three or four miles due west of Bloor and Yonge streets, along the Bloor subway line. But just east of the park is a long street running north–south: **Roncesvalles Avenue.** This is the commercial heart and soul of Toronto's Polish community, filled with butcher shop after butcher shop, each selling homemade sausages just like grandmother should have made, if she had had the skill and time. (Consider buying a few to grill in High Park.)

8 On the west side of the park is **Runnymede Road.** Here, and along Bloor Street West, you move both west and east across Europe: Both German and Ukrainian shops come into view, selling fine food and clothing.

9 **An Italian community.** From the College and Bathurst streets area, west to Dufferin Street and beyond, and north all the way to the city limits of Steeles Avenue, is the ever-widening Italian neighborhood, its numbers making Toronto one of the largest Italian communities outside the mother country. The streets here are filled with the passion and excitement of that great, vibrant Mediterranean culture—especially **St. Clair Avenue,** from Bathurst Street west to Dufferin Street. Here are many fine Italian restaurants and stores, including many that sell excellent ices and ice creams.

10 **A West Indian community.** West Indians and their fascinating food shops can be found along Eglinton Avenue, just east of Dufferin Street, and down along Bloor Street West near Christie Street. They can also be found along Bathurst Street, north from Bloor Street. Their snack bars selling *roti*—spicy Jamaican meat patties—can be found most everywhere in Toronto nowadays.

11 **An East Indian community.** East Indians are also fairly widely dispersed, although there is one quite concentrated row of Indian shops and restaurants—and movie houses—along Gerrard Street East, near Greenwood Avenue, a few miles east of Yonge Street.

12 **A Greek community.** The Danforth. This is a strange name for a street, but it is stranger still in its crazy-quilt ethnicity: Once English-settled (although it was named after Asa Danforth, an American contractor who cut a road in the area back in 1799), it is now Italian, Greek, East Indian, Latin American, and, increasingly, Chinese. But it is still called "Greek town," with its late-night taverns, all-night fruit markets, and some of the most tasty ethnic restaurants in Toronto.

There are now well over a quarter-million Greek Canadians; more than 150,000 of them live in Ontario, and more than half of those live in Metropolitan Toronto. They created such major Canadian enterprises as Devon Ice Cream and Diana Sweets restaurants, and they gave the world internationally acclaimed opera star Teresa Stratas. For more than a decade, in fact, Toronto provided a home and a professorship (at York University, in the northwest part of the city, near Finch and Keele) for exiled Andreas Papandreou, who has been Greece's socialist prime minister during much of the 1980s.

In the summer of 1982, 50 street signs in the Little Athens area of the Danforth, between Logan and Woodycrest avenues, went bilingual (English and Greek). When you've had a little too much souvlaki and Greek wine, the signs can help you find your way home.

What to See and Do with Children

Free Attractions The **Hilton,** at University Avenue and Richmond Street, and the **Harbour Castle Westin,** at the foot of Bay Street, both have outdoor, glass-enclosed elevators, which provide hair-raising rides and spectacular views of the city.

The **ferry boat** to the **Toronto Islands** offers a stunning panorama of downtown Toronto. The islands themselves offer swimming and biking (bikes can be rented) in the summer, skiing in the winter, and the delightful **Far Away Farm** in Centreville (*see* Tour 1).

The **Riverdale Farm** in Cabbagetown is a working farm with animals and a wading pond (*see* Tour 4).

High Park has a sweet little zoo, swimming, skating, picnicking, and more (*see* Parks and Gardens in Sites and Attractions).

Skating, skiing and **tobogganing** are all available for free in most of the major Toronto parks and ravines. And, still thinking winter, don't forget the beautiful skating rink in front of the New City Hall and the often-terrifying hills at Winston Churchill Park, High Park, Earl Bales Park, and Riverdale Park.

The **Children's Bookstore** in Mirvish Village can provide an hour or more of free fun for children. It's the largest store of its kind in the world, and it frequently holds weekend concerts and readings in the summer (*see* Tour 2).

The **David Dunlap Observatory** in Richmond Hill, just north of Metro Toronto, and the **McLaughlin Planetarium,** right next to the Royal Ontario Museum, both provide outer-space experiences for preteens and teens (*see* Museums and Observatories in Sites and Attractions).

Harbourfront nearly always has free events and activities, from painting and sculpting to concerts and plays. Just being on the waterfront can be a thrill for kids. Feeding the seagulls popcorn or hunks of bread is endlessly interesting, especially when the gulls catch the food in midair dives (*see* Tour 1)!

Boys and Girls House is a superior library for children. The Spaced-Out Library on the second floor will thrill all teenage fans of science fiction (*see* Libraries and Special Collections).

Ecology House, near Bloor Street and Spadina Avenue, has displays on everything from water conservation to solar heating and organic gardening (*see* Museums and Observatories in Sites and Attractions).

Modestly Priced Attractions **Apple, strawberry,** and **raspberry picking** are available within a short drive of downtown Toronto. Our favorite place is **Al Ferri's** (15 minutes west of the airport, near the corner of Mississauga Rd. and Steeles Ave.; tel. 416/455–8202). For a free list of places to pick fruits and vegetables in the vicinity of Toronto, phone 416/965–7701.

The Haida, at Ontario Place, is a giant World War II destroyer that children love to explore (*see* Theme Parks and Amusement Areas in Sites and Attractions).

The **Art Gallery of Ontario** has a hands-on room that is marvelously creative and entertaining. Right behind it is the fascinating, historic **Grange** house. In front of the gallery is a Henry Moore sculpture that kids love to climb (*see* Tour 2).

The **Royal Ontario Museum,** with its fantastic dinosaurs, towering totem pole, and other child-oriented exhibits, is ideal for kids from 3 to 18 (and their parents).

Casa Loma, that magical castle in the heart of Toronto, is much loved by all children. Even preschool kids will enjoy the great views from the towers and the long, creepy tunnel that leads to the stables (*see* Tour 4).

The Puppet Centre, near Yonge Street and Highway 401, has more than 400 puppets from all over the world.

More Expensive Attractions

The **Ontario Science Centre** is a must for children, especially age 5 and up; don't miss the free movies and the thrilling space, communications, laser, and electricity exhibits (*see* Museums and Observatories in Sites and Attractions).

The **CN Tower** and the **Tour of the Universe** in its basement are not cheap, but they're a real treat for everyone, especially kids. (*see* Tour 1).

Black Creek Pioneer Village is a great place for kids, where they can watch everything from a blacksmith shaping a horseshoe to a "19th-century woman" making candles (*see* Historic Buildings and Sites in Sites and Attractions).

In their respective seasons, there are numerous events that are great for children: most especially, the **Frostfest** and **Winterfest** (January); the **Fort York Festival** (May); **Caravan** and **International Festival** (June); **Caribana** and **International Picnic** (July); the **Canadian National Exhibition** (August); the **Bindertwine Festival** (September); the **Royal Winter Fair** and **Santa Claus Parade** (November); and the **Festival of Lights** (December).

From early April through September each year, the **Toronto Blue Jays** continue their eternal/infernal climb toward the American League pennant. Throughout the season, children 14 and under are offered various freebies, such as bats, baseball caps, and sports bags. For ticket information, phone 416/595–0077.

The **Toronto Maple Leafs,** the only leaves that fall from October through April, can provide the occasional hockey thrill at Maple Leaf Gardens (tel. 416/977–1641).

For theater and concerts, the **Young People's Theatre** (tel. 416/864–9732) often has excellent fare, and there are frequent performances for children at **Roy Thomson Hall** (tel. 416/593–4828) and the **Minkler Auditorium** (tel. 416/491–8877), which is up north, near Finch Street and the Don Valley Parkway.

Pricey but Worth It

Just north of the city is **Canada's Wonderland,** Toronto's frozen version of Disneyland. It's uninspired but can provide a decent day's entertainment. There are many rock concerts here at the Kingswood Music Theatre. In past years, Shoppers Drug Mart has offered reduced-rate tickets with purchases of more than a few dollars (*see* Theme Parks and Amusement Areas in Sites and Attractions).

African Lion Safari, about an hour's drive west of Toronto, can provide marvelous entertainment, especially if the giraffe puts its head through your car window. Half-price tickets are often available in shops around the city (*see* Theme Parks and Amusement Areas in Sites and Attractions).

Marineland, in Niagara Falls, is top-quality entertainment put on by underwater zoo crew. It's a world-class park, with thrilling amusement rides, dolphin shows, and aquariums (*see* Niagara Falls, Ontario, in Excursions).

Canada's Wild Water Kingdom, not far from the airport, Black Creek Pioneer Village, and Canada's Wonderland, is a welcome recent addition to every kid's wet cultural heritage: high water slides, river rapids, giant outdoor hot tubs, a fantastic wave pool, and a delightful area for younger children to splash around in. *Finch Ave. W. and Hwy. 427; tel. 416/794–0468. Admission: $13.95 adults; $11.95 children 4–9; $7.95 senior citizens. Open daily June 30–Labor Day; weekends late May–June 30 and Labor Day–Sept. 30; closed rest of year.*

The Metro Toronto Zoo

The Metro Toronto Zoo was built for animals, not people. The Rouge Valley, just east of Toronto, was an inspired choice of site when it was built in the 1960s, with its varied terrain, from river valley to dense forest, where mammals, birds, reptiles, and fish have been grouped according to where they live in the wild. In most of the regions, you'll find remarkable botanical exhibits in enclosed, climate-controlled pavilions. Don't miss the three-ton banyan tree in the Indo-Malayan Pavilion; the fan-shaped traveler's palm from Madagascar in the African Pavilion; or the perfumed flowers of the jasmine vines in the Eurasian Pavilion. The "round the world tour" takes some three hours and is suitable for any kind of weather, because most of the time is spent inside pavilions. It's been estimated that it would take four full days to see everything in the Metro Zoo, so study the map you'll get at the zoo entrance, and decide in advance what you wish to see most.

For the younger children, there is the delightful Littlefootland, a special area that allows contact with tame animals, such as rabbits and sheep. In the winter, cross-country skiers follow groomed trails that skirt the animal exhibits. Lessons and rentals are available. There is an electrically powered train that moves silently among the animals without frightening them. It can accommodate wheelchairs (available for free, inside the main gate), and all pavilions have ramp access.

Located on Meadowvale Rd., just north of Highway 401, in Scarborough, a 30-minute drive from downtown. Or take Bus 86A from the Kennedy subway station; tel. 416/392–5901 for taped information, 416/392–5900 for human contact. For animal contact, visit the zoo. Admission: $7 adults, $4 children ages 12–17 and senior citizens, $2 children 5–11. Family rates available, although expect all prices to increase slightly in 1990. The zoo is hardly cheap, but it's well worth the cost. Open daily except Christmas. Summer 9:30–7; winter 9:30–4:30.

Off the Beaten Track

Watching the Italian promenade. St. Clair Avenue West, running from Bathurst Street to Dufferin Street and beyond, remains the heart of this city's vibrant Italian community. On many evenings, especially Sundays, the street is filled with thousands of men and women promenading between *gelaterias*, eyeing each other, and generally enjoying their neighbors. You'll think you're in Rome.

Chinatown on a Sunday morning. Spadina Avenue, from College Street south to Queen Street, and Dundas Street, from Spadina all the way east to Bay Street, are bustling most of the time, but on Sunday mornings—all day, really—the activity is nonstop. A great time to browse, buy, and just plain enjoy.

Greektown on a Sunday. The Danforth (Bloor St. east of the Don Valley Parkway) has great Greek restaurants, gift shops, and hundreds of Greek-Canadians promenading. Welcome to the Mediterranean!

There's no hotel more romantic than the **Guild Inn** (*see* Lodging), and no view of Toronto more wonderful than from **Centre Island at sunset.**

4 Sites and Attractions

Historic Buildings and Sites

There are many attractive, even fascinating historic buildings and sites around the city of Toronto, a few of them rather far from the core of the downtown area. The following is a checklist for those who wish to make sure they see the most interesting ones. A number of these have been described before, in our Exploring chapter.

Black Creek Pioneer Village. Less than a half hour's drive from downtown Toronto is a rural, mid-19th-century village that makes one feel as if he or she has gone through a time warp. Black Creek Pioneer Village is a collection of over two dozen period buildings that have been moved to their current site: a town hall, weaver's shop, printing shop, blacksmith's shop, and a school, complete with dunce cap. The mill dates from the 1840s and has a four-ton wood waterwheel that still grinds up to a hundred barrels of flour a day.

Visitors watch men and women in period costumes go about the daily routine of mid-19th-century Ontario life—cutting tin, shearing sheep, tending gardens (weather permitting), fixing and even making horseshoes, baking bread, weaving, printing a newspaper, stringing apple slices, and dipping candles. Most pleasantly, these knowledgeable souls will explain what they're doing and how they do it, and they will answer all questions about pioneer farm life.

Free wagon rides, a decent restaurant, and many farm animals all contribute to a satisfying outing. And in the winter, there's also skating, tobogganing, and sleigh rides. *Generally open 10–4. Phone for seasonal events, reduced winter hours, and extended summer hours. Located in northwest Metro Toronto at Jane St. and Steeles Ave. By car, take Highway 401, then Highway 400 north to Steeles East, and follow the signs. By bus, take #35B from the Jane St. subway station in Toronto's west end and/or #608 from the Finch Ave. subway station. Tel. 416/661–6600 for a recorded message, 416/736–1733 for more information. Admission: $5 adults, $2.50 children and students, $3 senior citizens; expect rates to increase slightly in 1990. During the winter months, $1 adults, 50¢ children; 75¢ for sleigh rides.*

Campbell House. This lovely "living museum" is described in Tour 3 in the Exploring chapter.

Casa Loma. This dream castle is one of the highlights of any trip to Toronto (*see* Tour 4 in Exploring).

Colborne Lodge. Visit this grand 19th-century home in conjunction with a trip to High Park. An architect named John Howard built this Regency-style "cottage" on a park hill overlooking Lake Ontario more than 150 years ago. Visitors will see the original fireplace, bake oven, and kitchen, as well as many of Howard's own drawings and paintings. *Located on Colborne Lodge Dr., at the south end of High Park. By subway, take the Bloor St. Line west to the High Park station. Tel. 416/392–6916. Admission: $2.50 adults, $1.50 children, students, and senior citizens. Open Mon.–Sat. 9:30–5; Sun. and holidays noon–5.*

Enoch Turner Schoolhouse. This building, just a few blocks east of Union Station in the St. Lawrence area, helps us remember that free public education began only in the mid-19th century. Back in the 1840s, Toronto parents paid two-thirds of teachers' salaries, and the government picked up the rest. When the Ontario legislature passed an act in 1848 authorizing cities to provide free schools (paid for by property taxes), the Toronto City Council balked at the radical concept and closed down every public school in town. A brewer named Enoch Turner was outraged by the reactionary policy of the city elders, and he created Toronto's first free educational institution. Three years later, the politicians relented and absorbed the Enoch Turner Schoolhouse into the public school system of Toronto. And so, this small red-and-yellow brick building remains, looking frightfully like today's schoolrooms, except for the ancient desks. *106 Trinity St., near the corners of King St. E and Parliament St., tel. 416/863–0010. Admission free. Open weekdays 9:30–4:30.*

Fort York. This remarkable historical site is located in downtown Toronto, not far from Harbourfront and Ontario Place. It could well be combined with visits to either of those sites.

In 1813, a fierce battle took place between the Yankees and the Queen's Rangers regiment in what was then York (now, Toronto). **Fort York** was torched, but the Canadians rebuilt it just three years later, and it still stands, near the foot of Bathurst Street, in downtown Toronto. The eight buildings, with their brick, stone, and log frames, give visitors a good sense of what it was like to be a British soldier stuck out in the boondocks nearly two centuries ago.

You'll see the blockhouses, where dozens of men froze to death in their beds over the years, and the mess, where women still bake bread in the giant stone fireplace. There's a model of the famous battle from the War of 1812, and, year-round, men get rigged up in the uniforms of the era, call themselves the Fort York Guard, and perform 19th-century drills, complete with artillery salutes. Children will enjoy climbing on the various cannons, and tour guides are both knowledgeable and friendly. *By car, take Lakeshore Blvd. W to Strachan Ave. (pronounced "strawn") north, and head east on Fleet St. By subway, take the Bloor St. train west to Bathurst St., then the streetcar south to the Garrison Rd. exit. The Bathurst St. #511 streetcar also goes there. Tel. 416/392–6907. Admission: $4 adults, $2 children 5–12 and senior citizens. Open 9:30–5; Oct.–Apr., Sun. and holidays noon–5. Closed Jan. 1, Good Friday, and Dec. 25–26.*

Gibson House. It's the Little House in the Suburbs, convenient for people driving anywhere near Highway 401 and Yonge Street. The 10-room country house was built in 1851 by one of the supporters of William Lyon Mackenzie's 1837 rebellion. True, David Gibson's original home was burned to the ground by anti-Mackenzie men while the surveyor was off in a decade-long exile in the United States (during which time he assisted in constructing the Erie Canal), but when he returned to Toronto, he built this. As in Fort York and Black Creek, there are men and women in 19th-century costumes who demonstrate the cooking and crafts of the pioneers. *5172 Yonge St., about 1 mi north of Sheppard and Hwy. 401, tel. 416/225–0146. Admission: $1.50 adults, $1.25 students, 75¢ children and senior citizens, $3.50 families; senior citizens free on Wednes-*

days; expect all rates to increase by up to 10% during 1990. Open Tues.–Sat. 10–5, Sun. noon–5.

The Grange. This fine living museum is located just behind the Art Gallery of Ontario. In 1911, a prominent lady donated her historic house (1817) to what was then the Art Museum of Toronto. It's been restored as a "Gentleman's House" of the mid-1830s, and it should not be missed. The columned Georgian front and the delicately balanced wings that flow from the sides of its porch only hint at the joys of the interior: Carefully refurnished in English regency style, it is a virtual stage set for "Upstairs/Downstairs," complete with music room and a row of bells to call the servants from the basement kitchen. Costumed hostesses bake bread in the 19th-century brick ovens and give out slices, and children can dress up in aprons and bonnets. *317 Dundas St. W, just west of University Ave.; tel. 416/977–0414. Admission free with admission to the Art Gallery ($4.50 adults, $2.50 students and senior citizens, $9 families). Open Tues.–Sun. noon–4.*

Mackenzie House. This is in a deceptively modest row of houses, just blocks from the Eaton Centre. Its owner, William Lyon Mackenzie, was born in Scotland at the end of the 1700s and emigrated to Canada in 1820. He began a newspaper that so enraged the powers that be (they were known as "the Family Compact"—a powerful, smug group of politicians, *not* an economy car) that they broke into his print shop and dumped all his type into Lake Ontario. Undismayed, Mackenzie was elected the first mayor of Toronto, even designing the coat of arms of the new city. When he wasn't reelected in 1836, he gathered about 700 supporters and marched down Yonge Street to try to overthrow the government. They were roundly defeated, and Willie had to escape to the United States with a price on his head. When the Canadian government finally granted him amnesty, a dozen years later, Mackenzie was promptly elected to the legislative assembly—suggesting a daring on the part of Torontonians that few would imagine today—and began to publish another newspaper. By this time, though, Mackenzie was so down on his luck and cash that some friends passed the hat and bought him and his family the house we suggest you visit. His grandson, William Lyon Mackenzie King, became the longest-lasting prime minister of Canada.

This remarkable character enjoyed the place for but a few sickly and depressing years, as he died there in 1861. Today it has been lovingly restored as a National Historic Site and is operated as a museum and library. There are dozens of 19th-century furnishings and treasures, even the wild man's printing press. *82 Bond St., two blocks east of Yonge St. and a few steps south of Dundas St., tel. 416/392–6915. Admission: $2.50 adults, $1.50 students and senior citizens; group tours lasting 1 hr cost $2 per adult and $1.25 for senior citizens. Open 9:30–5, Sun. noon–5; afternoon tea daily 2–4 ($2.50 high tea; $1.50 regular).*

Montgomery's Inn. This restored inn—one of the few attractions in the west end of Toronto—was built in the early 1830s by an Irish immigrant, and it is a good example of the Loyalist architecture of the time. Costumed staff go about quilting, rug hooking, and cooking traditional foods. There are many tours, and a daily afternoon tea, 2–4:15. *4709 Dundas St., a brief* *walk from the Islington subway stop; tel. 416/394–8113. Admission: $1.50 adults, $1 students and senior citizens, 50¢ children, $3.50 families. Open weekdays 9:30–4:30, weekends 1–5.*

Old City Hall/New City Hall. *See* Tour 2 in Exploring.

Queen's Park. *See* Tour 3 in Exploring.

Spadina. Pronounced spa-*dee*-na, as the avenue should be but never is, it is filled with arts and artifacts of a prominent Toronto family. First built in 1866, it is now a glorious living tribute to the Victorian and Edwardian eras, featuring French porcelain vases, handsome furniture, crystal chandeliers burning softly with natural gas, fine paintings, and magnificent gardens. *285 Spadina Ave., next to Casa Loma; tel. 416/392–6827. Admission: $4 adults, $2 children and senior citizens. Open 9:30–5, Sun. and holidays noon–5.*

Todmorden Mills Historic Site. A number of the city's oldest buildings have been restored on their original sites, all in open parkland that is a marvelous place to picnic. The name Todmorden Mills comes from England, as did the settlers who built these structures. There are two pioneer houses, a brewery (1821), a paper mill (1825), and the old Don Train Station, built in 1891 to serve two once-great railroads, the Canadian National and Canadian Pacific. *67 Pottery Road, just off the Bayview Ave. Extension; tel. 416/425–2250. Admission: $1.50 adults, $1 students and senior citizens, 50¢ children. Open May–Dec., Tues.–Fri. 10–5; weekends and holidays 11–5. Closes Nov.–Dec. at 4.*

Union Station. The terminus for the Toronto subway system, it is a stunning building in its own right (*see* Tour 1 in Exploring.)

Museums and Observatories

As befits the largest city in Canada, as well as the capital of the province of Ontario, Metro Toronto has many major museums. These range from one of the world's great museums—the Royal Ontario Museum—to the superb Ontario Science Centre to the tiny but fascinating Museum of the History of Medicine.

Art Gallery of Ontario. This excellent collection is located in the heart of Chinatown (*see* Tour 2 in Exploring).

Bell Canada Building. Just north of the Old City Hall is a modest display of early telephones that go back to the times of Alexander Graham Bell, who actually invented the darned thing in a town just west of Toronto. You may enjoy seeing the phone book of 1879, which listed 30 houses in Toronto, as well as the offices of 18 doctors and a single dentist. *483 Bay St., down in the basement; tel. 416/581–4050. Admission free. Open weekdays 9–5.*

Beth Tzedec Museum. Located within an attractive Conservative synagogue of the same name, it is the only museum of Jewish artifacts in Toronto. It has special exhibits, as well as fine regular displays of ancient coins and glass, silver coins from ancient Greece and Rome, medieval Sabbath spice boxes, and even a centuries-old chair on which infant boys would be circumcised. Tours can be arranged. *1700 Bathurst St., about four blocks south of Eglinton or 3 mi northwest of the Royal*

Ontario Museum; tel. 416/781-3511. Admission free. Open Mon.–Thurs. 2–6, Fri.–Sat. 10–3.

Black Creek Pioneer Village. This magnificent "living museum" is described in Historic Buildings and Sites.

David Dunlap Observatory. Constructed in 1935, this is both a museum of photos of sunspots, nebulae, and galaxies and the largest observatory in all of Canada—and it is only 15 miles north of downtown! Visitors are admitted only in large groups on Saturday nights, from mid-April to early October, but individuals or small groups who call for reservations may join the next tour that has space. Visitors climb a ladder and peek through the 25-ton telescope at the planet, star, or moon that is "playing" that night. It can get extremely chilly under the unheated dome, even in midsummer, so dress warmly for your close encounter. *Located three km (1.8 mi) north of Highway 7, along Yonge Street. Drive past the large white dome on your right, and turn right on Hillsview Drive. By public transit, take the Yonge Street subway to Finch Avenue, and then the Yonge Street GO bus north. Tel. 416/884-2112. Admission free.*

Ecology House. This is an energy-efficient Victorian house designed and run by Pollution Probe, with demonstrations of water and heat conservation, waste management, solar greenhouses, hydroponic and organic gardening, and more. *12 Madison Ave., a block east of Spadina Ave., just north of Bloor St. W; tel. 416/967-0577. Admission free. Open Wed.–Sat. noon–5.*

H.M.C.S. *Haida*. On the grounds of Ontario Place, across from the Canadian National Exhibition, this World War II destroyer is now a floating museum. It is irresistible for children of all ages. *Tel. 416/965-6331. Nominal admission charge. Open summers 10–7.*

Hockey Hall of Fame and Museum. Open since 1961, this shrine has everything from the original Stanley Cup, donated in 1893, to displays of goalie masks, skate and stick collections, jerseys of the great players, and video displays of big games. If you wish to see Wayne Gretzky's feet cast in bronze, this is the place to catch them. *Exhibition Place, CNE grounds, tel. 416/595-1345. Admission: $3 adults, $1 students and senior citizens. Open mid-May–mid-Aug., Tues.–Sun. 10–7. Mon. 10–5. During the CNE in Aug. and early Sept., open daily 10–5. Other months, open Tues.–Sun. 10–4:30.*

Lakeview Generating Station. A living museum located in the west end, this giant thermal-electric station produces more power than Niagara Falls's stations. Visitors see coal converted to energy in furnaces towering 17 stories overhead. *Lakeshore and Dixie Rds., a 15-min drive west of downtown; tel. 416/222-2571. Tours weekdays 9:30–4:30. Children should be over 10.*

Marine Museum of Upper Canada. Exhibits cover the War of 1812, fur-trade exploration, and so on. On display are canoes, a diving suit, relics from sunken ships, and a wireless room from the 1930s. Outside the museum is a 1932 steam tugboat in dry dock. *Located inside Exhibition Place on the CNE grounds, near Dufferin St. and Lakeshore Blvd.; tel. 416/392-6827. Take Bathurst St. #511 streetcar from the Bathurst/Bloor subway stop. Admission, including a guided tour: $2.50 adults, $1.50* *students, $7 for a family. Open Mon.–Sat. 9:30–5, Sun. and holidays noon–5.*

McMichael Canadian Collection. Though 20 miles northwest of Toronto, this popular art gallery attracts more than 300,000 visitors a year. The building, constructed from native stone and hand-hewn timber, houses the art of the Group of Seven painters and some of their contemporaries. These talented young men turned to the Canadian landscape for inspiration in the early decades of this century. At a time when 19th-century British styles were still holding the colonies in an artistic stranglehold, this struggle to capture the passion and fury of the raw and powerful Canadian landscape was a great leap forward. In addition to seeing the paintings, you won't want to ignore the 100 acres of river valley around the gallery buildings—an ideal spot for picnics. *Drive west on Hwy. 401 to Hwy. 400, then north to the Kleinburg exit; tel. 416/893–1121. Admission: $3 adults, $1.50 students and senior citizens, $6.50 families. Free for senior citizens Wed. Open winter Tues.–Sun. 11:30–4:30; open daily May–Nov. 11–5 (phone to confirm hours).*

Metro Toronto Police Museum. Highlights are a replica of a 19th-century police station, an exhibit of counterfeit money, a display of techniques for taking identifications, a wide selection of firearms, and displays of some of the city's most infamous crimes. *590 Jarvis St., a few blocks east of Yonge St. and south of Bloor St.; tel. 416/967–2222. Admission free, but children must be 14 or older. Open Thurs.–Fri. 6–9* PM*, Sat.–Sun. 1–5.*

Museum of the History of Medicine. This is one of the most interesting little museums in Toronto. Founded in 1907, and part of the University of Toronto's Academy of Medicine, it has hundreds of objects on display, including an Egyptian mummy and the record of the recently performed autopsy on it, 300-year-old nursing bottles with chamois nipples, an English wheelchair from 1910, and a North American bleeding bowl from the 1780s. Everything from magical and religious artifacts to prints and photographs shows how people have practiced medicine for thousands of years. *288 Bloor St. W, a few minutes' walk west of the Royal Ontario Museum; tel. 416/922–0564. Admission free; nominal charge for guided group tours (minimum 10 people). Open weekdays 9:30–4.*

Ontario Science Centre. It has been called a museum of the 21st century, but it's much, much more than that. Where else can one stand at the edge of a black hole, work hand-in-clamp with a robot, or land on the moon? Even the building itself is extraordinary. Three linked pavilions float gracefully down the side of a ravine at Eglinton Avenue East, near the Don Valley Parkway, and each overflows with exhibits that make space, technology, communications, and life itself irresistible. A dozen mini-theaters show films that bring the natural world to life. Live demonstrations—of lasers, glassblowing, papermaking, electricity, etc.—take place regularly throughout the day, so check the schedule when you arrive at the center, and plan your time accordingly.

You need at least two hours to scratch the surface; you may want to spend an entire day. Children will love this place, probably more than any other in Toronto, but adults will be enthralled, too. There is a cafeteria, a restaurant, and a gift store with a cornucopia of books and scientific doodads. *770 Don Mills Rd., about 11 km (7 mi) from downtown. By car, head west from the Eglinton Ave. exit of the Don Valley Parkway. By public transportation, take the Yonge St. subway from downtown to the Eglinton station, and transfer to the Eglinton E bus. Get off at the Don Mills Parkway stop. Tel. 416/429–0193 for a recording, 416/429–4100 for further information. Admission: $5.50 adults, $4.50 youth, $1.75 children under 12, free for senior citizens, $12 for families. Weekdays are less crowded. Open daily 10–6; closed Christmas.*

Puppet Centre. *See* What to See and Do with Children in Exploring.

Redpath Sugar Museum. Located on the waterfront, a few blocks east of where the ferries depart for the Toronto Island, this museum has displays of sugar harvesting, vintage sugar tools, and an enjoyable 20-minute film, "Raising Cane." The curator is available to answer questions. *95 Queen's Quay E, by the water; tel. 416/597–0286. Admission free. Open weekdays 10–noon and 1–3.*

Royal Ontario Museum. This spectacular collection is described at length in Tour 3 in the Exploring chapter, as are its siblings, the **McLaughlin Planetarium,** the **Sigmund Samuel Canadiana Collection,** and the **George R. Gardiner Museum of Ceramic Art.**

Sports Hall of Fame. This is right next door to the hockey museum and honors every other sport known to man, woman, or child, from rowing to running. *Tel. 416/595–1046.*

Art Galleries

Toronto is a highly cosmopolitan art center, second only to New York in North America. Over 300 commercial art galleries are listed in the Yellow Pages, offering every kind of art for viewing and sale, from Picasso to Warhol, from representational to abstract, from Inuit to Indian. The following is a list of some of the best and most respected galleries. The entertainment section of the Saturday *Globe and Mail* has several pages of listings and reviews of current shows. Most galleries have free copies of the monthly booklet *Slate,* which includes a gallery guide to Toronto. Visitors may want to stroll from gallery to gallery in either of two major districts—the Yorkville area, and the Queen Street area, west of University Avenue. Most galleries are open Tuesdays through Saturdays, 10–5:30 or 6.

Yorkville. In the Yorkville area, just behind the exclusive Hazelton Lanes complex, one can find many important galleries.

Sable-Castelli Gallery (33 Hazelton Ave., tel. 416/961–0011) is the result of Jared Sable's amalgamation with the renowned Castelli galleries of Manhattan in 1974. Since then, he has exhibited established American artists such as Warhol, Oldenburg, Johns, and Rosenquist, as well as innovative young Canadian artists who use strong expressive imagery.

Waddington & Shiell Ltd., located in the same building as Sable-Castelli (tel. 416/925–2461), is a beautifully designed space for displaying expensive work from the United States and abroad, as well as that of several established Canadians.

One can see Dufy and Matisse, Noland and Olitski, as well as Inuit art.

Mira Godard Gallery (22 Hazelton Ave., tel. 416/964–8197), which came from Montreal to Toronto in 1972, carries such major French-Canadian artists as Borduas and Riopelle, as well as established Canadian artists like Alex Colville, Kenneth Lochhead, David Milne, Jean-Paul Lemieux, and Christopher Pratt.

Nancy Poole's Studio (16 Hazelton Ave., tel. 416/964–9050) is a small, intimate space, almost exclusively exhibiting Canadian contemporary painting and sculpture, generally representational. Her artists include Jack Chambers and the astonishing Canadian Indian wood-carver, Joe Jacobs.

Gallery Dresdnere (12 Hazelton Ave., tel. 416/923–4662), created by an ex-Montrealer, shows a fine selection of Canadian abstract and conceptual paintings, as well as graphics and wall hangings.

Glass Art Gallery is the only gallery of its kind in Canada. It is a thrilling showroom of stained glass, laminated and crystal sculpture, and other avant-garde work. *21 Hazelton Ave., tel. 416/968–1823. Open 11–6.*

Gallery One, on the next block (121 Scollard St., tel. 416/929–3103), is one of the mainstays for large-format abstract expressionists in Canada and the United States, as well as for representational landscape art from western Ontario and Inuit art. Color-field painters, from Larry Poons to Jules Olitski, are exhibited here.

Gallery Moos, on Yorkville Avenue, just a block down, was opened by German-born Walter Moos 30 years ago to promote Canadian art. He is a discerning, reliable dealer, whose gallery has Picassos, Chagalls, Miros, and Dufys, as well as such internationally admired Canadians as Gershon Iskowitz, Ken Danby, Sorel Etrog, and Jean-Paul Riopelle. *136 Yorkville Ave., tel. 416/922–0627. Open 11–6.*

The **Inuit Gallery of Eskimo Art** was started by the respected Av Isaacs to showcase fine art and crafts produced in the Canadian Arctic. It is the finest gallery of its kind anywhere. Prints, drawings, sculpture, wall hangings, and antiquities are all beautifully displayed. *9 Prince Arthur Ave., tel. 416/921–9985. One of the rare galleries to remain open on Mon. (10–6).*

Prime Canadian Crafts has crafts from across Canada, including avant-garde ceramics, functional teapots, wall sculpture, and jewelry. *229 Queen St. W, tel. 416/593–5750. Open Mon.–Sat. 11–6.*

Ydessa Gallery, recently moved to King Street, near Bathurst, is now, more than ever, a wonderful, major showcase for contemprary international art. *778 King St., 2 blocks west of Bathurst, tel. 416/941–9000. Open 1–5.*

Klonaridis, Inc., located north off Queen Street, is run by a young dealer of discerning taste who displays local talent and imports some of the newest and best from New York and elsewhere south of the border. A must place for those interested in new, exciting art. *179 John St., tel. 416/979–1090. Open Wed.–Sat. 11–5.*

Jane Corkin Photographic Gallery, in the same building, has proven that photography is a major art form. Featuring everyone from Andre Kertesz to Richard Avedon, this is one of the most fascinating galleries in town, showing hand-painted photos, documentary photos, and fashion photography. *Tel. 416/979–1980. Open Tues.–Sat. 10–5.*

The Isaacs Gallery (179 John St., tel. 416/595–0770), run by Av Isaacs, was a mainstay for Canadian abstract expressionists during the 1950s, giving tremendous support to nonobjective art when Canadians did not yet dare to buy it and other galleries did not show it. Many of those he has shown have become well-known: William Kurelek, Robert Markle, Michael Snow, Mark Prent, Gordon Rayner, Joyce Wieland, Greg Curnoe, Dennis Burton.

Carmen Lamanna Gallery (788 King St. W, tel. 416/363–8787), for many years the most avant-garde gallery in the city, specializes in conceptual and experimental art. It's not surprising that many of Lamanna's clients are curators of public and commercial galleries around the world.

Olga Korper (80 Spadina Ave., tel. 416/363–5268) is one of the most accessible and knowledgeable dealers in Toronto, and he is a trailblazer who has discovered many important artists. This is a fine place for beginning collectors to visit.

Wynick-Tuck Gallery, in the same building (tel. 416/364–8716), represents contemporary Canadian artists whose work expresses a wide range of untrendy, often imagistic concerns. Many of them have become well established, attesting to the gallery's influence.

Bau-Xi Gallery, across the street from the Art Gallery of Ontario (340 Dundas St. N, tel. 416/977–0600), was founded by Paul Wong, an artist and dealer from Vancouver. It provides a window on contemporary Canadian west coast art (some from Ontario, as well), much of it affordable.

Parks and Gardens

Toronto was originally a series of little villages, each one treasuring its tiny common or park. The metro area now has some 3 million souls, but residents still think in the old village way, saving from development as much parkland as is possible. The parks are more than just grass; they are great places to jog, bike, picnic, see flowers, even bird-watch. Some have skating rinks, tennis courts, and playing fields.

Edwards Gardens. Thirty-five acres of beautiful hillside gardens flow into one of the city's most popular ravines. Paths wind along colorful floral displays and exquisite rock gardens. Refreshments and picnic facilities are available, but no pets are allowed.

The great ravine walk begins at Edwards Gardens (entrance on the southwest corner of Leslie St. and Lawrence Avenue E). Head south through **Wilket Creek Park** and through the winding Don River valley. Pass beneath the Don Valley Parkway and continue along Massey Creek. After hours of walking (or biking, or jogging) through almost uninterrupted parkland, you'll end up at the southern tip of **Taylor Creek Park** on Victoria Park Avenue, just north of the Danforth. From here you can catch a subway back to your hotel.

High Park. Toronto's equivalent of London's Hyde Park or Manhattan's Central Park (but with no political ranting and few muggings) is three or four miles from downtown, but it is certainly worth a visit—especially in the summer, when there are many special events, including free productions of Shakespeare. One of the highlights is **Grenadier Pond,** a small lake in the southwest corner. Named for the British soldiers who used to drill on its frozen surface in the last century, it is home today to thousands of migrating birds. You can fish in its well-stocked waters, either from the shore or from a rented row-boat. There are Sunday afternoon concerts in summer and supervised skating in winter. The **High Park Zoo** is a far cry from the Metro Zoo, but it's a lot closer, and it's free. It's modest enough that even young children won't tire walking among the deer, Barbary sheep, peacocks, rabbits, and the only truly native Torontonians extant—raccoons. Other high lights of the park are a large swimming pool, tennis courts, fitness trails, and hillside gardens with roses and sculpted hedges.

Take the Bloor Street subway west to the High Park station, or the College Street streetcar to the eastern end of the park. There's limited parking along Bloor Street, just north of the park, and along the side streets on the eastern side.

Highland Creek ravines. Since these are almost in their natural state, they are considered the most beautiful in Toronto—ideal for cross-country skiing, biking, and jogging. There are two parks that follow Highland Creek, **Colonel Danforth Park** and **Morningside Park.** The Colonel Danforth trail begins south of Kingston Road, on the east side of Highland Creek bridge. Morningside Park is accessible off Morningside Avenue, between Kingston Road and Ellesmere Avenue. Both parks can be entered from the grounds of Scarborough College, 1265 Military Trail, in Scarborough. The **Toronto Field Naturalists** (tel. 416/968–6255) lead over 150 outings every year, mainly within these ravine systems.

Humber Valley. This parkland in Toronto's west end is well worth a hiking/jogging/biking tour. It stretches along the Humber River ravine, from north of the city limits (Steeles Ave.) all the way down to where the Humber flows quietly into Lake Ontario.

James Gardens, a lovely formal garden, can be reached from Edenbridge Drive, east of Royal York Road. Adjoining it to the south is **Scarlet Mills Park,** one of North America's only wild-flower reserves. Both parks are open daily until sunset, with lots of free parking.

Nordheimer Ravine. This can be approached from a path leading from Boulton Drive, in the shadow of Casa Loma. On your right is a view of the great mansions of Forest Hill; on your left is Casa Loma, rising above a steep bank of trees. The ravine eventually opens up like a flower, and you are soon at **Churchill Park,** which, as we've noted, has the best tobogganing in the city.

Queen's Park. This small, lovely park in the heart of the downtown area is discussed in Tour 3 in the Exploring chapter. It's not worth a special trip, but it's certainly worth remembering after a day of shopping or museum-hopping.

The **Rosedale ravines** are only a few minutes walk from the shopping mecca of Yonge and Bloor streets, in the very heart of the city. They are a series of peaceful ravines that cut through the luxurious, heavily wooded neighborhood of Rosedale. Walk north from the Castle Frank subway station along Castle Frank Road to **Hawthorn Gardens.** There you will find a short footpath to **Craigleigh Gardens.** Suddenly, this tiny, quiet park gives way to a ravine, and paths wind steeply down through a tangle of underbrush. From here you can go west, up Balfour Creek, across Mount Pleasant Road, and through **David Balfour Park** to St. Clair Avenue. Or you can walk northeast, past the Don Valley brickworks to **Chorley Park** and Mount Pleasant Cemetery, by way of the still-undeveloped Moore Park marshes. These marshes remain an excellent breeding ground for wildlife, though they lie within the core of a bustling city. Another way to explore this ravine is to start at Yonge Street and St. Clair Avenue. Walk east along St. Clair Avenue a few blocks, until you come to a bridge. On the north side of the street is a sign marked "nature trail." Believe it.

Scarborough Bluffs. This is the most scenic park along Lake Ontario, with breathtaking views from the high lakeside cliffs. **Cathedral Bluffs Park,** at the foot of Midland Avenue, also offers dramatic views.

Sherwood Park. Farther north, near Lawrence Avenue East and Mt. Pleasant Road, is one of the best-kept secrets in Toronto. Sherwood Park has one of the finest children's playgrounds in the city, a lovely wading pool, and a hill that seems to go on forever. Head up Mt. Pleasant Road, north of Eglinton Avenue, until you see a little street called Sherwood on the right. Go east a long block, and you're there. A ravine begins at the bottom of the hill. You can follow it across Blythwood Road, all the way to Yonge Street and Lawrence Avenue. There, subways and buses await you—and so do the beautiful rose gardens in **Alexander Muir Park.**

Sir Casimir Gzowski Park. Enjoy marvelous views of the Toronto Islands, Ontario Place, and the downtown skyline, and swim at nearby **Sunnyside Park.** Both lakefront parks are only a few blocks east of Bathurst Street, easily accessible by streetcar.

Sir Winston Churchill Park. Winter visitors—especially those with children—should try not to miss this park, located at Spadina Avenue, only a short walk from Casa Loma. In summer there's a sweet playground, a sandbox, a jogging track, and tennis courts. In winter there's a serious hill offering the most terrifying toboggan run in the city.

Tommy Thompson Park. This interesting place, known until 1985 as the **Leslie Street Spit,** is a peninsula that juts five kilometers (3 miles) into Lake Ontario. It was created from the sand dredged for a new port entry and the landfill of a hundred skyscrapers. (These Canadians don't waste a thing.) It has quickly become one of the best areas in the city for cycling, jogging, walking, sailing, photography, and bird-watching.

This strange, man-made peninsula immediately became the home (or stopover) for the largest colony of ring-billed seagulls in the world and for dozens of other species of terns, ducks, geese, and snowy egrets.

No private vehicles are permitted, but on weekends, mid-May to mid-October, two vans operate free of charge from the parking lot. In summer, a city bus travels through the park from the corner of Queen Street and Berkshire Avenue.

If you drive, go east along Queen Street to Leslie Street, then south to the lake. The park is open weekends and holidays 9–6.

The Toronto Islands. *See* Tour 1 in Exploring.

Theme Parks and Amusement Areas

African Lion Safari. This fabulous drive-through wildlife park is a full hour's drive from Toronto, but it should be considered by anyone with children and access to a car.

If the idea of a giraffe sticking its head into your backseat does not warm your heart, there are air-conditioned trams that carry as many as 3,000 visitors a day over a six-mile safari trail. Lions, tigers, cheetah, black bears, elephants, white rhinos, and zebras make this astonishingly uncommercial park truly special.

In addition to six large game reserves, there's a birds of prey flying demonstration, a parrot show, an elephant roundup, and even an *African Queen*-style boat that cruises past birds and primates. *Located near Cambridge, Ontario, due west of Toronto. Take Hwy. 401 west to Hwy. 6. Drive south to Safari Road, and turn right. Package tours are offered by Gray Coach. The trip takes about an hour. Tel. 519/623–2620. Admission, including the boat and railway cruises: $10.95 adults, which will probably increase to $11.95 in 1990, $8.95 youth ages 13–17, $6.95 children ages 3–12 and senior citizens. You may want to pack a picnic, but food is available. Open Apr.–mid-Oct. 10–4, 4:30, or 5. Weekends only in early Apr.*

Black Creek Pioneer Village. This recreation of a 19th-century Ontario community is a joyous outing for the entire family. *See* Historic Buildings and Sites.

Canada's Wonderland. Yogi Bear, Fred Flintstone, Scooby Doo, and other Canadian cultural heroes are part of a $160-million theme park overflowing with games, rides, restaurants, and shops. The entertainment ranges from Broadway-style productions to pop and rock performances to dolphin shows. Canada's first world-class theme park lacks the warm evocativeness of Disneyland; and because it's here in the Frozen North, its season runs only from late April to early October. Yet the park is remarkably close to Toronto—barely 30 minutes from downtown, and only 15 minutes from the airport—and a visit here can easily be combined with a trip to Black Creek Pioneer Village.

Children will love it here, but adults should stay away unless they've been longing for brassy entertainment, stomach-churning rides, and eateries such as Yee Ribb Pytt, which serves French Fryes and Shrymps. Indeed, families should consider packing a picnic lunch and eating at the few tables (reluctantly) provided, just outside the park.

Teens and many adults will be delighted to know that on the grounds of Canada's Wonderland is the high-quality **Kingswood Music Theatre** (tel. 416/832–8131), which has excellent pop and rock acts through the summer that cost only $7 above the park admission. The open-air facility has 5,200 reserved seats under a covered pavilion and 8,800 additional seats on the sloping lawn.

The low-cost GO express buses leave regularly from the Yorkdale and York Mills subway stations. By car, take Hwy. 401 to Hwy. 400; drive north about 10 minutes to Rutherford Road, and follow the signs. Tel. 416/832–7000. Admission: $21.95 adults, $9.95 children 3–6 and senior citizens over 60. Grounds admission alone, which does not include rides, is 13.95 adults. Those who plan to return several times should consider an individual season pass, $37.95; a family season pass, $109.95 for 4 people; $27.50 for each additional person. These prices invariably go up 10% each year. Visitors should check newspapers, chain stores and hotels for half-price tickets. Open spring and fall weekends 10–8; late May–Labor Day, daily 10–10.

The Canadian National Exhibition (the CNE or "the Ex"), at the foot of Dufferin Street and Lakeshore Boulevard, attracts over three million people each year. It began back in 1879 as an agricultural show, and remnants of that tradition can still be found in the livestock exhibits. But in its second century, the Ex is a noisy, crowded, often entertaining collection of carnies pushing five-dollar balloons, tummy-turning midway rides, sexist beauty contests, live bands, horticultural and technological exhibits, and (sometimes) top-notch happenings.

Parades, dog swims, horse shows, grandstand shows with such talent as Bill Cosby, Kenny Rogers, and Whitney Houston—the Exhibition has something for all. It's often vulgar and brassy, the snacks overpriced and greasy, the rides too short and too expensive. But it can also be an enjoyable way to spend an afternoon—after all, the world's largest annual exhibition must have *something* still going for it! *Lakeshore Blvd. W at Strachan ("strawn") Ave. or off Dufferin St., just south of King. Tel. 416/393–6000. In 1990, the CNE will run Aug. 15–Sept. 3. Open daily 8 AM–1 AM; buildings, open 10–10. Admission: about $7 adults; senior citizens free until noon and about $2 thereafter; less than $1 for children 13 and under. Tickets to grandstand shows available from the box office, as well through Ticketmaster (tel. 416/872–2277). Check local newspapers for special daily events. Never take a car to the Ex; the parking is insufficient and always terribly overpriced. Many buses and streetcars labeled "Exhibition" travel across the city into the CNE grounds. Tel. 416/393–6000.*

Centreville. A charming, modest, and low-priced amusement area for younger children, it is located on Centre Island, just a 10-minute ferry ride from the foot of Bay Street (*see* Tour 1 in Exploring).

Harbourfront. A brilliant collection of parks, marinas, theater, dance, restaurants, boutiques, festivals, and more, situated just east of Ontario Place, along the waterfront (*see* Tour 1 in Exploring).

Marineland. A park full of quality rides and dolphin/killer whale shows, about 90 minutes southwest of Toronto (*see* Niagara Falls, Ontario, in Excursions).

Ontario Place. Highlights of this waterfront complex, built on three man-made islands, include the **Cinesphere** (a dome with a six-story movie screen enclosed); several interesting shows in pods that float above the waters of Lake Ontario; the ***Haida,*** a destroyer from the Second World War that is fun to explore; and, best of all, the outdoor **Forum,** where free nightly concerts by everyone from the Toronto Symphony to world-famous rock stars take place (free once you've paid your way into the park, that is). Here, too, you will find the **Children's Village**—complete with water games, towering tube slides, and a moon walk. This is one of the most creative playgrounds in the world, and a must for children 3–14. Children's theater, puppet shows, clowns, and magicians are also included with admission. The eateries are uneven, and the Imax films at the massive Cinesphere tend to be all medium and no message (though still a thrill). But Ontario Place is still a major summer draw to the waterfront, and irresistible to those in their early teens and younger. *South of Lakeshore Blvd., across from CNE grounds. Tel. 416/965–7711. Open daily mid-May–mid-Sept. 10 AM–1 AM; Sun. 10–10. Admission: $6 adults and "juniors"; $2 children under 13; $3 senior citizens, but free on Wednesdays. Bumper boats, pedal boats, miniature golf, the Haida warship, and a few other attractions have an additional charge of under $2.*

Throughout much of the winter, the Cinesphere has been offering 70 mm films such as ET. *Check daily newspapers for times, and remember that one has not truly lived until one has seen* Indiana Jones *surrounded by snakes on a 60′ by 80′ screen.*

Canada's Wild Water Kingdom. This recent collection of waterslides, river-rapids ride, and more is not far from Black Creek Pioneer Village and Canada's Wonderland, just northwest of Toronto (*see* What to See and Do with Children in Chapter 3).

Libraries and Special Collections

Boys and Girls House. When it opened in 1922, this was the first library in the British Empire that was devoted entirely to children's books. It's still one of the best. (40 St. George St., tel. 416/393–7746). **The Osborne and Smith Collections of Early Children's Books,** located in the same building, is a world-renowned collection of children's literature. Dr. Edgar Osborne, a British librarian, presented his private collection of about 2,000 children's books to the Toronto Public Library in 1949; today there are more than 21,000. The collection includes letters written and illustrated by Beatrix Potter, and the oldest book is a fairy tale printed in 1476. There are regular lectures and changing exhibits on everything from fairy tales to Christmas customs of the Victorians. *Tel. 416/393–7753. Open weekdays 10–6, Sat. 9–5; July–Aug., closes weekdays at 4 PM.*

Metropolitan Toronto Library. One of the most beautiful and accessible public libraries in the world (*see* Tour 3 in Exploring).

The Spaced-Out Library. This is the largest public collection of science-fiction material in the world. Although only a small percentage of the volumes is allowed to circulate, the collection includes more than 20,000 books, many of them in foreign languages, and close to 10,000 magazines, including a complete collection of *Galaxy. 40 St. George St., on the 2nd floor of Boys and Girls House; tel. 416/393–7748. Open weekdays 10–6, Sat. 9–5.*

Thomas Fisher Rare Books Library. Scholars and lovers of antique books may find this place of particular interest. Part of the University of Toronto, it has tomes and manuscripts going back to the early Middle Ages. *120 St. George St., just a few blocks west of University Ave. and the Royal Ontario Museum and just south of Bloor St.; tel. 416/978–5285. Open weekdays 9–4:45.*

5 Sports and Fitness

Participant Sports

A wide range of sports is available for each of Toronto's four distinct seasons. From Lake Ontario to the skiing hills just outside the city and the beautiful lakes and parks beyond, a thousand sports and recreational activities are available.

Contact the Ministry of Tourism and Recreation (Queen's Park, Toronto, Ont. M7A 2R2) for pamphlets on various activities. For information on sports activities in the province, phone 800/268–3735 from anywhere in the continental United States and Canada (except the Northwest Territories and the Yukon). In Toronto, contact Ontario Travel (tel. 416/965–4008).

A number of fine **conservation areas** circle the Metro Toronto area, many less than a half-hour from the downtown area. Most have large swimming areas, sledding, and cross-country skiing, as well as skating, fishing, and boating. Contact the Metro Conservation Authority (tel. 416/661–6600) and ask for their pamphlet.

Bicycling There are over 18 miles of street bike routes cutting across the city and dozens more along safer paths through Toronto's many parks (*see* Parks and Gardens in Sites and Attractions). Bikes can be rented on the Toronto Islands. The **Martin Goodman Trail** is a 12–mile strip that runs along the waterfront all the way from the Balmy Beach Club in the east end, out past the western beaches southwest of High Park. Phone the *Toronto Star* (tel. 416/367–2000) for a map.

Metro Parks Department (tel. 416/392–8186) has maps that show bike (and jogging) routes that run through Toronto parkland. **Ontario Cycling** (tel. 416/495–4141) has maps, booklets, and information.

Boardsailing Equipment can be rented in various areas of the waterfront. Try along Bloor Street West, near the High Park subway station.

Boating Grenadier Pond in High Park, Centre Island, Ontario Place, Harbourfront, and most of the Conservation Areas surrounding Metro Toronto rent canoes, punts, and/or sailboats.

Bowling Don't laugh; Toronto has 5-pin, a marvelous tradition unknown to most Americans. This sport of rolling a tiny ball down an alley at five fat pins—each with a different numerical value, for a possible (impossible) score of 450—is perfect for children, even as young as three or four. **Bowlerama** has lanes all over the city; look in the yellow pages for locations. This can provide an entertaining few hours on a rainy day.

Fishing One does not have to go very far from downtown Toronto to catch trout, perch, bass, walleye, salmon, muskie, pike, and whitefish. Contact Communication Services, Wildlife Information, Ministry of Natural Resources (Queen's Park, Toronto M7A 1W3, tel. 416/965–4251).

Within Metro Toronto itself, fishing is permitted in the trout pond at Hanlon's Point on Toronto Island, as well as in Grenadier Pond in High Park. And the salmon fishing just off the Scarborough Bluffs, in Toronto's east end, is extraordinary! Every summer there is a Great Salmon Hunt, with cash prizes. Check the *Toronto Star*, which sponsors it, for details.

There are over 100 charter boats on Lake Ontario (about $60 for a half-day). Contact **Ontario Travel** (tel. 416/965–4008). Be warned, though: Some fish caught in this province have such high levels of mercury in them that you can take your temperature at the same time that you eat them. It's sad, but water pollution (including acid rain) has taken its toll upon the edibility of many fish in Ontario.

Golf The season lasts only from April to late October. The top course is **Glen Abbey** (tel. 416/844–1800), where the Canadian Open Championships is held. Cart and green fees will cost up to $75 on weekends, but this course is a real beauty.

Less challenging courses—and much closer to the heart of the city—include the **Don Valley Golf Course,** just south of Highway 401 (Yonge St., tel. 416/392–2465); the **Flemingdon Park Golf Club** (Don Mills Rd. and Eglinton Ave., tel. 416/429-1740). For other courses, contact Metro Parks (tel. 416/367–8186) or Ontario Travel (tel. 416/965–4008).

Horseback Riding There are two stables within the city limits. **Central Don Stables,** in Sunnybrook Park (Leslie St. and Eglinton Ave., tel. 416/444–4044), has an indoor arena, an outdoor ring, and nearly 12 miles of bridle trails through the Don Valley. **Eglinton Equestrian Club** (near Don Mills Rd. and John St., tel. 416/889–6375) has two indoor arenas.

Just north of the city, in Richmond Hill, the **Rocking Horse Ranch** (tel. 416/884–3292) offers scenic western trail rides year-round. For booklets detailing riding establishments across the province, call **Ontario Travel** (tel. 416/965–4008) or **Equestrian Ontario** (tel. 416/495–4125). The disabled will be pleased to hear of the **Community Association for Riding for the Disabled** (tel. 416/667–8600), which offers riding in a park near Black Creek Pioneer Village. Children as young as four years old can ride here, thanks to the **Variety Club** (tel. 416/961–7300).

Hunting There is little hunting within a few hours' drive of Toronto, and even that is limited to the fall: deer, moose, and black bear. The waterfowl season is longer, extending from fall into the winter. Contact Public Information Centre, Room 1640, Ministry of Natural Resources (Queen's Park, Toronto M7A 1W3, tel. 416/965–4251), or write the Ontario Federation of Anglers and Hunters (Box 1269, Campbellford, Ontario).

Ice Skating Toronto operates some 30 outdoor artificial rinks and 100 natural-ice rinks—and all are free! Among the most popular are in Nathan Phillips Square, in front of the New City Hall, at Queen and Bay streets; down at Harbourfront (which has Canada's largest outdoor artificial ice rink); College Park, at Yonge and College streets; Grenadier Pond, within High Park, at Bloor Street and Keele Street; and inside Hazelton Lanes, that classy shopping mall on the edge of Yorkville, on Avenue Road, just above Bloor Street. *Tel. 416/392–7259.*

Jogging The **Martin Goodman Trail** (*see* Bicycling) is ideal. Also try the boardwalk of The Beaches in the east end; High Park in the west end; the Toronto Islands; or any of Toronto's parks.

Roller Skating The one major stadium in Toronto is **The Terrace** (70 Mutual St., at Dundas St., just east of Yonge St., tel. 416/363–8741)—only a few blocks from Eaton Centre.

Sailing This can be a breeze, especially between April and October. Contact the Ontario Sailing Association (tel. 416/495–4240).

Skiing
Cross-country Try Toronto's parks and ravines; High Park; the lakefront along the southern edge of the city; Tommy Thompson Park; Toronto Islands; and, perhaps best of all, the inspired concept of Zooski, out at the stunning Metro Toronto Zoo, where one can ski past lions, leopards, and other furry friends. Check the yellow pages for ski equipment rentals; there are many places. Only Zooski charges a fee; all other places are free.

Downhill Although there are a few places where one can get a taste of this sport within Metro Toronto, such as **Earl Bales Park,** on Bathurst Street, just south of Sheppard Avenue, and **Centennial Park Ski Hill** in Etobicoke (tel. 416/394–8754), the *best* alpine hills are a good 30–60 minutes north of the city. These include **Blue Mountain Resorts** in Collingwood, Ontario (tel. 416/869–3799), the **Caledon Ski Club** in Caledon (tel. 416/453–7404), **Glen Eden Ski Area** in Milton (tel. 416/878–5011), **Hidden Valley** in Huntsville (tel. 705/789–2301), **Hockley Valley Resort** in Orangeville (tel. 519/942–0754), and **Horseshoe Valley** in Barrie (tel. 705/835–2790). Phone 416/963–2992 for daily reports on lifts and surface conditions.

Sleigh Riding and Tobogganing **Black Creek Pioneer Village** (tel. 416/661–6610 or 416/661–6600), north of 401 along Highway 400, at Steeles Avenue, is open winter weekends 10-4 for skating, tobogganing, and horse-drawn sleigh rides. The best parks for tobogganing include **High Park,** in the west end, and our favorite, **Winston Churchill Park,** at Spadina Avenue and St. Clair Avenue, just two blocks from Casa Loma. It is sheer terror.

Swimming The beaches of Lake Ontario are studies in extremes: The water can be bitter cold, even through the summer, while the sand can raise blisters on the hottest days of the year. Many beaches are too polluted for safe swimming; phone the city's public health department (tel. 416/392–7466) for the latest report.

In the east end, **Beaches Park,** south of Queen Street and east of Coxwell Avenue, is lovely, thanks to the lengthy boardwalk, local canoe club, public washrooms, and tennis courts. Even closer to the downtown area—only a 20-minute streetcar-ride away, along Queen Street—are **Woodbine Beach Park** and **Ashbridges Bay Park,** both fine for sunbathing and boat-watching (*see* The Beaches in Tour 4 in Exploring).

To the west of the downtown area is another fine area, **Sunnyside Beach,** which has a pool, snack bar, jungle gym, and washrooms.

The most pleasing beaches—and certainly the ones with the best views—are on the **Toronto Islands** (*see* Tour 1 in Exploring). Remember, though, that Lake Ontario is rarely warm enough for sustained swimming, except for a few weeks in late August.

Public swimming is available in 16 indoor pools, 12 outdoor pools, and 15 community recreation centers; call the Toronto Department of Parks and Recreation (tel. 416/392–7259) for hours and locations.

Tennis The city provides dozens of courts, all free, and many of them floodlighted. Parks with courts open from 7 AM to 11 PM, in season, include the famous High Park in the west end; Stanley Park, on King Street West, three blocks west of Bathurst Street; and Eglinton Park, on Eglinton Avenue West, just east of Avenue Road. Call the Ontario Tennis Association (tel. 416/495–4215).

Hotel Health Facilities Nearly every major hotel in the Metro Toronto area has a decent indoor swimming pool; some even have indoor/outdoor swimming pools. The best include the **Sheraton Centre,** at Queen and Bay streets, and the **Inn on the Park,** at Eglinton Avenue near Leslie Street. Many also have health clubs, with saunas and Nautilus equipment.

Spectator Sports

Toronto has always been an exciting sports city, but since the Toronto Blue Jays made their debut—in a snowstorm!—in 1977, the place has gone wild. (Indeed, while the Blue Jays lolled about in the basement of the American League for their first five years, nearly 8 million fans poured into the ugly, uncomfortable Exhibition Stadium, down at the CNE grounds.) With the June 1989 opening of the extraordinary new SkyDome, you can just imagine how revved up the city will be.

Auto Racing For the past several years, the **Molson Indy** (tel. 416/595–5445) has been roaring around the Canadian National Exhibition grounds, including the major thoroughfare of Lakeshore Boulevard, for three days in mid-July. You'll pay over $75 for a three-day "red" reserved seat, but general admission for the qualification rounds, the practice rounds, and the Indy itself, can be as cheap as $10–$40, depending upon the day. Considering that this ancient tradition began in only 1986, the Molson Indy has already become Toronto's international showcase to the motor racing world. And with the cars reaching speeds of up to 200 mph, you'd better hurry down.

Then, there is **Mosport,** about 60 miles northeast of Toronto, where motorcycle and formula racing are held; the Can-Am is in June and September. *Take 401 east to Exit 75, then drive north to the track. Tel. 416/665–6665.*

Less than a half-hour drive away is the **Cayuga International Speedway** (tel. 416/765–4461), where international stock-car races are held from May through September.

Baseball As noted, the **Toronto Blue Jays** have developed into one of baseball's most dynamic teams, and are all the more popular since their move into the SkyDome in the summer of 1989. *For ticket information, tel. 416/595–0077; to charge tickets, 595–1362.*

Canoeing and Rowing The world's largest **canoeing and rowing regatta** is held every July 1, as it has been for over a century, on Toronto Island's Long Pond. *Canoe Ontario, tel. 416/495–4180.*

Football Although the Canadian Football League has been teetering on the brink of dissolution, the **Toronto Argonauts** have, in recent years, developed into annual contenders. Americans might find the three downs and 110-yard field to be rather quaint, but the game is much like their own. *Tel. 416/595–1131 for tickets and information.*

Golf The permanent site of the **du Maurier Canadian Open** golf championship is Glen Abbey, a course designed by Jack Nicklaus. This tournament is one of golf's Big Five and is always played in the last week in June. *Less than a 45-min drive* *west, along the Queen Elizabeth Way (QEW). Tel. 416/844–1800.*

The Ladies Professional Golf Association tour comes to Toronto's St. George's Golf and Country Club for the **du Maurier classic,** the last week in July. *1668 Islington Ave., in Toronto's west end. Phone Ticketmaster, tel. 416/872–1212.*

Hockey The **Toronto Maple Leafs** play 40 home games each season (Oct.–Apr.), usually on Wednesday and Saturday nights, in the big, ugly Maple Leaf Gardens. There are always tickets available at each game—at least from scalpers in front of the stadium on Carlton Street, a half-block east of the corner of Yonge and College streets. Call the office (tel. 416/977–1641) at 9 AM sharp on the day of the game you wish to see.

Horse Racing

Harness Racing The **Greenwood** track, built in 1874, is where the best trotters and pacers do their stuff, at three annual meetings. *Tel. 416/675–6110. Spring gathering runs Jan.–mid-Mar.; summermeeting, late May–Sept.; the brief winter meeting, the last two weeks in Dec.*

Thoroughbred Racing There are four major racetracks handled by the Ontario Jockey Club (tel. 416/675–6110)–two in the Toronto area; one down in Fort Erie, near Buffalo; and another about two dozen miles west of Toronto.

Greenwood Race Track is one of the premier harness tracks in North America and is the home of many of Canada's greatest trotting and pacing events, including the North American Cup. It is located in the city's east end, a 10-minute streetcar ride from downtown, at Woodbine Avenue and Queen Street East, near the lakeshore. *Tel. 416/698–3131. Winter meeting runs late Oct.–early Dec.; spring meeting runs mid-Mar.–late Apr.*

Woodbine Race Track is the showplace of Thoroughbred racing in Canada. *Located 30-min northeast of downtown Toronto, not far from the airport, at Hwy. 27 and Rexdale Blvd.; tel. 416/675–6110. Horses run late Apr.–early Aug.; then Sept.–Oct.*

Mohawk is in the heart of Ontario's Standardbred breeding country, and it features a glass-enclosed, climate-controlled grandstand and other attractive facilities. *A 30-min. drive west of Toronto, along Hwy. 401, past the town of Milton; tel. 416/854–2255.*

Fort Erie, in the Niagara tourist region, is one of the most picturesque racetracks in the world, with willows, manicured hedges, and flower-bordered infield lakes. It has racing on the dirt as well as on grass, with the year's highlight being the Prince of Wales Stakes, the second jewel in Canada's Triple Crown of Racing. *Tel. 416/871–3200 from Toronto, 716/856–0293 from Buffalo.*

Royal Horse Show This highlight of Canada's equestrian season is part of the Royal Winter Fair each November. *The CNE grounds, Dufferin St., by the waterfront. Tel. 416/393–6400.*

Ice Canoe Racing Every January, five-man/woman teams haul canoes across the ice floes off Harbourfront.

Soccer Although Toronto keeps getting and losing and getting a professional soccer team, one can catch this exciting sport, as well as collegiate football, in the very handy **Varsity Stadium.** *Bloor*

St. W at Bedford, a block west of the Royal Ontario Museum and University Ave. Tel. 416/979–2186.

Tennis The finest players in the world gather at the tennis complex on the York University campus, near Finch Avenue and Keele Street, each summer, for the **Player's International Canadian Open.** The York campus is not far from Black Creek Pioneer Village, the McMichael Gallery, and Canada's Wonderland. *For tickets, phone Tennis Canada, tel. 416/665–9777, or Ticketmaster outlets, tel. 416/872–1212.*

6 Shopping

Introduction

Toronto prides itself on having some of the finest shopping in North America; and, indeed, most of the world's name boutiques can be found here, especially along the Bloor Street strip (between Yonge Street and Avenue Road) and in the Yorkville area, which covers the three streets immediately north of and parallel to the Bloor Street strip.

Although some Canadians have traditionally frowned on the concept of discount stores as vulgar and beneath them, there are many moderately priced stores around the city and a lively off-price clothing trade. Because of the weakness of the Canadian dollar, visitors obtain what amounts to an immediate discount on any purchase.

Toronto has a large artistic and crafts community, with many art galleries, custom jewelers, clothing designers, and artisans. From sophisticated glass sculpture to native and Inuit art, the many beautiful objects you'll find are ideal for gifts or for your own home. Among traditional crafts, available at antique and specialty stores, are quilts, wood carvings, and pine furniture.

Food items that are fairly easy to transport as gifts include wild rice, available in bulk or in gift packages, and maple syrup in jars or cans.

If you can afford it, fur coats and hats are a popular item with visitors from outside Canada. You can buy from a high-fashion outlet such as Creed's (on Bloor Street west of Yonge Street) or directly from a furrier in the Spadina Avenue garment district. Beaded Indian slippers and moccasins are also popular souvenirs. Distinctive **Hudson Bay** wool blankets, available only at The Bay, are an enduring Canadian tradition. The unique Tilley hat, sold by mail order or in the **Tilley Endurables** boutique at Queen's Quay Terminal, is an ideal present for sailors and adventurers: It's advertised as having been retrieved intact after being eaten by an elephant, and comes with a lifetime guarantee and owner's manual.

The better record stores stock a good selection of Canadian musicians, from Maureen Forrester and Liona Boyd to Anne Murray, Leonard Cohen, Kate and Anna McGarrigle, the Nylons, and Stringband, as well as French-Canadian stars like Robert Charlebois. Similarly, good bookstores will introduce you to Canadian authors such as Margaret Atwood, Robertson Davies, Timothy Findley, Margaret Laurence, Alice Munro, and popular historian Pierre Berton.

Most stores accept MasterCard and Visa without minimums, though if you charge a purchase under $5 you won't be too popular. Major stores also accept American Express. You'll find American cash generally accepted, although not always at the most favorable rate of exchange.

Most stores are open late on Thursdays; some, like the Eaton Centre and Simpsons downtown, are open late every weekday. Liquor stores are unlikely to be open late more than one night a week, perhaps Friday, although beer stores stay open later.

The biggest sale day of the year is Boxing Day, the first business day after Christmas, when nearly everything in the city, including furs, is half price. In fact, clothing prices tend to drop even further as winter fades. Summer sales start in late June and continue through August.

Shopping Districts

The **Yorkville Avenue/Bloor Street area** is where you'll find the big fashion names, fine leather goods, important jewelers, some of the top private art galleries, upscale shoe stores, and discount china and glassware. Streets to explore include Yorkville Avenue, Cumberland Street, and Scollard Street, all running parallel to Bloor Street, and Hazelton Avenue, running north from Yorkville Avenue near Avenue Road. Hazelton Lanes, between Hazelton Avenue and Avenue Road, and the adjacent York Square are among the most chi-chi shopping areas in Canada, and they are headquarters for café society during the brief annual spell of warm weather. Back in the 1960s, Yorkville was Canada's hippie headquarters, a mecca for potheads, runaways, and folk musicians. Goodbye Dylan, hello Gucci.

On **Bloor Street** you'll find **Creed's** and **Holt Renfrew**—both very-high-end clothing stores (Holt's has men's and children's departments as well)—Harry Rosen for men, Georg Jensen, and shoe shops like Boutique Quinto and David's.

The **Eaton Centre** is a very large galleria-style shopping center downtown, on Yonge Street between Queen and Dundas streets. With scores of large and small stores and restaurants, all sheltered from the weather, it's one of the city's major tourist attractions. Generally speaking, the lower levels are lower priced and the higher levels are more expensive. In the immediate area are Sam the Record Man, probably Toronto's most comprehensive record/CD store; Simpson's department store; a smaller shopping center called **The Atrium on Bay,** which is immediately north of the Eaton Centre and not tremendously interesting; and an assortment of cut-price consumer electronics stores on Yonge Street.

Queen Street West, starting just west of University Avenue and continuing past Spadina Avenue, creeping ever westward past Bathurst Street, is a trendy area near the Ontario College of Art. Here you'll find young, hip designers; new and used bookstores; vintage clothes; two comic book stores, including the biggest in North America (**Silver Snail,** #367; see also Dragon Lady Comic Shop at #200); and the more progessive private galleries. People-watching is fun here, too. The action is spreading onto John Street and other cross streets, and there's a rather interesting assortment of shops in **Village by the Grange,** a development on McCaul Street south of Dundas Street, across from the Art Gallery of Ontario.

Harbourfront includes an antique market that's Canada's biggest on Sundays, when there are around 200 dealers. (390 Queen's Quay W, tel. 416/364–7500. Open Tues.–Sat. 10–5, Sun. 5–5.) The **Queen's Quay Terminal** is a renovated warehouse that now houses a collection of unique boutiques, craft stalls, patisseries, and so on; it's a great place to buy gifts.

There's a free shuttle bus from Union Station, or it's a fairly easy walk. Parking is expensive.

Mirvish Village, a one-block assortment of bookstores, antique shops, and boutiques, on Markham Street south of Bloor Street, has the advantage of being open Sundays. (Harbourfront is, too.) If you're in Mirvish Village any other day, though (preferably not Saturday, which is unbearably crowded), check out **Honest Ed's** bargain house at Bathurst and Bloor streets, the truly silly deep-discount store that financed the revival of London's Old Vic theater. It's a good place to buy film for your camera, by the way. The strip of Bloor Street running east from Honest Ed's to Spadina Avenue is a vibrant mix of discount bookstores, casual clothing and health food shops, pubs frequented by students from the University of Toronto, cafés, and Hungarian restaurants; it makes a delightful walk, particularly in the evening.

Another good bet for summer Sundays is **The Beaches,** on Queen Street East, starting at Woodbine Avenue. Here you'll find lots of casual clothing stores, gift and antique shops, and bars and restaurants, all with a resort atmosphere: A boardwalk along the lake is just to the south. Take the Queen Street streetcar; parking can be a hassle.

Spadina Avenue, from Wellington Street north to College Street, has plenty of low-price clothing for the whole family, as well as fur and leather factory outlets. **Winner's,** south of King Street, is a good discount outlet for women and children. **Evex Luggage Centre**, 369 Spadina Avenue, south of College, has good discount luggage, handbags, and leather accessories.

Downtown Toronto has a vast underground maze of shopping warrens that burrow in between and underneath the office towers. The tenants of the **Underground City** are mostly the usual assortment of chain stores, and the shopping is rather dull; also, directions are poorly marked. The network runs roughly from the Royal York Hotel near Union Station north to the Eaton Centre.

If you're venturing to the suburbs, there's a large shopping center at **Yorkdale,** easily reached by subway but pointless if you've been to the Eaton Centre. The area also has a number of off-price outlets for which a car is necessary; check ads in the *Toronto Star*.

For the visitor with time to explore outside the central area, **Little Italy,** on St. Clair Avenue West (roughly between Lansdowne and Westmount), has some high-fashion Milanese clothing stores like Christian Boutique (#1236), LaScala Men's Wear (#1190), Gente Boutique (#1228), and the more casual Cheeky (#1180).

Department Stores

The major department stores have branches around the city and flagship stores downtown. They accept major credit cards and have liberal return policies. However, service tends to be very slow and uninformed compared with that of boutiques, and the stores generally lack the cachet of American chains like Bloomingdale's or Macy's. The big names are **Eaton's,** in the

Albert Britnell, **65**
Allery, **15**
All the Best Breads, **64**
Art Metropole, **3**
Atomic Age, **14**
Atrium on Bay, **60**
Back Store, **64**
Bakka Sci. Fi., **21**
Ballenford Books, **46**
Beaches, The, **74**
Big Carrot, **72**
Bob Miller Book Room, **34**
Book Cellar, **45, 64**
Book City, **4, 66, 72**
Boomer, **27**
Boutique Quinto, **40**
Bragg, **7**
Brown's (clothing), **6, 35**
Brown's (shoes), **39, 62**
Can-Do Bkst., **25**
Children's Bkst., **1**
Christie's, **48**
Clotheslines, **53**
Cookbook Store, **58**
Creed's, **54**
David's, **49**
David Mirvish Books, **1**
David Wood Food, **64**
Early Learning, **17**
Eaton Centre, **61**
Edward's Books, **13, 64,72,74**
Evex Luggage, **11**
Fab, **22**
Fashion Crimes, **16**
Fenton's Foods, **67**
Fetoun, **47**
Filigree, **64**
Friends of Terpsichore, **73**
Glad Day Bkshp., **59**
Glass Art Gallery, **42**
Holt Renfrew, **55**
Honest Ed's, **1**
Hudson Bay, **68**
Isaacs Gallery, **28**
I.X.L., **32**
Jane Corkin, **28**
Just Game, **74**
Kensington Market, **8**
La Mode de Vija, **1**
Lichtman's News, **50, 63,64**
Little Italy, **1**
Longhouse Bk.Shop, **1,5**

Toronto Shopping

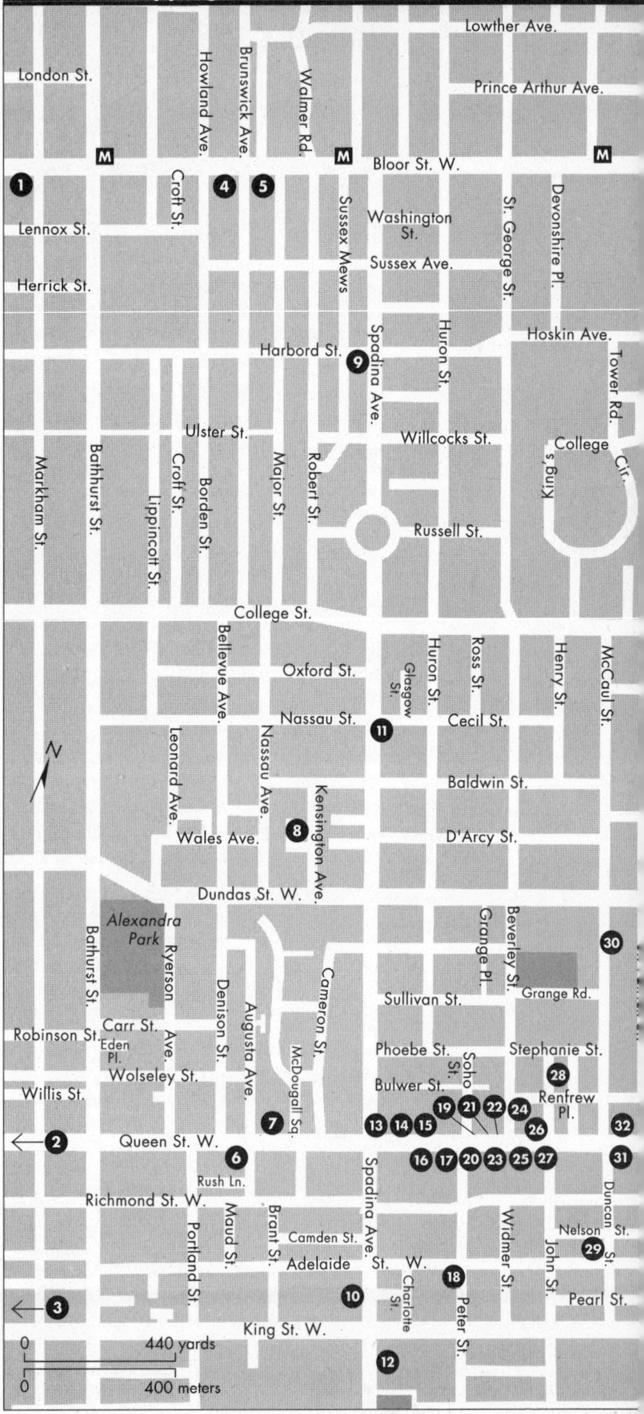

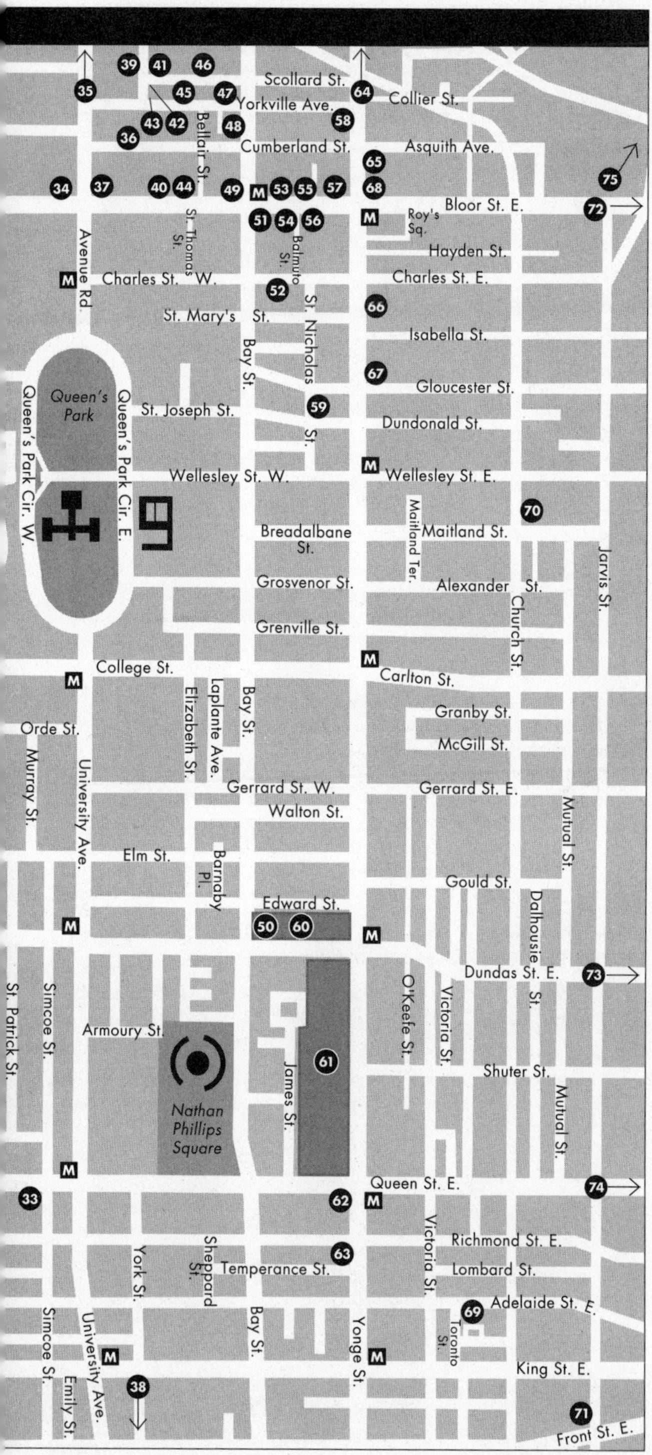
Scollard St.
Yorkville Ave.
Collier St.
Cumberland St.
Asquith Ave.
Bellair St.
Bloor St. E.
Roy's Sq.
Hayden St.
Avenue Rd.
St. Thomas St.
Balmuto St.
Charles St. W.
Charles St. E.
St. Mary's St.
St. Nicholas St.
Isabella St.
Bay St.
Queen's Park
Queen's Park Cir. W.
Queen's Park Cir. E.
Gloucester St.
St. Joseph St.
Dundonald St.
Wellesley St. W.
Wellesley St. E.
Maitland Ter.
Maitland St.
Breadalbane St.
Grosvenor St.
Alexander St.
Jarvis St.
Church St.
Grenville St.
College St.
Carlton St.
Orde St.
Granby St.
McGill St.
Laplante Ave.
Elizabeth St.
Murray St.
University Ave.
Gerrard St. W.
Gerrard St. E.
Walton St.
Mutual St.
Elm St.
Barnaby Pl.
Gould St.
Edward St.
Dalhousie St.
Dundas St. E.
O'Keefe St.
Victoria St.
St. Patrick St.
Simcoe St.
Armoury St.
James St.
Nathan Phillips Square
Shuter St.
Queen St. E.
Richmond St. E.
York St.
Sheppard St.
Temperance St.
Lombard St.
Adelaide St. E.
Toronto St.
Yonge St.
King St. E.
Emily St.
Front St. E.

Eaton Centre; **Simpson's,** on Yonge Street between Queen Street and Richmond Street; and **The Bay** (The Hudson Bay Company), at Yonge and Bloor streets. Of the three, Simpson's is probably the most upscale, and The Bay the most downscale.

Specialty Shops

Antiques and Galleries Yorkville is the headquarters of the establishment antique dealers, including **Navarro Gallery** (33 Hazelton Ave., tel. 416/921–0031). There are several other pockets around town, including a strip along Queen Street East, roughly between Sherbourne Street and George Street.

The Allery (322½ Queen St. W, tel. 416/593–0853) specializes in antique prints and maps.

Art Metropole (788 King St. W, tel. 416/367–2304) specializes in limited-edition, small-press, or self-published artists' books from around the world. These works often hover between visual arts and literature. There's also a range of serious art periodicals and ephemera. It's a fascinating destination for those interested in what's happening on the fringes of the artistic community.

Ballenford Architectural Books (98 Scollard St., tel. 416/960–0055) has Canada's largest selection of architectural titles and a gallery with usually interesting exhibits of architectural drawings and related work.

Jane Corkin Gallery (179 John St., north of Queen St.; tel. 416/979–1980) specializes in photography. In the same building is **Isaacs Gallery,** owned by Av Isaacs, godfather of many of the established Canadian artists. The more avant-garde galleries include **Cold City** (30 Duncan St.), **YYZ** (1087 Queen St. W), and **Mercer Union** (333 Adelaide St. W). Also check out **Toronto Photographers Workshop** and the other galleries at 80 Spadina Avenue, where you'll usually find at least one opening on a Saturday afternoon.

Glass Art Gallery (21 Hazelton Ave., tel. 416/968–1823) often has interesting Canadian and international exhibitions.

Prime Canadian Crafts (229 Queen St. W, tel. 416/593–5750) has an ever-changing array of merchandise.

Quasi Modo (789 Queen St. W, next door to Dufflet Pastries; tel. 416/366–8370) has a quirky collection of 20th-century furniture and design. You never know what will be on display: vintage bicycles, Noguchi lamps, a corrugated cardboard table by Frank Gehry. They'll order you any lamp available.

Sawtooth Borders (5 Macpherson Ave., tel. 416/961–8187) sells good-quality antique quilts.

20th Century (23 Beverley St., just north of Queen St.; tel. 416/598–2172) is for serious collectors of 20th-century design, particularly furniture, lamps, jewelry, and decorative arts. Many of the pieces are museum quality, and the owners are extremely erudite.

Auctions **Christie's Auctioneers** (94 Cumberland Ave., tel. 416/960–2063).

Sotheby's (Canada) Inc. (9 Hazelton Ave., tel. 416/926–1774).

Books Toronto is rich in bookstores selling new books, used books, best-sellers, and remainders. If you just need a current magazine or a paperback for the plane, there are the ubiquitous chains—Coles, Classic Bookshops, and W.H. Smith. Otherwise, we recommend:

The **Albert Britnell Book Shop** (765 Yonge St., just north of Bloor St.; tel. 416/924–3321) has been a Toronto legend since 1893. The shop is now run by the third generation of the family. You will find both care and a superb search service that are rare anywhere. Marvelous, British-like ambience; great browsing.

The **Book Cellar** (1560 Yonge St., above St. Clair Ave., tel. 416/967–5577; 142 Yorkville Avenue, near Avenue Rd., tel. 416/925–9955) offers a fine choice of classical records, as well as international political and intellectual journals.

Book City has three locations (501 Bloor St. W, near Honest Ed's; Carrot Common, 348 Danforth Ave., near Chester Station; and 663 Yonge St., south of Bloor St.). It's strong on good remaindered books, has a knowledgeable staff, and offers a fine choice of magazines. It is usually open late into the evening.

The **Children's Bookstore** (604 Markham St., in Mirvish Village; tel. 416/535–7011) is simply magical: beautiful, large, with readings and concerts—the best-stocked bookstore of its kind on this child-obsessed globe. The staff knows and loves children and the literature they long for and need. They also have a superior collection of children's records, many of them Canadian.

David Mirvish Books/Books on Art is just down the block (596 Markham St., tel. 416/531–9975). A gorgeous place, overflowing with quality books and many remainders. Best price in town for the Sunday *New York Times*.

Edward's Books and Art is now at four locations (356 Queen St. W, near Spadina Ave.; 2179 Queen St. E, in The Beaches; 387 Bloor St. E, at Sherbourne St.; and 2200 Yonge St., south of Eglinton Ave.). All are open Sundays. This is one of the loveliest minichains in the city. It advertises huge discounts on best-sellers and remainders in every Saturday's *Globe and Mail*, as does David Mirvish.

Lichtman's News and Books is at several locations (144 Yonge St. near Adelaide St.; the Atrium on Bay St., near Dundas St.; and 1430 Yonge St., south of St. Clair Ave.). There's a good selection of books, but Lichtman's is best known for its selection of magazines and its newspapers from around the world, often only a day old.

Longhouse Book Shop (recently relocated to 497 Bloor St. W, just west of Bathurst St., as well as Mirvish Village, tel. 416/921–9995) stocks only Canadian titles, handsomely shelved or piled high on pine tables: over 20,000 back titles and new publications. The respect and love for Canadian writers and writing is palpable here.

Bob Miller Book Room (180 Bloor St. W, just northwest of the Royal Ontario Museum; tel. 416/922–3557) has the best literature section in the city and a staff that has been with Bob for decades.

Pages Books and Magazines (256 Queen St. W, tel. 416/598–1447) has a wide selection of international and small-press literature; fashion and design books and magazines; and books on film, art, and literary criticism.

Old Favourites Bookshop (250 Adelaide St., west of University Ave.; tel. 416/977–2944) has over a quarter-million used books, magazines, and journals at fair prices.

This Ain't the Rosedale Library (483 Church St., south of Wellesley Ave.; tel. 416/929–9912) stocks the largest selection of baseball books in Canada, as well as a good selection of fiction, poetry, photography, design, rock, and jazz books. The staff is well-read and can offer intelligent advice when asked.

Special-Interest Bookstores

Bakka Science Fiction Book Shoppe (282 Queen St. W, tel. 416/596–8161) is the largest sci-fi and fantasy bookstore in the country (8,000 new and 3,000 used titles), with rare books and posters as well.

Can-Do Bookstore (311 Queen St. W, tel. 416/977–2351) stocks over 17,000 how-to titles for the mad, obsessed do-it-yourselfer.

The **Cookbook Store** (850 Yonge St., north of Bloor St.; tel. 416/920–2665) has the city's largest selection of books and magazines on cooking and wine.

Friends of Terpsichore (396 Dundas St. E, tel. 416/960–5817) specializes in dance subjects.

Glad Day Bookshop (598a Yonge St., tel. 416/961–4161) is Toronto's leading gay book store.

Open Air Books and Maps (25 Toronto St., just east of Yonge and King Sts.; tel. 416/363–0719) offers over 10,000 travel guides, oodles of atlases and road maps, specialized travel books, and titles on nature and food.

Sleuth of Baker Street (1543 Bayview Ave., south of Eglinton Ave.; tel. 416/483–3111) is the best place for mysteries and detective fiction.

Theatrebooks (25 Bloor St. W, tel. 416/922–7175) has an astounding collection of plays from around the world and large sections on every other theatrical topic.

Toronto Women's Bookstore (73 Harbord St., near Spadina Ave.; tel. 416/922–8744) carries the latest feminist works on women's political and legal issues, divorce, childbirth, etc. Reading lounge upstairs.

China, Flatware, and Crystal

There are a few well-known outlets, but the best-known discounter, and bride's best friend, is **William Ashley** (50 Bloor St. W, just off Yonge St.; tel. 416/964–2900). They'll ship anywhere.

Clothing

Atomic Age (350 Queen St. W, tel. 416/977–1296) features the hottest young Toronto designers. (Also in the neighborhood are other stores for the young and zany: **Fab** at #274, **290 Ion** at #290, **B Scene** at #352, **Fashion Crimes** at #395, **Strange** at #319, **Boomer** for men at #309, **Metropolis** at #265 and **I.X.L.** at #198.)

Brown's (1975 Avenue Rd., south of Hwy. 401; tel. 416/489–1975) provides classic clothing for short men and women. There's also a store for men only (545 Queen St. W, tel. 416/368–5937). An offshoot is **Muskat & Brown** (2528 Yonge St., tel. 416/489–4005) for petite women.

Clotheslines (50 Bloor St. W, 2nd floor; tel. 416/920–9340) features designs by owners Shelley Wickabrod and Bernard McGee.

Fetoun (97 Scollard St., tel. 416/923–3434) is one of the latest high-fashion emporiums for the nouveau riche. If you go to a lot of charity balls, this is the place to shop.

La Mode de Vija (601 Markham St., in Mirvish Village; tel. 416/534–6711) sells discount designer clothing with names like Anne Klein at good prices.

Sportables (55 Bloor St. W, tel. 416/967–4122, and Queen's Quay Terminal, tel. 416/366–7410) offers a good assortment of well-made casual wear in natural fibers.

Sublime (156 Cumberland Ave., tel. 416/962–7303) attracts the keenest fashion buyers in Toronto. Usually an excellent assortment of zany hats and avant-garde designs for men and women, from New York, Milan, and Toronto. Service is attentive and friendly, as it should be at these prices.

Vintage Furs (39a Charles St. W, at Bloor and Bay Sts.; tel. 416/960–5020) sells second-hand furs for men and women.

Willie Wonderful has several suburban locations. It's a reliable source for discounted clothing for women and children. Check the large ads in the Thursday *Star*.

Food Markets

Kensington Market (northwest of Dundas St. and Spadina Ave.; tel. 416/593–9269) is an outdoor market with a vibrant ethnic mix. Saturday is the best day to go, preferably by public transit, as parking is difficult.

St. Lawrence Market (Front St. and Jarvis St., tel. 416/392–7219) is best early on Saturdays, when, in addition to the permanent indoor market on the south side of Front Street, there's a farmer's market in the building on the north side. The historic south market was once Toronto's city hall, and it fronted the lake before extensive landfill projects were undertaken.

Specialty Food Shops

David Wood Food Shop (1110 Yonge St., tel. 416/968–6967) is Toronto's mini–Fortnum and Mason and is the neighborhood grocer to Toronto's old money.

Fenton's Food Shop (2 Gloucester St., just east of Yonge St.; tel. 416/961–8485) is a downtown mecca for the gourmand.

The Big Carrot (on Danforth Ave., near Chester subway station; tel. 416/466–2129). A new and pricey health-food supermarket, complete with organic butcher shop.

Just Game (1386 Bayview Ave., near Moore Ave.; tel. 416/481–1616) stocks a wide variety of game.

All the Best Breads and All the Best Cheese (1099 and 1097 Yonge St., tel. 416/928–3330) are just what they say.

Footwear

Boutique Quinto (110 Bloor St. W, tel. 416/928–0954) has the wildest shoes in town for men and women.

David's (66 Bloor St. W, at Bay St.; tel. 416/920–1000) has a somewhat more subdued but always elegant collection.

Brown's (Hazelton Lanes, Simpson's downtown, and other locations, tel. 416/968–1806) has an excellent selection of well-made shoes, handbags, and boots.

Marek, the Best of Europe (110 Bloor St. W, tel. 416/923–5100), is located in a lane running between Cumberland Street and Yorkville Avenue. It has an interesting assortment of shoes, as well as belts and other leather goods; it also has shirts, an outstanding selection of men's ties, and other wearing apparel.

Gift Ideas

The Back Store (8 Price St., tel. 416/924–BACK) has everything for a friend with an aching spine.

Early Learning (387 Queen St. W, tel. 416/598–2135) sells European and Japanese playthings.

Filigree (1210 Yonge St., tel. 415/961–5223) has a good assortment of linens, as well as drawer liners, silver frames, and other Victorian pleasures. In the neighborhood are other gift shops selling fine glass and antiques.

Bragg (446 Queen St., west of Spadina Ave.; tel. 416/366–6717) has an amusing assortment of vintage bric-a-brac, china, cards, and jewelry.

Jewelry

Secrett Jewel Salon (150 Bloor St. W, tel. 416/967–7500) is a reputable source of unusual gemstones and fine new and estate jewelry; local gemologists consider it the best in town.

Time Out

Here are a few suggestions for places to rest those tootsies while shopping:

Eaton Centre area. If the Centre's restaurants and fast-food joints don't appeal to you, walk two blocks north to *The Bangkok Garden* (18 Elm St.) for delicious Thai food in a luxurious atmosphere. The related bar, *The Brass Flamingo,* offers less expensive light meals, all of which are good. For an inexpensive meal, get a fabulous home-style burger at *Lick's* (Yonge St. at Dundas Sq., opposite the Eaton Centre); they're also in The Beaches, and at Yonge Street and Eglinton Avenue. Kids will enjoy the singing counter help.

Queen Street West. We recommend *The Bam Boo* (#312), a unique Thai-Caribbean experience, courtyard service in summer; *The Queen Mother* (#206), a neighborhood favorite with wholesome meals and fabulous desserts, all at reasonable prices; *The Peter Pan* (#373, at Peter St.); and the *Parrot Express* (#254), for gourmet pizza and other goodies to stay or go.

Bloor Street/Yorkville. *The Copenhagen Room* (corner of Bloor St. and St. Thomas St., near Georg Jensen) is a Toronto stalwart, if you like Danish open-faced sandwiches. Next door, in the Windsor Arms Hotel (St. Thomas St.), is *The Courtyard Cafe,* a popular hangout for visiting movie stars. For Canadian ingredients interestingly prepared, try *Metropolis* (838 Yonge St., north of Bloor St.).

Spadina Avenue. For spicy Chinese food, it's *The Great Wall* (444 Spadina Ave., south of College St.). For falafel and gingery Jamaica sweet-potato pudding, check out *Tiger's Coconut Grove* (12 Kensington Ave., in the market).

Bargaining

Toronto is *not* the Middle East, but one might haggle at flea markets, including the Harbourfront Antique Market, and perhaps in the Chinatown and Kensington Market/Spadina Avenue areas.

Refund Information

Visitors, including Canadians from other provinces, can receive a refund on the 8% Ontario sales tax for purchases over $100, as well as on the 5% sales tax on hotel and motel bills, provided they leave within 30 days. It's worthwhile if you do a significant amount of shopping. There's a form to be sent in with your receipts after you leave Ontario. You can get the form at Pearson Airport, at visitors' information booths like the one outside the Eaton Centre, at Traveller's Aid in Union Station, or from the merchants themselves.

7 Dining

by Joanne Kates

Restaurant critic for the Toronto Globe and Mail, *Joanne Kates in 1988 won both the best restaurant critic and best food writer awards in the Canadian food writing association. She is the author of four books, including her own cookbook and a Toronto restaurant guide.*

A decade ago visitors to Toronto enjoyed a varied mix of ethnic restaurants, but good food could not be found in the middle ground of gastronomy—between the Italian sandwiches and the Dover sole. Today Toronto is a city of bistros.

The "bistroization" of Toronto is due in part to a new generation of chefs, the first wave of young people who are just now fanning out across the city, opening neighborhood restaurants that are a little cheaper, slightly less ambitious, and thus more accessible than those of their teachers. There are Chris Klugman (a Michael Stadtlander alumnus) at Bistro 990, two Jamie Kennedy protégés at Le Fave's, and Susur Lee, who was influenced by Stadtlander, at Lotus.

What the bistros serve is another matter. That old tired imitation Continental menu, which Toronto's upper crust dined out on since before the Beatles, is finally dead. We are no longer stuck eating less than perfect imitations of what they do in Paris and Rome. The new bistros are eclectic, as likely to borrow from Bangkok as they are from Los Angeles. Furthermore, their clever mentors have taught the new generation of young chefs to do things that have heretofore been forbidden in kitchens; think for themselves, create dishes based on what dazzles them in the morning market, and use local ingredients and spontaneity of approach.

As a result, we are beginning to enjoy a Toronto cuisine that is based on the present rather than the past. The food is becoming simple. Sauces, if they exist at all, are quiet little *beurre blancs* that sit under the main event and do not obscure it. Toronto eats more and more grilled foods, because the more frequently people eat out (which Torontonians do more than any other Canadians), the more healthful they want it. Hence the turn to stripped-down plates: grilled fish or meat and vegetable, a little garlic or fresh thyme for excitement. Toronto restaurants' great strength is this simplicity—what home cooking should be but so rarely is. Twenty years ago the nuclear family was Toronto's haven in a heartless world. Today it's our favorite bistro.

The most highly recommended restaurants in each category are indicated with a star ★.

Category	Cost*
Very Expensive	over $35
Expensive	$27–$34
Moderate	$15–$26
Inexpensive	under $15

**per person without tax, tip, or drinks*

The following credit-card abbreviations are used: AE, American Express; CB, Carte Blanche; DC, Diners Club; MC, MasterCard; V, Visa.

Afternoon Tea

Inexpensive **The King Edward Hotel.** Those who wish for privacy should go to tea at the unfashionable, not quite delicious, but very beautiful King Eddie. It's served every afternoon from 3 to 5:30 PM in the small lounge just off the lobby. The rugs are thick enough to trip over, and the furniture is either antique or expensive or both. Chairs built of fat bamboo speak of better days for the Empire. There are little loveseats, glass tables, and good strong English breakfast tea in a Rosenthal Classic Rose Collection pot, *avec* silver strainer. The scones are tired, the small tea sandwiches are so thin as to be anorexic. Still, other than the frequent refills of hot water for the teapot, tea at the King Eddie fulfills only the most illusory notions of gentility, which is, after all, what afternoon tea is about. *37 King St. E, just east of Yonge St.; tel. 416/863–9700. Tie and jacket optional. Reservations recommended. AE, CB, DC, MC, V.*

Windsor Arms. Just a block from the Royal Ontario Museum, "Upstairs, Downstairs" comes deliciously to life. The Fireside Lounge is a comfy, cozy drawing room that has the welcome patina of its years. You sit on a couch or a Queen Anne chair, by an equally antique coffee table, and the tea lady brings English breakfast or Prince of Wales. From the silver tray, there are first-rate smoked salmon, chicken, cucumber, and sometimes watercress sandwiches. Then come scones—very fresh, very buttery. Next, a pastry, such as crumbly, cinnamony Linzer torte, made on the premises and generally faultless. The Windsor Arms has the right stuff at teatime. *22 St. Thomas St., near Bay and Bloor Sts.; tel. 416/979–2341. Tie and jacket optional. No reservations. AE, CB, DC, MC, V. Open 3–6PM.*

Bistros

Expensive

★ **Bistro 990.** This is a gorgeous homage to a French provincial bistro. Owner Tom Kristenbrun studied hard to come up with the right idea. Chef Chris Klugman (ex-Panache, ex-Karin, ex-Stadtlander's) has given up his habitual green mango sauce and chrysanthemum butter for something a little more accessible—country cooking *à la française*. There are thick soups, marinated mackerel, duck terrine, hearty stews, sweet french fries, kidneys with fresh artichokes, and buttery desserts. This is Gallic bistro bliss. *990 Bay St., tel. 416/921–9990. Dress: informal. Reservations recommended. AE, MC, V.*

★ **Brownes Bistro.** In one night, you can count a dozen mink coats. Full-length dark ranch. What does a person who spends $17,000 on a coat want in a restaurant? Apparently she wants an impeccable bistro that avoids the tarted-up Paris look. Everything at Brownes is breathtakingly simple, from the white paper on the tables to the small black-and-white ceramic tiles. The monochromatic room is colored only by dark wood paneling and one fuchsia azalea at the bar. Lack of pretension is elevated to art. Former Cordon Bleu cooking teacher Beverly Burge had a reputation for strictest adherence to *la cuisine classique*. Breeding tells. Brownes's pizza may be the best in Toronto. The *gnocchi* are unexceptional. The bouillabaisse has perfect, sweet little fresh scallops, but a blandness of broth. There are seven main courses, and three of them are lamb. Brownes gives full glory to lamb's heretofore neglected parts, such as lamb shanks (braised till they soften like butter and served in their own heart-warming broth, slightly thickened, with fennel, potatoes, and carrots). A lemon curd and a darkly dense chocolate cake, served with crème fraîche and chocolate sauce, are both very fine. The price of under $70 for two, with wine—a real bargain—makes Brownes the hottest show in town. *2 Woodlawn Ave. E, tel. 416/924–8132. Tie and jacket optional. Reservations recommended. AE, CB, DC, MC, V. No lunch; closed Sun.*

Joso's. Because properly cooked fish is rare in Toronto, you put up with certain annoyances at Joso's, the city's best seafood restaurant. Joso Spralja exhibits tasteless sculpture throughout his restaurant. But his Adriatic way with fish is dazzling: a drizzle of extra-virgin olive oil, a fast trip on a hot grill. Sweet little squids come hot and golden; sea bass is thick and firm, never overcooked; seafood salad is incredibly tender and fragrant from its olive oil bath. Joso even dares, and succeeds, at risotto. For all this pleasure, tacky decor and insouciant service are a small price to pay. *202 Davenport Rd., tel 416/925–1903. Dress: informal. Reservations recommended. AE, MC, V.*

★ **Palmerston.** In an unfashionable area, in a plain gray dining room, one of this country's great chefs, Jamie Kennedy, continues his magic. Osso buco—basically stewed veal shank—is perfectly cooked and is garnished with fresh emerald peas and little explosions of fresh lemon. The potato au gratin with the pink baby lamb is *chèvre*-scented. The lake trout with *beurre blanc* is grilled to moist perfection. A warm salad is made from ruby salmon covered in tangiest vinaigrette, with lots of cracked black pepper and a bed of *radicchio*. The food is fun to eat, except for some of the desserts; stick with Kennedy's homemade ice creams—they are faultless, especially the dark chocolate. And his patio offers the utterly simple—pork, fish, hamburger—done to utter perfection. Haute bistro comes to Toronto. *488 College St., at Palmerston Ave.; tel. 416/922–9277. Jacket optional. Reservations recommended for dinner. AE, CB, DC, MC, V. No lunch during winter months; closed Sun.*

Moderate

★ **BamBoo.** Inside a funky little inner courtyard decorated by a bohemian hand—fishnets on the walls, a stand of Muskoka bamboo, fading signs, all bordered by a thatched roof, à la South Pacific—is a relentlessly low-tech club cum restaurant that rebukes glitz-crazed Toronto with a smile up its sleeve. More and more ordinary people are going to the BamBoo for one purpose only: to eat food that jumps up joyously on the tongue. You can eat in the club area (240 seats, barnlike but warm) or in the small funky dining room off to the right. On weekends guests line up for both the food and the live Caribbean music, which starts at 10 PM. Chef Wendy Young makes a hot-and-sour soup that has more oomph than anything in Chinatown. Much of the food is spicy. The callalloo, a creamed spinach and coconut soup, is the very weapon that blocked sinuses require. BamBoo's single most popular dish, Thai spicy noodles, comes in three modes, mild, medium, and wow! Mild is a superlative ungreasy wok fry of rice noodles with peanuts, bean sprouts, chicken, shrimp, tofu, egg, Vietnamese fish sauce, chilies, sugar, garlic, and fresh lime juice. Chicken wings are marinated overnight in ginger, mustard, soy sauce, oyster sauce, sesame oil, pepper, and paprika; deep-fried into hot juicy submission; and served with a pretty spectacular garlic chili vinegar dipping sauce. This is not artistic Thai cooking; things are more casual and more multi-ethnic—but portions are large, the flavors assertive, and the cooking rather like the best of fresh home cooking. *312 Queen St. W, tel. 416/593–5771. Dress: informal. No reservations. AE, MC, V. Closed Sun.*

Tipplers. Right in midtown, this charmer sells more than 30 wines by the glass, and such wines: Chateauneuf-du-Pape, Bourgogne Aligote, decent Chablis, and Mersault. But there's more than wine: Boston bluefish is grilled to perfection and strewn with a spicy sauté of red peppers and zucchini. Big fat shrimp are zinged with garlic and grilled fast. Chicken breasts are painted with three different kinds of hot mustard and then grilled. The soups, especially the cream of mushroom, are dreamy. *1276 Yonge St., near Summerhill Ave.; tel. 416/967–9463. Jacket optional. Reservations for lunch only. AE, CB, DC, MC, V. No lunch Sat.*

Inexpensive

Emilio's. Located about five blocks from the Toronto City Hall, this once-unassuming lunchtime sandwich deli expanded and upgraded several times, got a liquor license, and is now fabulous. The artsy and unaffected atmosphere provides a garden effect. The turnip-and-leek soup is creamy, the caviar Provençale a classic. The sea bass is fantastic: barely cooked, then smothered in little shrimp pieces, uncooked bright green scallions, and a light reduction of cream. Desserts are by the superlative Dufflet. *127 Queen St. E, near Jarvis St.; tel. 416/366–3354. Dress: informal. Reservations recommended for dinner. AE, V. Closed Sun. Summer outdoor dining.*

Brunch

Moderate
★

Kensington Kitchen. Its clientele is the self-consciously unchic University of Toronto people who live in the area and appreciate the ask-nothing ambience. The reigning sensibility belongs to Said Mukayesh, who leans heavily toward the healthy, so his interpretation of Middle East cooking includes whole-wheat pita; and if there's rice, it's brown. But none of this prevents Mukayesh from serving wickedly wonderful spinach-and-cheese ravioli in a dense cream sauce. Ingredients are fresh and always prepared with affection and care. Where else do you get velvety *baba ghannoush*, *lubya* (green beans in a thick sauce of cinnamon and cardamom), divinely garlicky fried eggplant, and assertive cream soups? The *tabbouleh* (cracked wheat salad with parsley, tomato, and cucumber) is delicate, and the falafel in pita is a class act. Two people could lunch splendidly for $10. *124 Harbord St., south of Bloor St.; tel. 416/961–3404. Dress: informal. Reservations not necessary. MC, V.*

Inexpensive

The Boulevard Cafe. Don't worry about being underdressed; the neighbors are countercultural, but charming. The tables are made out of hand-painted ceramic tiles; wall hangings from South America announce the Peruvian theme. Brunch varies from week to week, but there are always Peruvian specialties, ranging from scrambled eggs with hot peppers to more exotic fare. There is also French toast or other simple egg dishes, plus a titillating collection of coffees: Borgia, Colombian, Peruvian, etc. *161 Harbord St., tel.416/961–7676. Dress: informal. Reservations not necessary. MC, V. Summer outdoor dining.*

Cafés

Inexpensive

The Amsterdam. This is everything you would expect a good dining room not to be: It's rowdy, noisy, a symphony of heavy metal, a deliberately down-scale barn of a place. But like a Maserati in overdrive, it goes. And when Gary Hoyer cooks—about one-third of the time—the kitchen can sing and dance. He personally smokes the meats and fish. His fresh-smoked tuna, the marriage of sushi and lox, is cold-smoked so that it won't cook. He grills *chèvre* and piles on the sweet baked fennel vinaigrette. He grills shrimp till they barely burst their pink skins and spreads them with a rather erotic roasted garlic puree. His daube of beef is steak sautéed with red wine, tomatoes, and a lot of garlic. It's astonishingly reasonable, too. *133 John St., near Queen St. and University Ave.; tel. 416/595-8201. Dress: informal. Reservations recommended. AE, MC, V.*

L'Express Café. Just across from the charming Parrot bistro on Queen Street West, is a café that since the fall of 1987 has been serving good casual food with some dispatch. For under $5, they take the ordinary (chicken salad, ham and cheese) and annoint it with goat cheese or roasted red peppers in oil, laid lovingly between slices of impeccable Italian bread. The pizzas and savory tarts are enough to justify its existence. (The former is simple and robust; the latter, a texture of gossamer, thanks to the 35% cream.) The leek and *chèvre* tart with a touch of curry is one of the most inventive dishes. *254 Queen St. W, in walking distance of New City Hall; tel. 416/596-0205. Dress: informal. No reservations. AE, MC, V, for orders over $10. Closed Sun.*

Chinese

Moderate

Champion House. In our never-ending quest for the perfect Peking duck, we tried this popular Toronto restaurant. A brass gong is hit when your duck enters the dining room, and groans of delight circle the table: The combination of the sweet, crackling duck skin with sharp onions and jazzy sauce is the ultimate fulfillment of the pleasure principle. Then comes the refreshing and light duck salad, the pungent duck in a hot sauce full of ginger, star anise, and chilies, and the duck soup. "Ants climbing up a tree" (alias bean starch noodles and minced pork in brown sauce) and scallops with chilies and peanuts are both first rate. Order the Peking duck (for 4) in advance. *478 Dundas St. W, at Spadina Ave.; tel. 416/977-8282. Dress: informal. Reservations recommended. AE, CB, DC, MC, V. Closed Tues.*

New World. There is probably very little that could induce you to penetrate the wilds of Scarborough on a wintry night, but this place can. Again and again and again. Do not miss the New World's *shui kow* soup—a sea of fine stock afloat with freshly made dumplings of chopped shrimp, Chinese mushrooms, and barbecued pork—and the fresh abalone that comes in its shell accompanied by one pristine broccoli floret in a translucent sauce made from beef stock reduced with oyster sauce. It's not on the menu, but the password is, "Kam Wong said we could have it." New World is frankly Cantonese. There is a lick and a promise in the direction of Szechuan, but the cook's heart is on the sea. Big fat indelicate West Coast oysters

Metropolitan Toronto Dining

Arlequin, **15**
Astoria Shish Kabob, **24**
Brownes Bistro, **20**
Cafe Creole, **1**
Camarra's, **2**
Centro, **19**
Costa Basque, **16**
Dufflet Pastries, **5**
Eating Counter, **28**
Ellas, **26**
Filippo's Gourmet Pizzeria, **8**
Grano Cafe, **21**
Jerusalem, **10**
Joso's, **7**
Le Fave's, **13**
Lotus, **6**
New World, **29**
Odyssey, **27**
Patachou Patisserie, **9**
Pearl Court, **25**
Pronto, **22**
Scaramouche, **14**
Sisi Trattoria, **17**
Stelle, **3**
Tipplers, **18**
Trapper's, **23**
Trattoria Giancarlo, **4**
United Bakers, **11**
Yitz's Deli, **12**

Earl Bales Park
401
Ave.
York Mills Rd.
Allen Expwy.
Avenue Rd.
Yonge St.
Leslie St.
Lawrence Ave. E.
Don Mills Rd.
Don Valley Pkwy.
Wigmore Park
Eglinton Ave. E.
Sunnybrook Park
Laird Dr.
Oakwood Ave.
Mount Pleasant Rd.
EAST YORK
404
Davenport Rd.
O'Connor Dr.
Taylor Creek Park
Dupont St.
Bayview Ext.
Broadview Ave.
Pape Ave.
Greenwood Ave.
Coxwell Ave.
Woodbine Ave.
Bathurst St.
DOWNTOWN
Bloor St. E.
Gerrard St. E.
Parliament St.
Dundas St. W.
Dundas St. E.
Leslie St.
Queen St. E.
Eastern Ave.
King St. W.
Lake Shore Blvd. E.
0 1 mile
0 1500 meters

Amsterdam, **42**
BamBoo, **37**
Barolo, **54**
Beaujolais, **41**
Bistro 990, **48**
Boulevard Cafe, **31**
Champion House, **36**
Eating Counter, **34**
Emilio's, **53**
Karin, **47**
Kensington Kitchen, **33**
King Edward Hotel, **51**
La Fenice, **43**
Le Bestingo, **40**
Le Cafe, **45**
Lee Garden, **35**
Nami, **52**
Nekah, **50**
Palmerston, **30**
Parrot, **38**
Parrot Express, **39**
Renaissance Cafe, **32**
Vegetarian Restaurant, **49**
Windsor Arms, **46**
Young Lok, **44**

Downtown Toronto Dining

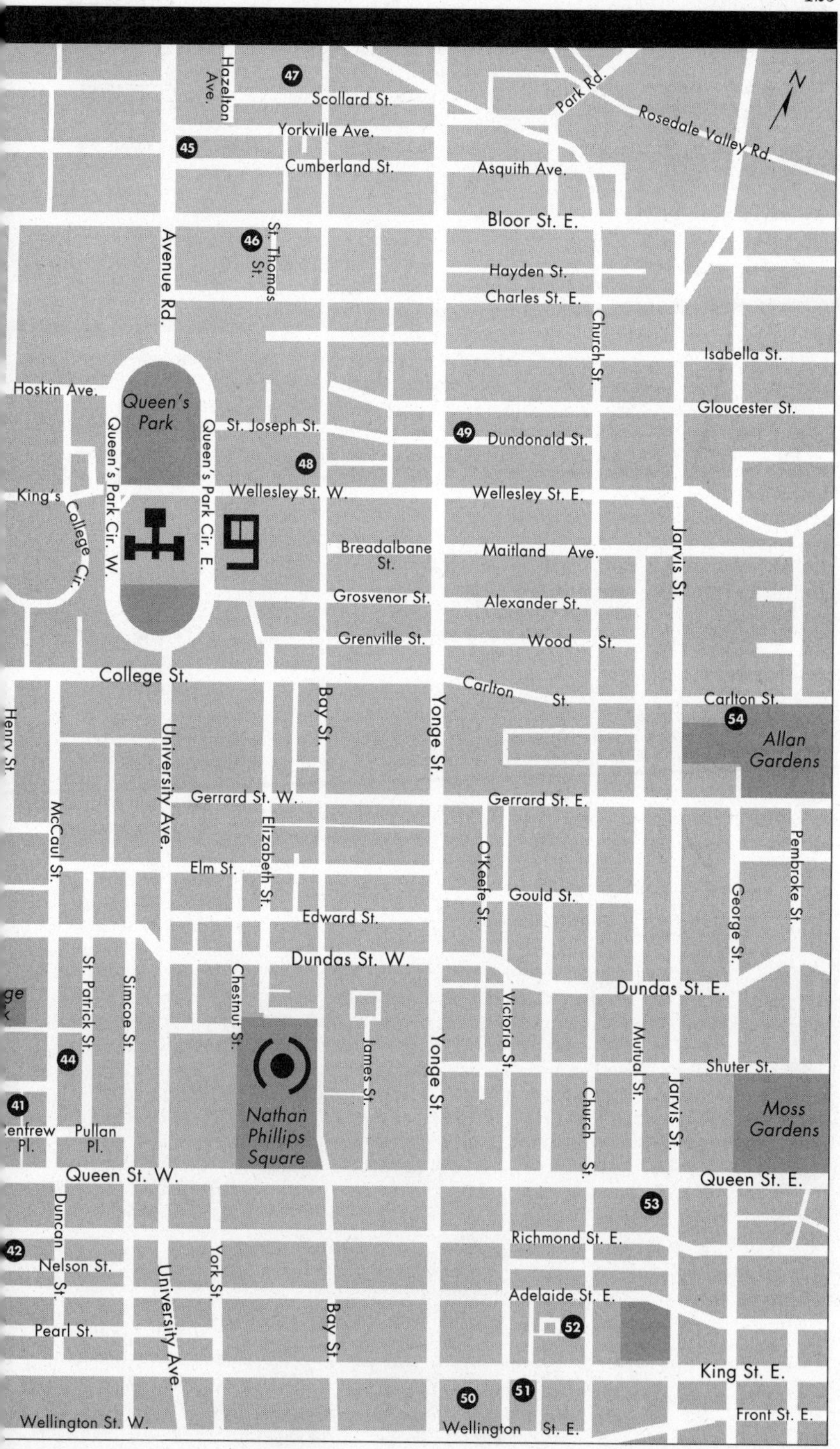
Hazelton Ave.
47
Scollard St.
Yorkville Ave.
45
Cumberland St.
Asquith Ave.
Park Rd.
Rosedale Valley Rd.
N
Bloor St. E.
46
St. Thomas St.
Avenue Rd.
Hayden St.
Charles St. E.
Church St.
Isabella St.
Hoskin Ave.
Queen's Park
Gloucester St.
St. Joseph St.
49
Dundonald St.
48
King's College Cir.
Queen's Park Cir. W.
Queen's Park Cir. E.
Wellesley St. W.
Wellesley St. E.
Jarvis St.
Breadalbane St.
Maitland Ave.
Grosvenor St.
Alexander St.
Grenville St.
Wood St.
College St.
Carlton St.
Carlton St.
54
Allan Gardens
Henry St.
Bay St.
Yonge St.
University Ave.
Gerrard St. W.
Gerrard St. E.
McCaul St.
Elizabeth St.
O'Keefe St.
Pembroke St.
Elm St.
Gould St.
George St.
Edward St.
Dundas St. W.
Dundas St. E.
St. Patrick St.
Simcoe St.
Chestnut St.
Victoria St.
Mutual St.
44
James St.
Yonge St.
Shuter St.
41
Nathan Phillips Square
Church St.
Jarvis St.
Moss Gardens
Pullan Pl.
Queen St. W.
Queen St. E.
53
Duncan St.
Richmond St. E.
42
Nelson St.
York St.
University Ave.
Adelaide St. E.
Bay St.
52
Pearl St.
King St. E.
50
51
Wellington St. W.
Wellington St. E.
Front St. E.

come properly (barely) cooked in their own shells, dressed up with black beans, fresh coriander, and chives. Chicken cubes and scallops in phoenix nest are not to be missed. And I have never tasted fish so fresh in hot pots, nor eaten a hot pot crowned with soft shell crab and oyster. No reservations are taken for the hot-pot tables, so go early. This place is a treasure. *3600 Victoria Park Ave., tel. 416/498–1818. Dress: informal. Reservations advised on weekends. AE, MC, V.*

Young Lok. Upwardly mobile and still delicious, this is a handsome restaurant in the very attractive Village by the Grange. The menu is biblical in scope, ranging from old tired Cantonese clichés to the fiery stars of the Szechuan kitchen. The clear soups are great; the panfried pancakes with scallions is a bargain appetizer and wonderful: cheap, greasy, and oniony. The main courses are almost all terrific: Sautéed shrimp with ginger and scallion is crunchy on the outside, sweetly juicy on the inside. Fresh lobster in black bean sauce is a perfect juxtaposition of sweet flesh and salty beans. Vegetarians' hodgepodge, a Young Lok classic, has a variety of crunchy vegetables. Mandarin crispy duck is for all unrepentant grease lovers. *122 St. Patrick St., at Dundas St., just south of the Art Gallery; tel. 416/593–9819. Dress: informal. Reservations recommended. AE, CB, D, MC, V. Dim sum weekends 10:30 AM–3 PM. Summer outdoor dining.*

Inexpensive

Eating Counter. There's one not far from the Art Gallery of Ontario and another in the east end; both have glorious Chinese seafood. They are the darlings of the Cantonese-style cognoscenti, who line up on weekends for the food, not for the Formica-table-Pepsi-sign ambience, you can be sure. The delights include the extremely fresh lobster with ginger and green onions, a variety of sizzling hot-plate dishes with barely cooked vegetables, and sweet and tangy barbecued specialties. Most of the items described by Chinese characters on the wall are not listed in English, so ask the waiter what's fresh that day. *23 Baldwin St., near Dundas St., tel. 416/977–7028; 2183 Danforth Ave., near Woodbine Ave., tel. 416/690–5666. Dress: informal. Reservations recommended. No credit cards.*

Lee Garden. From October till May, it has a Mongolian fire pot on every table, with people dipping bounteous piles of fish, meat, and morsels in raw egg. With the summer, it switches to Szechuan and Hakka dishes, ideal for the heat. This place is better and cheaper, and has lighter and more inventive food, than most other Szechuan places on Spadina Avenue. The soups are excellent, and the Hakka dish—shrimp with eggplant—is pretty and very original. The pièce de résistance is baked shrimp with pepper. The decor is dreadful, the food, scrumptious. *358 Spadina Ave., south of College St.; tel. 416/593–9524. Dress: informal. Reservations taken at door. V. No lunch; closed Mon.*

★ **Pearl Court.** This is the most recent of the good Chinese restaurants to hit the big time. Make sure you take a number as you join the crowd outside the door; by the way, you might end up sitting near the door, with its chilling draft. All this for superlative, barely cooked, fat, fresh oysters sizzling on a hot iron plate with black pepper and green onion. Or fresh kiwi clams, each one steamed with a half-teaspoon of minced garlic. Garlic is a central theme here. So is fresh coriander. Lemon grass accents the oxtail in a fine citrusy stew pot. Chicken in paper is a platter of little paper packets, each holding a little morsel of pink tender chicken steamed in soy with five–spice powder. Skip the soups, which are bland, and consider the oysters. *598 Gerrard St. E, near Broadview Ave.; tel. 416/463–8773. Dress: informal. V.*

Creole

Expensive **Cafe Creole.** This is the most impressive restaurant on the airport strip, and it's an extravaganza that only money could buy. The chef studied with the great Paul Prudhomme, of K-Paul's Louisiana Kitchen fame. The room is almost too big for intimacy—it seats 165 people—but the brick, the potted herbs on every table, the pale pink arches, and the petit-point chairs are lovely. First, the salad bar: new potatoes mayonnaise, marinated leeks, vegetables à la Greque, tricolor pasta salad. The crayfish popcorn is a sweet-batter fry, as addictive as ice cream. The red beans are a soupy garlic seduction; the dirty rice is true to Louisiana, each grain distinct, the sweet and hot peppers and chicken gizzards in careful harmony. The lobster Creole comes tender, barely cooked, in a fine tomato and sweet-pepper sauce. For dessert: K-Paul's superlative never-too-sweet potato pecan pie, and gravity-defying bread pudding with mellow whiskey sauce. *In the Skyline Hotel, 655 Dixon Rd. at Martingrove Rd., near the airport; tel. 416/244–5200. Dress: jacket optional. Reservations required. AE, CB, DC, MC, V.*

Delis

Inexpensive ★ **United Bakers.** For nearly seven decades, this noisy, crowded, Formica restaurant served the Jews of Spadina—and all other nationalities with the wisdom to head for the old needle-trade area—with great Jewish food. Just a few years ago, it sadly closed its doors, but not before the third generation of Ladovskys—Philip and Ruth—opened a branch in a small plaza, a few miles northwest of downtown Toronto. The soups are wonderful, with the cabbage soup and the barley bean soup among the best. The cheese blintzes, sweet and sour pike, gefilte fish, whitefish and carp, toasted bagels with lox and cream cheese—all are superb. Don't miss the vegetarian chopped liver—this is, after all, a dairy restaurant. *In Lawrence Plaza, corner of Bathurst St. and Lawrence Ave. W; tel. 416/789–0519. Dress: informal. No reservations taken. MC, V.*

Yitz's Famous Deli. Grown-ups can enjoy the food here, and kids are welcomed, too. The cabbage borscht is thick and sublime, and there's a superb hot, piquant corned beef on rye, with new dills and a latke (potato pancake) with applesauce. It's not the last word in elegance, but it's good civilized food in pleasant surroundings. The thick, round fries can be excellent, and the various sandwiches and the chicken and meat platters are of good quality—and quantity. *346 Eglinton Ave. W, corner of Avenue Rd.; tel. 416/487–4506. Dress: informal. Reservations not necessary. AE, MC, V.*

French

Very Expensive ★

Le Bistingo. Certain gifts from Chef Claude Bouillet's kitchen are among the finest flavors Toronto can offer: His open ravioli filled with shrimp and scallops is astonishing—toothsome pasta sheets laid over and under with soft, sweet seafood, all bathed in the lightest of *buerre blancs* thinned with fish stock. The house signature appetizer, duck liver sautéed until just pink and soft and napped in a very tart raisin sauce, is fabulous. Among main courses the fish dishes shine. A perfectly cooked fat red snapper sits on a wondrously astringent bed of stewed endive, surrounded by *beurre blanc* cleverly thinned with vermouth. Those in the know order a hot dessert with dinner, and are thus seduced by fresh-from-the-oven buttery puff pastry cradling caramelized apples, then bathed in a foam of Calvados sabayon. As if that were not enough, there are sauternes by the glass (or real champagne) to wash it all down. *349 Queens St. W, tel. 416/598–3490. Tie and jacket optional. Reservations required. AE, DC, MC, V.*

Expensive ★

Beaujolais. The menu here does not cater to every little frisson of fashion. It is rather more solid than that. Of course they engage in natural acts with sun-dried tomatoes, goat cheese, and red pepper. Their warm salads (one day salmon, another day duck liver) are often dressed in shallot/red wine/vinegar reductions that make the uptown vinegar and oil seem commonplace. But partners Barbara Gordon and Bob Bermann do not shift every time the wind blows, which is to their credit. Bermann still cooks the duck La Cachette that Gordon invented at her restaurant of that name in Vancouver. The leg is marinated and slow-roasted (as it requires in order to be tender), and the breast is fast-grilled into pink sweetness. The restaurant offers The Grand Beginning for $7.50, a wondrous assortment of appetizers; not a mediocre taste on that plate. This is a wonderful and important place; it's one of the five best restaurants in this town. What other restaurant has The Grand Dessert, which includes superb apple crumble pie, tart lemon pie like a cloud on the tongue, dense chocolate cake, and two kinds of homemade ice cream? *165 John St., tel. 416/598–4656. Dress: informal. Reservations preferred. AE, MC, V. No lunch Sat.; closed Sun.*

Scaramouche. This is Toronto's most luxurious French restaurant, with a stunning view of downtown Toronto, gorgeous ambience, and delicious food. The superb service, the tasteful luxury of the room, the amazing wines (who else offers Chateau d'Yquem by the glass?), and the carefully prepared food all add up to understated elegance. No particular dish dazzles and none disappoints. Your guinea fowl will be juicy, your salmon perfectly cooked, your lamb pink, and your sauces limpid. New money seeks Thai/Italian/Californian taste treats—old money dines at Scaramouche. *1 Benevenuto Pl., tel. 416/961–8011. Jacket optional. Reservations recommended. Valet parking. AE, MC, V.*

Moderate

Arlequin. There are no velvet banquettes or chandeliers here; merely a very clever small dining room with a gently stated theme: the harlequin. The waiter brings garlic toast and tapenade (a puree of olives, olive oil, capers, and anchovies)—the Provençal national spread. Scallops are marinated in lime juice and white wine and are covered in a layer of tomato and carrot cubes. Also featured are roast lamb with potatoes and sautéed tomatoes; fresh grouper with a strong anchovy sauce; tender rabbit, thyme-scented on a bed of basil and spinach. The desserts are among the best in Toronto. *134 Avenue Rd., near Davenport Rd.; tel. 416/928–9521. Jacket optional. Reservations recommended for dinner. AE, CB, D, MC, V. Closed Mon.*

Greek

Moderate ★ **Astoria Shish Kabob House.** Out in Greektown, a 10-minute subway ride east from Bloor and Yonge streets, are some superior ethnic restaurants. This one is a delightful Danforth Avenue escape (Bloor St. changes its name east of the Don Valley Parkway), where hardly anything is served but terrific Greek-style charcoal-barbecued foods, the best of which are the barbecued quails, the sweet little birds prepared with a hint of lemon. They're so tender you can eat the bones. Also try the moussaka and Greek salad with a baklava chaser. *390 Danforth Ave., near Chester Ave.; tel. 416/463–2838. Dress: informal. No reservations taken. AE, MC, V.*

The Odyssey. Here is a place, not far from the others, where there's Greek salad good enough to bring out all the clichés about the gods and goddesses on Mount Olympus; there is also creamy moussaka, and roast lamb with all the wonderful, greasy pan juices anybody having an existential crisis could want. You can drink retsina (if you like the taste of resin) and then wake yourself up for the drive home with the murkiest, sweetest, thickest Greek coffee there is. *477 Danforth Ave., near Logan Ave.; tel. 416/465–2451. Dress: informal. Reservations recommended. AE, MC, V.*

Inexpensive **Ellas.** You can get informal, delicious Greek food here, making your choices from the steaming food on the stove. The fish is always flaky and sweet, the roast lamb fork-tender, the potatoes moist. A good place to take the kids: it's noisy and informal, and the service is fast. For Mom and Dad, Ellas can provide dolmades, taramasalata, shish kebab, spanakopita, and feta salads. *702 Pape Ave., at Danforth Ave.; tel. 416/463–0334. Dress: informal. Reservations recommended. AE, MC, V.*

Iberian

Moderate **Costa Basque.** Food is taken extremely seriously in Basque country, and this eaterie has more visual integrity than any other restaurant in Toronto; even the building looks Mediterranean—no mean feat on Avenue Road north of Bloor Street. Avoid the Parisian clichés (such as the mousseline of shrimps and scallops in pimiento purée) and go for the sweet fruits of the Basque kitchen—calamari, for instance, which are deep-fried fast and hot, so their batter is innocuous and ungreasy. Happily, the tomato sauce is zinged with chilies. The farmer Basque soup is a down-home tomato and vegetable broth; in the manner of all good peasant cooking, the vegetables are overcooked (and cut too small) and the broth is real. Ditto for the Mediterranean fish soup. The quails—boned and filled with sweetbreads—are far better than the paella. And the *bacalao* is a tribute to the homeland: Salt cod has been simmered with tomatoes, a lot of roasted sweet red peppers, crunchy little slices of garlic, and white wine until it possesses the sweetness of land and sea. Grouper à la Basque is also delightful. Reserve a balcony table and think of the Pyrenees. *124 Avenue Rd., near Davenport Rd., in walking distance of the Royal Ontario Museum, tel. 416/968–0908. Jacket optional. Reservations recommended on weekends. AE, CB, DC, MC, V. No lunch Sat.; closed Sun.*

Italian

Expensive

★ **Barolo.** For 14 years Michael Pagliaro worked under Luigi Orgera of La Fenice (*see* below), learning everything the master had to teach. And he learned it well. Barolo serves the nouvelle Italian cooking that grills scallops just until their fat and juicy hearts run sweet, that puts plump capers and red pepper purée on tuna, that lovingly prepares wild mushrooms in the fall, gilding them in the sauté pan, then bedding them down on a splendid variety of garden greens. With every dessert there are enough fresh berries and fine butterfat to bring strong epicures to their knees. *193 Carlton St., tel. 416/961–4747. Jacket optional. Reservations advised. AE, MC, V.*

★ **Centro.** Franco Prevedello spent blood, sweat, and $2 million on dreamlike art deco lighting, etched glass, 18-foot ceilings with fat white columns, oxblood leather armchairs, Rosenthal china worth $45 a plate, and the most exciting Italian wine cellar in Toronto. The food can be heavy and overcomplicated—*agnolotti* with too much cream; overcooked poached salmon—but every day it moves closer to inspired Italian country style, with such specialties as poached skate in a mustardy coriander vinaigrette; a fat juicy roasted capon breast garnished with fresh pecans and lemon-pepper garlic mayonnaise; and espresso ice cream scented with Sambuca. *2472 Yonge St., tel. 416/483–2211. Jacket optional. Reservations recommended. AE, MC, V. No lunch; closed Sun.*

★ **Pronto Ristorante.** There's black mink, fat glistening pearls, and a conversation about Swiss bank accounts at the bar, where people with reservations at eight are waiting to be seated at nine. The mirrored ceiling and walls, the open kitchen, and the ceramic tile create a charming kaleidoscopic effect; it's so noisy and busy here that one is free to be casual. Chef Mark McEwan is in his element here. He makes liberal use of the grill, charring red and yellow peppers, zucchini, summer squash, meat, and fish. One night, he grilled very fresh striped bass hot and fast till it was barely cooked, set it in a puddle of wonderfully astringent grapefruit butter, and painted on a rainbow of grilled vegetables. He grills salmon till it's pink perfection and tosses it with roasted yellow peppers, cream, and *tagliatelle*. Pronto is a kitchen in superb control; even the waiters are charming. *692 Mount Pleasant Rd., south of Eglinton Ave.; tel. 416/486–1111. Jacket optional. Reservations required. AE, CB, D, MC, V.*

Moderate–Expensive

Sisi Trattoria. A proper trattoria—just 34 seats and unpretentious in the extreme. The ceiling is low, the pipes are exposed (not on purpose). The only thing that's high is the price—$100 for two with wine and the essential etceteras. The only decor is a few glued-on plaster ornaments. But I am drawn back again and again to Sisi's hot-blooded kitchen, her chorus of oil and wine, lemon and garlic, her gifts from the sea. Fresh sardines sit fragrant on the mesquite grill, sweet and earthy. Sisi's husband, Leo Schipani, grills fresh succulent oyster mushrooms and a slice of slightly aged *romanelle* cheese (from Italy) till they both crunch and explode in the mouth. His spaghetti Palermo is a carnival of anchovies, capers, black olives, tomato, parsley, and *pecorino* cheese. His linguine Saraceni is superior as well. The cuisine is southern Italian, a rarity in Canada. *116A Avenue Rd., above Bloor St.; tel. 416/962–0011. Jacket optional. Reservations required. AE, V. Closed Sun.*

Moderate **Trattoria Giancarlo.** Out past College and Bathurst streets, a restaurant wasteland, is this airy, warm, sweet little 40-seater, with exposed brick wall, fine music, and big black-and-white floor tiles. The appetizers are splendid, particularly the cream of butternut-squash soup with feathery snippets of fennel tops. The main courses are superbly diverse, from squid in their ink to pressed grilled chicken, quail in light tomato sauce, pink and tender lamb chops, and *zuppa di pesce.* The menu changes every month, creating a moveable feast. *41–43 Clinton St., tel. 416/533–9619. Dress: informal. Reservations recommended. AE, V. No dinner Thurs. and Fri., closed Sun. and Mon.*

Inexpensive **Camarra's.** Pizza heaven, in northwest Toronto. The dough has always been high and soft, with the delightful bite of a leavened dough. And on top are only good ingredients—real Italian plum tomatoes, not the canned tomato sauce of too many Toronto pizzerias. Very casual. *2899 Dufferin St., 1 mi south of the 401; tel. 416/789–3222. Dress: informal. No reservations required. AE, MC, V. No lunch Sun.; closed Tues.*

★ **La Fenice.** This is the most authentic Italian restaurant in Toronto. Luigi Orgera is a ballerina in the kitchen, the Nureyev of the grill. Who else in Toronto has fresh *porcini* in October? Who else grates heavenly slivers of fresh white truffle on pasta? The antipasto trolley is more Rome than Toronto: mint-scented grilled eggplant; roasted zuccini; tangy salad of shrimps and squid; roasted sweet red peppers anointed in extra-virgin olive oil; and more. His *risotto al mare* is a tiny perfect stew of clams and mussels; the spaghetti is tossed with sweet chunks of sun-dried tomatoes, southern Italy incarnate. In fish, one can expect red and white snapper, yellowtail, and porgy, all as fresh as fish can be in this city. *319 King St. W, near John St.; tel. 416/585–2377. Dress: informal. Reservations required. AE, MC, V. No lunch Sat.; closed Sun.*

Filippo's Gourmet Pizzeria. Pizza is the fast food that was supposedly invented by prescient Neapolitan cooks who anticipated the two-income family with no time to cook. It is best kept simple. Resist Filippo's designer pizza called La Yuppie (with salmon and goat cheese). The normal pizzas, such as the Calabrese, with huge green olives, roasted red peppers, spicy soprossata sausage, mozzarella, and tomato sauce, are excellent—crunchy on the outside, soft-hearted on the inside. Salads are large and crispy. You can eat in or take out. *744 Clair Ave. W, tel. 416/658–0568. Dress: informal. No reservations required. AE, MC, V.*

Japanese

Moderate ★ **Nami.** Just steps from the Eaton Centre sits this very fine restaurant, with a beautiful, spare Japanese ambience. Here, you will find *robata:* sushi for the squeamish, cooked on a gas barbecue (sushi is served, too). Lunches are less carefully prepared; this solid restaurant is for long, slow, shoeless evenings in the tatami rooms. *55 Adelaide St. E, near Yonge St.; tel. 416/362–7373. Dress: informal. Reservations recommended for lunch and weekends. AE, D, MC, V. No lunch Sat.; closed Sun.*

Nouvelle

Very Expensive ★ **Nekah.** Michael Stadtlander is probably the best cook in Canada. Other chefs copy; he creates. At Nekah, a spare and elegant room, he offers two six-course fixed-price menus for $60 each, and the menu changes nightly. Creamless vegetable purées come on handcrafted pottery bowls, crystalline consommés are served in black lacquer. Next there might be free-range chicken in fresh chervil jelly, or warm salad of raw oysters and barely grilled halibut, strewn with inoki mushrooms, white radish shred, and tiny tendrils of raw beet, in a barely-there miso dressing. The silver is Rosenthal, the glasses are crystal, and the drinking water comes from an Ontario spring. Meat courses represent field and forest in the form of splendid venison, buffalo, and Toronto's best collection of wild mushrooms. Desserts are made-to-order extravaganzas—fresh fig fritters, warm puff pastries, glazed crepes with the house ice creams. Statdlander's technique is superb, his touch delicate. Nekah is the most exciting restaurant in Toronto this year. *32 Wellington St. E, tel. 416/867–9067. Jacket and tie optional. Reservations advised. AE, MC, V.*

Expensive **La Fave's.** When two Palmerston stalwarts defected from Jamie Kennedy's kitchen to take over the former Antoine's in 1988, it was feared that the students would not match the master. They do not, but they come very close. Chef Michael Pawlick's touch is sure and delicate. He fries sweetbreads golden; poaches scallops till they melt; grills tuna, barely pink, and sets it on a magical *beurre blanc* of fresh thyme. His desserts are ethereal, especially the white chocolate gratin that is smooth as silk. Co-owner Peter Le Fave's gracious service matches Pawlick's culinary gentility. *553 Eglinton Ave. W, tel. 416/489–1834. Jacket optional. Reservations recommended. AE, MC, V.*

Lotus. This tiny homemade room, with no decor to speak of, is hotter than Szechuan garlic eggplant. Chef Susar Lee, who apprenticed in classical French cuisine at Hong Kong's Peninsula Hotel and a number of better Toronto eateries, calls the shots here, with every plate bearing his signature. One night, a thick, gutsy hot-and-sour soup with the favorite undertone of the late '80s: coriander. Another night, a fresh, sweet duck liver fried barely unto pinkness, dressed in pumpkin-seed oil and plum wine, and garnished with poached pear and Japanese basil. Lee buys as much organic meat and vegetables as is possible, and no factory chicken could ever taste as strong and real as his free-range bird stuffed with fresh apricots, raisins, and ginger, in black cherry sauce. Desserts include homemade tropical ice creams, baked fruits atop limpid coconut custards, and buttery pastries made from whole-wheat flour. This is French

Chinese cooking, a true hybrid. *96 Tecumseth St. at King St., west of Bathurst St.; tel. 416/368–7620. Jacket optional. Reservations recommended. AE, MC, V. No lunch; closed Sun.*

Trapper's. Visitors can be forgiven for believing that Canada lacks a national cuisine, but there is a culinary heritage, and Trapper's introduces it deliciously. They use farmhouse chutneys and purêed beets, Canadian cheddar, and the most flavorful Ontario lamb, grilled fast and hot over charcoal. Sauce at Trapper's is more likely to be raisin and brandy than butter and cream. That which is not blessed by the charcoal grill is more likely to be jumpfried, a technique borrowed by the Chinese that involves heating the pan to the smoking point and tossing meat, shrimp, or vegetable in briefly, to seal in the flavor. The technique produces dream-like textures, sweet inside, crispy outside, and intense flavors. If this is Canadian, raise the flag! *3479 Yonge St., tel. 416/482–6211. Jacket optional. Reservations recommended. AE, MC, V.*

Moderate–Expensive

Karin. On the plate is deep-fried arugula in a pool of white-chocolate peppermint sauce, garnished with papaya seeds and julienne of kiwi. The radicals of gastronomy crave new thrills like this, and they enjoy offbeat combinations and the ethnicity of exotic ingredients. Iconoclasts such as the chefs at Karin take the ordinary—the potato, the onion, the squash—and caress it with technique and garnish. They leave the kitchen daily to prowl Kensington Market and Chinatown for ingredients. Here, one can encounter rabbit and sweetbread married with wild leeks and cocoa *papardelle* (cocoa noodles—really!). The plainer works are still rigorously interesting: Tenderest beef striploin sits on a walnut and meat sauce, beside red onion, pear, and walnut flan. Split-pea soup is perfumed with roasted garlic. Shark is glazed with Japanese sherry. Guinea fowl comes with fresh, barely cooked okra and kumquats. The menu changes daily. *80 Scollard, near Bay and Bloor Sts.; tel. 416/964–0197. Dress: informal. Reservations recommended. AE, MC, V. No lunch Sat.; closed Sun.*

Patisseries

Inexpensive

Dufflet Pastries. For the best desserts in Toronto, bar none, check this one out. Dufflet Rosenberg has been supplying her inspired creations to dozens of the city's restaurants since 1974, but you can buy direct—it's cheaper and fresher. The chocolate orange Bavarian, the cranapple pie, the Linzer torte, the chocolate oatmeal cookies, the hazelnut chocolate balls and hazelnut cheesecake: All could give a diet doctor heart failure. And her chocolate mud cake (a deep, dark cake spiked with bourbon and coffee and iced with even darker semisweet chocolate) is one of the cakes that made Dufflet famous. Don't miss her two other classics: the toasted almond meringue torte and the chocolate fudge cake. *787 Queen St. W, near Bathurst St.; tel. 416/368–1812. Dress: informal. Reservations not necessary. No credit cards. No lunch; closed Sun.*

Patachou Patisserie. Up in a tiny plaza at Bathurst Street and Eglinton Avenue is this little place that feels like a neighborhood café on the Right Bank in Paris. (And now there's a more central branch on Yonge St., several blocks south of St. Clair Ave.) The brioches are as light and as buttery as any in Paris; the croissants and *pain au raisin* will make you long for France (you can eat them here or take them out). The *salade niçoise* is fine, and the *salade composée* at lunchtime is a treat—choose from three delicious salads. The Diplomate Pudding is superb, the Sacher torte good, the assorted fruit tarts a visual symphony that tastes as good as it looks. And the apple butter tart—quite incredible. *875 Eglinton Ave. W, tel. 416/782–1322; 1097 Yonge St., tel. 416/927–1105. Dress: informal. No reservations required. No credit cards. Closed Sun. at Eglinton Ave. W location only.*

Quick Meals

Moderate

Le Cafe. Every hotel, even the Four Seasons, needs a coffee shop, but what other one serves freshly squeezed strawberry juice? The effect of the rough brick walls, gas lights, and greenery is calm, pastoral, and warm. The dinner menu goes from Spanish omelet and chicken salad to some real exotica, such as the salad of snow peas, shrimps, and baby corn with sesame oil; and squab brushed with Meaux mustard, grilled, and then baked with bread crumbs. Cold dishes and grilled foods are best; desserts from the hotel kitchen are wondrous, especially the luscious pastries. *21 Avenue Rd., just above Bloor St.; tel. 416/964–0411. Jacket optional. Reservations not required. AE, CB, MC, V.*

Inexpensive

Grano Cafe. Franco Prevedello has served as godfather to a winner, helping a young couple, the Martellas, create a basic café—southern Italian style—the prettiest all-day café in Toronto. You order your meal at the bar, and Robert brings it. The soups and antipasti are dreams come true, the soups thick and strong, with fresh thyme and good stock. And some of the antipasti are as good as what you'd get in Bologna: Strips of zucchini are marinated with sweet oregano; a hint of caraway flavors the thin chewy strips of eggplant in oil. Grano's pizzas are so attractive because bread is the secret love at Grano (which means grain). All day the baker toils in the cellar under the café, and all day the breads come upstairs, fragrant and warm: The two most wonderful are the *foccaccia* and the oatmeal buttermilk bread. Avoid the steam-table stuff. *2035 Yonge St., below Eglinton Ave., tel. 416/440–1986. Dress: informal. No reservations accepted. MC, V. Closed Sun.*

★ **Jerusalem.** This is the ultimate family restaurant: the broadloom is dark red with a brown pattern, so accidents by children can go practically unnoticed. Service is fast. The bustle and noise are enough to camouflage the most unruly youngsters. And the food will not deliver a crisis to the taste buds. Jerusalem serves a rich variety of wonderful Middle Eastern foods—the most tender falafel in town, rich fried tomatoes with garlic, *sam bousek* (a deep-fried dough packet of ground meat and pine nuts), very sweet charcoal-grilled shish kebab, and ungooey baklava. *955 Eglinton Ave. W, tel. 416/783–6494. Dress: informal. Reservations not required. AE, MC, V.*

Vegetarian

Moderate

★ **The Parrot.** For a long while, this was Toronto's only vegetarian restaurant serving very fine food; and although meat was added to the menu in 1983, superlative veggie meals continue to be offered. The *cappellini primavera* is a delectable rainbow of pasta and vegetables. Try the baked *chèvre* with olive oil and

Parmesan fritters in tomato sauce. And the *gnocchi* are the finest I've ever eaten. *325 Queen St. W, near University Ave.; tel. 416/593–0899. Dress: informal. Reservations requested. AE, MC, V. No lunch Sat.–Mon.*

Inexpensive

Renaissance Cafe. A modest restaurant with a limited but cosmopolitan menu—the likes of ratatouille and curries. The daily brunches are pleasant. *509 Bloor St. W, near Bathurst St.; tel. 416/968–6639. Dress: informal. Reservations recommended. AE, MC, V.*

The Vegetarian Restaurant. For the uninitiated, there are lovely omelets, soups, and salads; for the adventuresome, soyburgers and soy pâté. It's now in a new location, in a cheerfully renovated Victorian house, with cafeteria-style service. *4 Dundonald St., just east of Yonge St.; tel. 416/961–9522. Dress: informal. No reservations. MC, V. No lunch Sun.*

8 Lodging

Places to stay in this cosmopolitan city range, as one might expect, from luxurious hotels to budget motels to a handful of bed-and-breakfasts in private homes.

Prices are cut nearly in half over weekends and during special times of the year (many Toronto hotels drop their rates a full 50% in January and February).

If you are traveling with children or are planning to do a good deal of sightseeing, you should consider staying in the downtown area (south of Bloor Street, east of Bathurst Street, west of Jarvis Street). This is where you will find Harbourfront, the CN Tower, Eaton Centre, the Toronto Islands, the SkyDome, Chinatown, and most of the finest shopping and restaurants. If you are staying only a day or two, and are mainly interested in visiting the zoo, the Ontario Science Centre, and Canada's Wonderland, then look into some of the places listed below as Off the Beaten Track or along the airport strip.

Accommodation Toronto (tel. 416/596–7117), a service of the Hotel Association of Toronto, is an excellent source for finding the room and price you want. Don't forget to ask about family deals and special packages.

The most highly recommended properties in each category are indicated with a star ★.

Category	Cost*
Very Expensive	over $175
Expensive	$125–$174
Moderate	$70–$124
Inexpensive	under $70

**for a double room*

The following credit-card abbreviations are used: AE, American Express; CB, Carte Blanche; DC, Diners Club; MC, MasterCard; V, Visa.

Downtown

Very Expensive

★ **Chestnut Park Hotel**. One of the newest—and biggest—additions to Toronto's hotel scene, this handsome 16-floor hotel with glass-enclosed atrium lobby could hardly be more convenient: just steps behind City Hall and a few short blocks from Eaton Centre. The 522 guest rooms, which include 21 for the disabled, are all well decorated, with finely crafted furniture and desks; many have queen- and king-size beds. Recreational facilities include a large heated indoor pool, sauna, Jacuzzi, health club and gymnasium, and a children's creative center. A business center makes the hotel attractive for executives. In addition, the Chestnut Hill will be connected by a walkway from the mezzanine level to a Museum of Textiles, where some 15,000 textiles from around the world will be displayed—the only museum of its kind in Canada. *108 Chestnut St., M5G 1R3, just north of Nathan Phillips Square; tel. 416/977–5000. AE, CB, DC, MC, V.*

★ **Four Seasons Toronto.** It's hard to imagine a lovelier or more exclusive hotel than the Four Seasons, which is usually rated among the top two dozen hotels in the world and one of the top three in North America. The location is one of the most ideal in the city: on the edge of Yorkville, a few meters from the Royal Ontario Museum. The 379 units are tastefully appointed. Maids come twice a day, and there are comfortable bathrobes, oversized towels, fresh flowers, and a fine indoor/outdoor pool. Even the special family rates, however, will not drop the cost much below $200 a night. Yet, during such slow months as January through March, sometimes into April, rooms on weekends have been offered for less than $80 per night (per person), and there is reason to believe that this tradition will continue into 1990. *21 Avenue Rd., M5R 2G1, a block north of Bloor St.; tel. 416/964-0411 or 800/332-3442. AE, CB, DC, MC, V.*

Harbour Castle Westin. This was a Hilton International hotel until 1987, when Westin and Hilton suddenly switched ownership of their major downtown Toronto hotels. A favorite with conventioneers, it's located just steps from Harbourfront and the Toronto Island ferry. It's a bit inconvenient to the city's amenities except for those directly on the lakeshore, but it enjoys the best views of any hotel in the city. There's a shuttle bus service to downtown business and shopping, and the swimming pool, squash courts, and health club are among the best in town. Its nearly 1,000 rooms are well-appointed and tastefully modern, and the frequent family and weekend rates help bring its regular price down by as much as a third. *1 Harbour Sq., M5J 1A6, tel. 416/869-1600 or 800/228-3000. AE, CB, DC, MC, V.*

King Edward Hotel. After too many years of neglect, this Edwardian classic was finally purchased and thoroughly renovated by a group of local investors. Some of the restorations were less than sensitive; the kitschy platform with pergola in the dining room desecrates one of Toronto's great interiors. Still, it's a treat having this splendid structure restored to its pink marble grandeur, and, under the British Trusthouse Forte group, it again attracting the well-heeled clientele it so manifestly deserves. There's a nonsmoker's floor, and family and weekend rates are available. Facilities include a health club. *37 King St. E, M5C 1E9, tel. 416/863-9700 or 800/225-5843. AE, CB, DC, MC, V.*

Sutton Place Hotel. This 33-story tower, located close to the various ministries of the Ontario provincial government, is a favorite with lobbyists, lawyers, and the like. Service is more personal than you would think, because many of the floors have luxury apartments, not hotel rooms. Being next to Wellesley Street means that it's in walking distance of Queen's Park, the Royal Ontario Museum, and many other midtown attractions. Facilities include a pool, health club, 24-hour room service, and special floors for nonsmokers. Family and weekend rates are available. *955 Bay St., M5S 2A2, tel. 416/924-9221. AE, CB, DC, MC, V.*

Expensive

Delta Chelsea Inn. The 977 rooms on the south side of Gerrard Street began as a budget hotel. Prices have crept up, but they're still reasonable by downtown standards. The Chelsea is much favored by tour operators, and the elevators, which were meant to serve the apartment building this was originally intended to be, can be hard to catch when all the buses are leaving at once. On the positive side, all guest rooms were redone in 1987, and the hotel has a creative, supervised day care service for children ages 3–8, open from 9:30 AM to 10 PM. Facilities include a pool and sauna. The Chelsea was offering rooms for as low as $50 per night, on weekends, in early 1989. *33 Gerrard St., M5G 1Z5, at the corner of Yonge St.; tel. 416/595–1975 or 800/268–1133. AE, CB, DC, MC, V.*

Hotel Admiral. This small, intimate hotel is exquisitely situated on the edge of Lake Ontario, overlooking Harbourfront. It has only 157 rooms and 17 handsomely furnished suites. The lacquered wood shines and the polished brass gleams in the stunning lobby. The Promenade Deck on the 5th level, surrounding the outdoor heated swimming pool, allows for fabulous views of the bustling harbor. There's frequent courtesy shuttle bus service for the downtown area. *249 Queen's Quay W, M5J 2N5, tel. 416/364–5444. AE, CB, DC, MC, V.*

Hotel Plaza II. This relatively small, modern, 256-room hotel is one that Torontonians tend to forget. It's part of the Hudson Bay complex, near the busy intersection of Yonge and Bloor streets. All rooms were redone six years ago. Facilities include a pool and a sauna. Weekend rates are available. *90 Bloor St. E, M4W 1A7, tel. 416/961–8000 or 800/323–7500. AE, CB, DC, MC, V.*

Park Plaza Hotel. It may lack a pool, but it has one of the best locations in the city: a short distance from the Royal Ontario Museum, Queen's Park, and Yorkville (one of the city's great shopping areas). The 350 units are well-appointed in a plush, old-fashioned way, and they seem to coast by on their old-shoe familiarity to regular Toronto visitors who have been staying in them since the days when there was much less choice. The roof lounge was once described by novelist Mordecai Richler as "the only civilized place in Toronto." In late 1988, two years of renovations began. Additions will include a 550-seat ballroom, a business center, a palm court, and a restaurant in the lobby, all designed by Zeidler Roberts Partnership, the same architects who were responsible for the Eaton Centre and Ontario Place. *4 Avenue Rd., M5R 2E8, at the corner of Bloor St. W; tel. 416/924–5471 or 800/268–4927. AE, CB, DC, MC, V.*

Royal York. It may still be, as it was for decades, the largest hotel in the British Commonwealth. With some 1,500 rooms and some 13 restaurants, it's unarguably a monster of a place. The service is necessarily impersonal, and there's always a convention of some sort going on. Still, it's venerable, comfortable, close to the financial core of the city, and rarely booked solid. Ask for one of the recently renovated rooms. The Imperial Room serves the likes of Peggy Lee and Tony Bennett with dinner. *100 Front St. W, M5J 1E3, tel. 416/368–2511 or 800/828–7447. AE, CB, DC, MC, V.*

Sheraton Centre. This 1,430-room conventioneer's tower is located across from the New City Hall, just a block from Eaton Centre. The below-ground level is part of Toronto's labyrinth of shop-lined corridors, and there are more shops on the ground floor and second floor. The restaurants' reach seems to exceed their grasp, but the Long Bar, overlooking Nathan Phillips Square, is a great place to meet friends for a drink. There's a nonsmoking floor and various special rates and packages. Facilities include a huge indoor/outdoor pool, hot tub, sauna, and workout room. *123 Queen St. W, M5H 2M9, tel. 416/361–1000 or 800/325–3535. AE, CB, DC, MC, V.*

Toronto Hilton International. As noted above, this hotel, located in the financial district, recently switched ownership

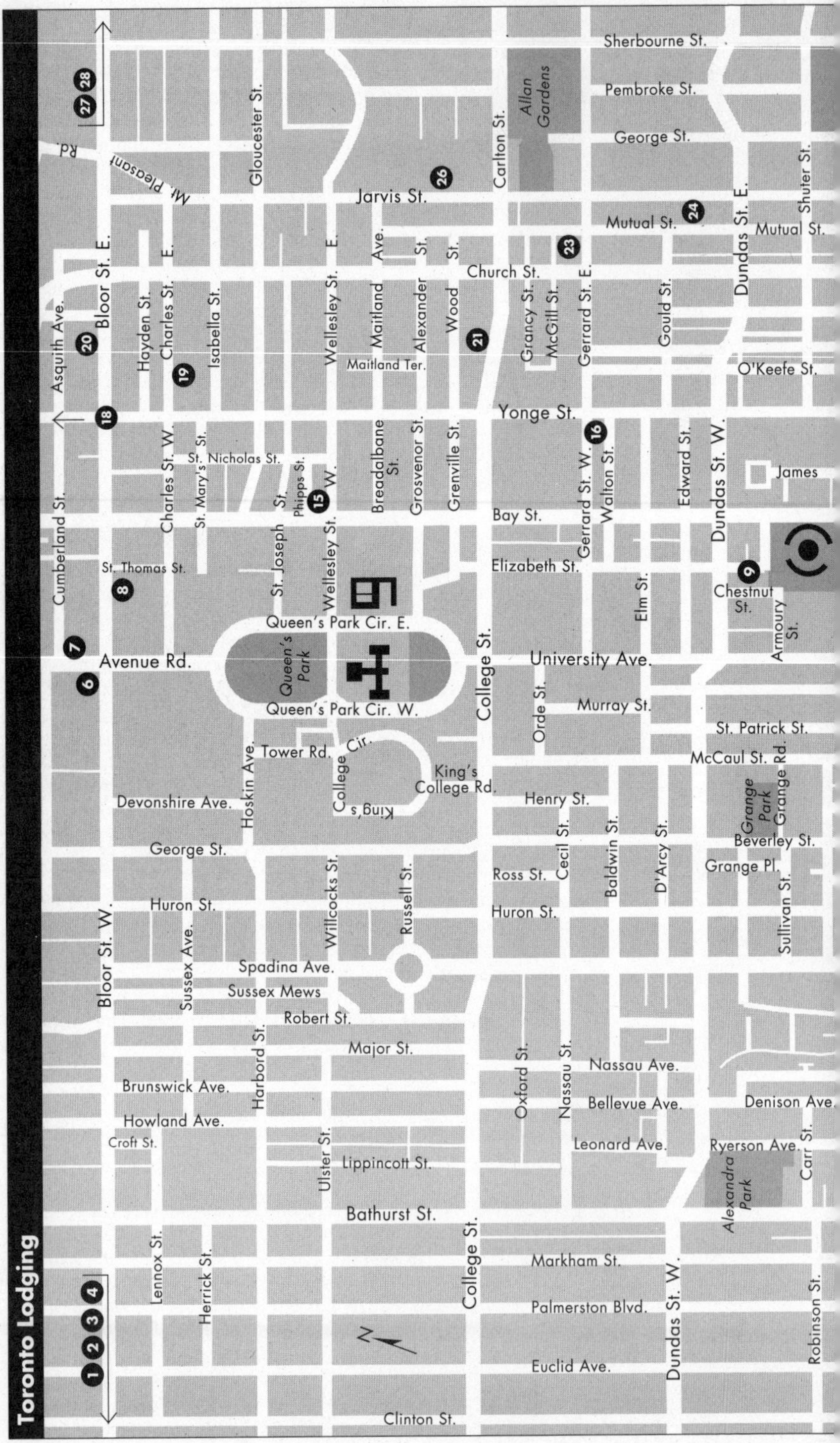
Toronto Lodging
Sherbourne St.
Pembroke St.
George St.
Allan Gardens
Carlton St.
Jarvis St.
Mutual St.
Shuter St.
Dundas St. E.
Church St.
Gould St.
Gerrard St. E.
McGill St.
Grancy St.
O'Keefe St.
Yonge St.
Wood St.
Alexander St.
Maitland Ave.
Maitland Ter.
Wellesley St. E.
Gloucester St.
Mt. Pleasant Rd.
Bloor St. E.
Asquith Ave.
Hayden St.
Charles St. E.
Isabella St.
Cumberland St.
Charles St. W.
St. Mary's St.
St. Nicholas St.
Phipps St.
St. Joseph St.
Wellesley St. W.
Breadalbane St.
Grosvenor St.
Grenville St.
Bay St.
Gerrard St. W.
Walton St.
Edward St.
Dundas St. W.
James
Elizabeth St.
Elm St.
Chestnut St.
Armoury St.
St. Thomas St.
Avenue Rd.
Queen's Park Cir. E.
Queen's Park
Queen's Park Cir. W.
College St.
University Ave.
Orde St.
Murray St.
St. Patrick St.
McCaul St.
Grange Rd.
Grange Park
Tower Rd.
College Cir.
King's College Rd.
King's College Cir.
Hoskin Ave.
Devonshire Ave.
Henry St.
Cecil St.
Baldwin St.
D'Arcy St.
Beverley St.
Grange Pl.
George St.
Ross St.
Huron St.
Sullivan St.
Bloor St. W.
Sussex Ave.
Willcocks St.
Russell St.
Spadina Ave.
Sussex Mews
Robert St.
Harbord St.
Major St.
Oxford St.
Nassau St.
Nassau Ave.
Brunswick Ave.
Bellevue Ave.
Denison Ave.
Howland Ave.
Croft St.
Leonard Ave.
Ryerson Ave.
Ulster St.
Lippincott St.
Alexandra Park
Carr St.
Bathurst St.
Lennox St.
Herrick St.
Markham St.
Palmerston Blvd.
Robinson St.
Euclid Ave.
Clinton St.
N
1 2 3 4 6 7 8 9 15 16 18 19 20 21 23 24 26 27 28

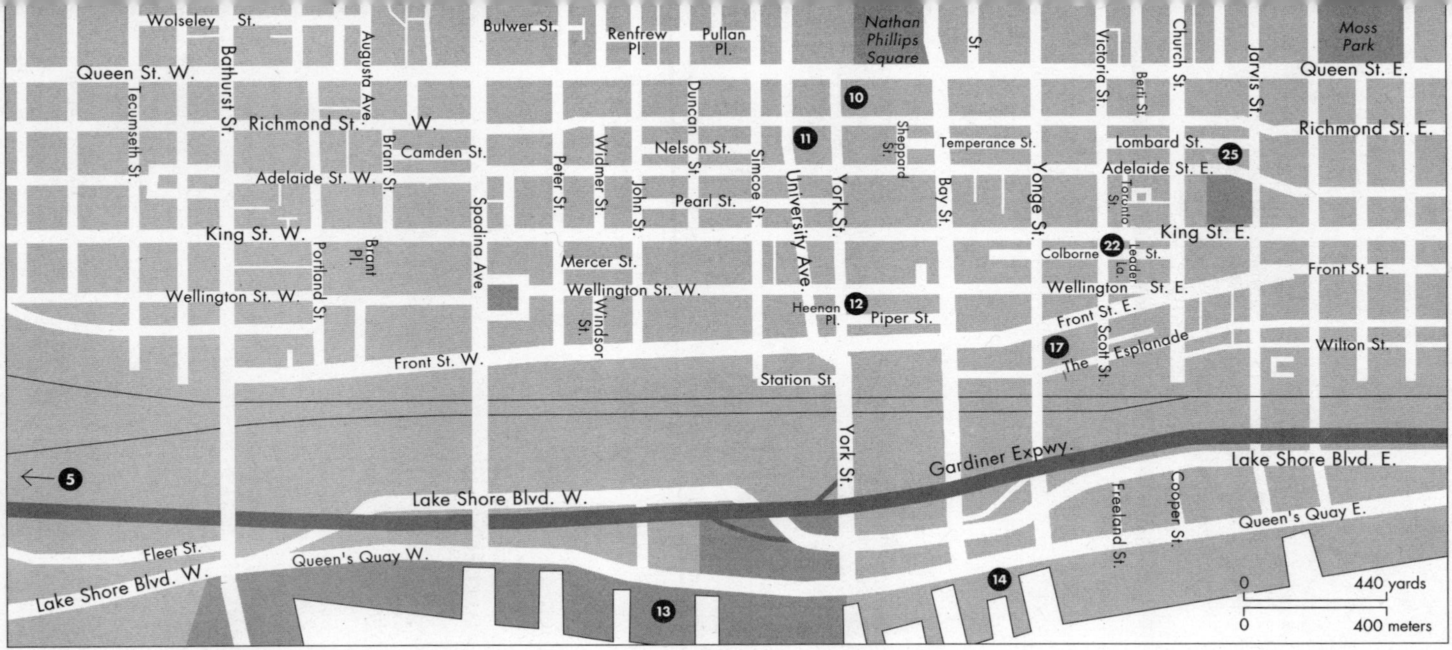

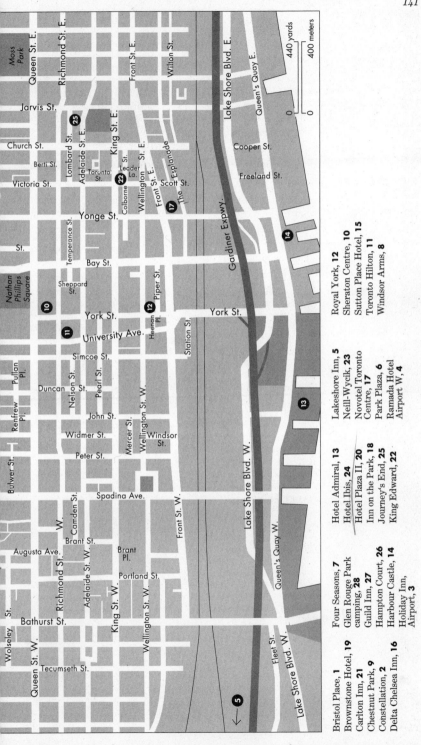

Bristol Place, **1**
Brownstone Hotel, **19**
Carlton Inn, **21**
Chestnut Park, **9**
Constellation, **2**
Delta Chelsea Inn, **16**
Four Seasons, **7**
Glen Rouge Park camping, **28**
Guild Inn, **27**
Hampton Court, **26**
Harbour Castle, **14**
Holiday Inn, Airport, **3**
Hotel Admiral, **13**
Hotel Ibis, **24**
Hotel Plaza II, **20**
Inn on the Park, **18**
Journey's End, **25**
King Edward, **22**
Lakeshore Inn, **5**
Neill-Wycik, **23**
Novotel Toronto Centre, **17**
Park Plaza, **6**
Ramada Hotel Airport W, **4**
Royal York, **12**
Sheraton Centre, **10**
Sutton Place Hotel, **15**
Toronto Hilton, **11**
Windsor Arms, **8**

with the Westin. The 600 rooms are newly renovated, and its nearness to the financial district, New City Hall, the CN Tower, and more makes it a convenient base for most visitors. The indoor/outdoor pool is modest, but the view of the city from the glass-enclosed elevators is a thrill. There are family plans and weekend rates, as always, and children can stay free. *145 Richmond St. W and University Ave., M5H 3M6, tel. 416/869–3456. AE, CB, DC, MC, V.*

★ **Windsor Arms.** Katharine Hepburn, Peter Ustinov, the Rolling Stones, and scores of other celebrities patronize this very small 81-room inn that nestles behind its ivy on a quiet, outdoor-café-lined side street just steps from the high-ticket shops of Bloor Street. One of the three Canadian members in the prestigious French *Relais et Châteaux* association, the Windsor Arms is also one of the few downtown hotels anywhere to meet that group's standards for "calm, comfort, and cuisine." No pool. No conference facilities. Just a superb kitchen (patronized by thousands of Torontonians who enjoy the hotel's four restaurants) and rooms fit for a country inn. Rates have risen since 1988, placing the hotel on the top end of the Expensive category. *22 St. Thomas St., M5S 2B9, tel. 416/979–2341 or 800/668–8106. AE, CB, DC, MC, V.*

Moderate

Brownstone Hotel. This intimate hotel—110 units in all—has some of the charm of a private club. You could not be closer to the center of town and still get a quiet night's sleep. Ask for one of the recently renovated rooms. No additional charge for children under 14. Rates include Continental breakfast, newspaper, and membership in health club two blocks away. *15 Charles St. E, M4Y 1S1, tel. 416/924–6631 or 800/263–8967. AE, CB, DC, MC, V.*

Carlton Inn. Some 535 reasonably priced rooms right next door to Maple Leaf Gardens and convenient to the Carlton/College streets subway stop. A favorite with budget travelers and sales people with tight expense accounts. Ask for one of the renovated rooms. *30 Carlton St., M5B 2E9, tel. 416/977–6655 or 800/268–9076. AE, CB, DC, MC, V.*

Lakeshore Inn. This 12-story hotel is one of the more pleasant properties of the many that are strung out along Lake Ontario, just outside the city. There are 143 rooms—ask for one that was recently redecorated—two restaurants, a lounge, and a pool. Family and weekend rates are available. *2000 Lakeshore Blvd. W, M6S 1A2, tel. 416/763–4521. AE, CB, DC, MC, V.*

Novotel Toronto Centre. This moderately priced hotel—part of a popular French chain—opened in December 1987. There are 266 modest, modern rooms on nine floors in the heart of downtown, in walking distance of Harbourfront and the CN Tower. Facilities include an indoor pool, whirlpool, exercise room, and sauna. *45 The Esplanade, M5E 1W2, tel. 416/367–8900 or 800/221–4542. AE, CB, DC, MC, V.*

Inexpensive

Hotel Ibis. This recent hotel belongs to one of Europe's leading chains. It is centrally located, just a few blocks from the New City Hall and Eaton Centre. As it proudly declares, "No bellhops, doormen, or concierges. No gushing fountains. And no room service with fancy silver trays." What it does have are 294 comfortable rooms with bare necessities (as well as 10 others specially designed and equipped for the disabled). There's no pool, but arrangements can be made with a nearby health club for a nominal fee. And there is a complimentary breakfast buffet. *240 Jarvis St., M5B 2B8, tel. 416/593–9400. AE, CB, DC, MC, V.*

Journey's End Hotel. Rooms are clean and Spartan in this 16-story chain hotel located in the downtown core area, a 10-minute walk from Eaton Centre. No pools, saunas, or convention rooms, but prices (starting at $69 for doubles) are reasonable for the area. *111 Lombard St., M5C 2T9, tel. 800/668–4200. AE, CB, DC, MC, V.*

Neill-Wycik College-Hotel. This is an attractive alternative for young people or families on a tight budget. From early May through late August, the college residence becomes Toronto's best hotel value. Rooms are private, but guests must share facilities with five or six other hotel guests. A cafeteria serves breakfast 6:30–11:30. There's a great view of the city from the cedar roof deck. Where else can a visitor find a room so close to Eaton Centre for $30–$40—with no cost for children under 17, and weekly discounts of 10%? *96 Gerrard St. E, M5B 1G7, tel. 416/977–2320. AE, CB, DC, MC, V.*

Toronto Bed & Breakfast. More than two dozen private homes are affiliated with this service, most of them scattered across Metro Toronto. Rooms cost as little as $45 a night and include breakfast. *Tel. 416/961–3676.*

Off the Beaten Track

Very Expensive

Inn on the Park. This is another classy member of the Four Seasons chain. It is located across the street from the Ontario Science Centre, just off Don Valley Parkway, only a 10-minute drive from downtown Toronto. The only resort in the city, it offers guests 600 acres of parkland, miles of cross-country ski trails, swimming, biking, jogging, and access to tennis, racquetball, squash, and horseback riding. Children ages 5–12 can disappear all day into a supervised program, complete with swimming, arts and crafts, and other activities. There are 568 modern rooms and 11 suites. *1100 Eglinton Ave. E, M3C 1H8, tel. 416/444–2561 or 800/332–3442. AE, CB, DC, MC, V.*

Moderate

Guild Inn. Modern units are built around a 1930s country inn on some 90 acres of forest, gardens, and woodland trails, a 20- to 30-minute drive from downtown Toronto. Facilities include a heated outdoor pool, a tennis court, and dining room. Guests have a choice of 13 traditional rooms in the original building or 67 modern rooms in the newer wing. *201 Guildwood Pkwy., Scarborough M1E 1P6, tel. 416/261–3331. AE, MC, V.*

The Airport Strip

Few hotels along the airport strip offer anything more than your standard, no-surprises rooms and meals. Most have pools, pay TV, and weekend rates, and their prices vary greatly.

Expensive

Bristol Place. This has long been considered the ritziest of all the hotels along the airport strip, and, thanks to a $2-million facelift in 1987, it is more attractive than ever. All 287 bedrooms and suites have been redone. Bedrooms have mahogany armoires, tables, desks, and minibars. Special packages ("Honeymoon," "Blue Jays," "Canada's Wonderland," etc.) help keep prices down. *950 Dixon Rd., M9W 5N4, next to the airport; tel. 416/675–9444. Facilities: indoor and outdoor* *pools, saunas, health club with exercise equipment, children's play area. AE, DC, MC, V.*

Moderate–Expensive **Constellation Hotel.** Just off the junction of Highway 27N and Dixon Road, not far from the airport, this is one of the classier hotels in the area: There is a stunning, seven-story, glass-enclosed lobby; a fully-equipped health club, including saunas and a delightful indoor/outdoor swimming pool; quality dining; and very impressive service. There are senior-citizen discounts and numerous, low-priced weekend packages to nearby Canada's Wonderland and more. Special floors for executives and nonsmokers; 900 modern rooms; children under 16 free. *900 Dixon Rd., M9W 1J7, tel. 416/675–1500. AE, CB, DC, MC, V.*

Moderate **Holiday Inn, Airport.** This location has indoor/outdoor pools with whirlpool and sauna, playgrounds, pleasant public areas, and those never-threatening rooms. There are more than 450 rooms in all and numerous weekend packages. *970 Dixon Rd., M9W 1J9, tel. 416/675–7611. AE, DC, MC, V.*

Ramada Hotel Airport West. This location has standard hotel amenities and lovely landscaped grounds. 300 rooms, eight suites, a nice heated pool, and saunas. Senior discounts and good weekend package plans are available. *5444 Dixie Rd., L4W 2L2, tel. 416/624–1144. AE, CB, DC, MC, V.*

Executive Apartments

Since 1977, the Canadian firm **ETA Suites** (formerly called Executive Travel Apartments) has been supplying corporate clients with short-term furnished apartment suites in 17 cities across North America and Europe. These can be rented for a minimum of three nights, with discounts for weekly and monthly reservations. Why are they so interesting? Well, in Toronto, the apartments have fully equipped kitchens, regular maid service, direct-dial phones, and vastly more space and privacy than a conventional hotel room. Prices range from less than $100 for a studio to under $200 for a two- or three-bedroom suite—far less than a single room in some of Toronto's finest hotels. And complimentary limo service to the downtown business district is sometimes included in the rate. *1101 Bay St., Suite 1805, M5S 2W8, tel. 416/923–3000.*

Family Farms

It's daring and different, but families with children might find it exciting to stay on a farm, not far from the city of Toronto. Including bed-and-breakfast, rates range from as low as $35 to $60 a night for two on weekends, to about $200 per person for a week. For further information of family farm vacations—in both summer and winter—write, enclosing a big envelope and a 60¢ stamp, to **Ontario Vacation Farm Association** (R.R. 2, Alma, Ont., N0B 1A0; tel. 519/846–9788).

Camping

This is a very citified area; the only location offering tent and trailer camping within Metro Toronto is **Glen Rouge Park,** 25 acres in the city's northeast end. Its attractions include nature trails, horseback riding, and proximity to the city's fabulous zoo. For a list of licensed private campgrounds and trailer parks, write to Travel Information, Ministry of Industry and Tourism, Third Floor, Hearst Block, Queen's Park, Toronto M7A 2E5. A list of provincial parks and recreation and conservation areas is available from Provincial Parks Information, Whitney Block, Queen's Park, Toronto M7A 1W3.

9 The Arts

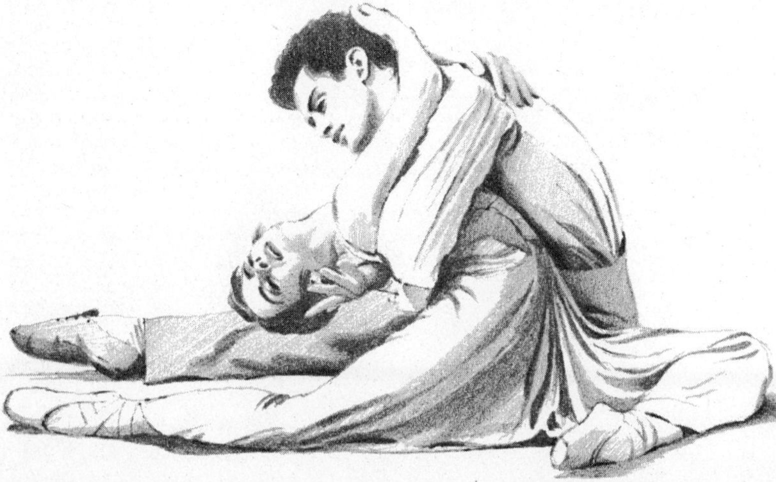

Toronto is the capital of the lively arts in Canada. True, Winnipeg has a very fine ballet, and Montreal's orchestra is superb. But in nearly every aspect of music, opera, dance, and theater, Toronto is truly the New York City of the North.

It was not always this way; before 1950—barely four decades ago—Toronto had no opera company, no ballet, and very little theater worthy of the title "professional." Then came the Massey Report on the Arts, one of those government-sponsored studies that usually helps put sensitive subjects on the back burner for several more years, but in this case, all Heaven broke loose: Money began to come from a variety of government grants; two prominent Canadian millionaires passed to their reward, and their death taxes were put toward the creation of a Canada Council, which doled out more money; the Canadian Opera Company, CBC television, and the National Ballet of Canada were born; and a number of little theaters began to pop up, culminating in an artistic explosion throughout the 1970s, in every aspect of the arts.

The reasons for this explosion were many: massive immigration from more culturally nourished countries of Eastern and Central Europe, as well as from England; a growing sense of independence from the mother country; a recognition that if Canada was not to develop its own arts, then the damned Yankees would do it for them; and, in general, a growing civic and cultural maturity.

Some of Toronto's impressive growth in the lively arts was sheer chance; after all, who can explain the miracle of pianist Glenn Gould's birth in this city, or the fact that ballet master Barishnikov decided to defect here and later came often to teach and dance with the National Ballet of Canada?

But it would not be fair to pass it off as simply as that. Toronto was like an awkward, gawky teenager for many decades, it's true, but there were always a number of cultural events happening; the city did not suddenly give birth to art overnight, like Athena bursting out, fully clothed and mature, from the head of Zeus.

The best places to get information on cultural happenings are in the Friday editions of the *Toronto Star* (their "What's On" section is superlative); the Saturday (weekend) *Globe and Mail* (whose entertainment section is the most critically solid); the free, weekly *Now* Magazine; as well as *Toronto Life*. For half-price tickets on the day of a performance, don't forget the **Five Star Tickets booth,** located in the Royal Ontario Museum lobby during the winter and, at other times, at the corner of Yonge Street and Dundas Street, outside the Eaton Centre. The museum booth is open daily noon–6, and Tuesday and Thursday to 7; the Yonge and Dundas booth is open—in good weather—Monday–Saturday, noon–7:30, and Sunday, 11–3. Tickets are sold for cash only, all sales are final, and a small service charge is added to the price of each ticket. The booth outside the Eaton Centre also gives out piles of superb brochures and pamphlets on the city.

Concert Halls and Theaters

The **Roy Thomson Hall** (just below the CN Tower) has become since 1982 the most important concert hall in Toronto.

It was to have been named the New Massey Hall, since it was replacing the much-loved original, which had served Toronto since 1894. But then the family of billionaire newspaper magnate Lord Thomson of Fleet gave the largest single donation ($4.5 million of its $43-million cost) and gave his name to the hall instead. Critics were silenced by the beauty of the hall's design and the sensitivity of its acoustics. It is the home today of the Toronto Symphony and the Toronto Mendelssohn Choir, one of the world's finest choral groups. It also hosts orchestras from around the world and popular entertainers from Liza Minelli to Anne Murray. *60 Simcoe St., at the corner of King Street W., a block west of University Ave.; tel. 416/593-4828. Tickets $10–$40 (best seats rows H and J in the Orchestra and row L upstairs). Rush seats are sold the day of a performance, beginning two hours before show time. Daily tours, highlighting the acoustic and architectural features of the stunning structure, take place Mon.–Sat., 12:30 PM (cost: $2). Tel. 416/593–4822 to confirm.*

Massey Hall has always been cramped and dingy, but its near-perfect acoustics and its handsome, U-shape tiers sloping down to the stage have made it a happy place to hear the Toronto Symphony, or almost anyone else in the world of music, for nearly a century. The nearly 2,800 seats are not terribly comfortable, and a small number are blocked by pillars that hold up the ancient structure, but it remains a venerable place to catch the greats and near-greats of the music world. *178 Victoria St. at Shuster, just a block north of Queen St. and a few feet east of the Eaton Centre; tel. 416/593–4828. Best seats are rows G–M, center, and in the balcony, rows 32–50.*

The Edward Johnson Building, in the Bloor Street/University Avenue area, houses the **MacMillan Theatre,** and it is an important place to hear avant-garde artists and the stars of the future. Because it's run by the faculty of music of the University of Toronto, the academic year also brings serious jazz trios and baroque chamber works—at little or no cost. The U of T newspaper, **The Varsity,** found across campus, often lists concerts planned for this special place. *Located behind the McLaughlin Planetarium, just to the south of the Royal Ontario Museum subway exit; tel. 416/978–3744.*

The **O'Keefe Centre** has become the home of the Canadian Opera Company and the National Ballet of Canada. It is also home to visiting comedians, pre-Broadway musicals, rock stars, and almost anyone else who can fill it. When it was built in 1960, its 3,167 seats made it the largest concert hall on the continent. The acoustics leave much to be desired, and its cavernous nature makes almost anything but the most lavish opera or musical seem dwarfed, but you still feel as if you are attending a cultural event. The city owns the building now and offers half-price seats to students and senior citizens for many of its shows. *1 Front St. E, a block east of Union Station; tel. 416/872–2262. Tickets $20–$50. Try for seats close to A47–48; avoid the very front rows, such as AA, BB, etc.*

About 50 yards east of the O'Keefe is the **St. Lawrence Centre for the Arts.** Since 1970, it has been presenting everything from live theater to string quartets and forums on city issues. The main hall, the luxuriously appointed **Bluma Appel Theatre,** hosts the often brilliant productions of the **Canadian Stage Company** and **Theatre Plus.** Classical and contemporary plays are often on a level with the best of Broadway and London's West End. *Front St. at the corner of Scott St., a block east of Yonge St., two blocks from Union Station; tel. 416/366–7723. Tickets $10–$25. Try for rows E–N, seats 1–10.*

The other important theater in the city is the **Royal Alexandra,** which has been the place to be seen in Toronto since its opening in 1907. The plush red seats, gold brocade, and baroque swirls and curlicues all make theater-going a refined experience. It's astonishing to recall that all this magnificence was about to be torn down in the 1960s, but was rescued by none other than "Honest Ed" Mirvish of discount-store fame. He not only restored the theater to its former glory but also made it profitable. *Les Misérables,* which opened in March 1989, is scheduled to continue its run here through at least the summer of 1990. *260 King St. W, a few blocks west of University, two blocks to the southwest of the CN Tower; tel. 416/593–4211. Tickets $20–$50. Avoid rows A and B; try for rows C–L center. For musicals, try the first rows of the first balcony.*

Since the summer of 1989, the gigantic **SkyDome** has been opening its doors (and roof, in good weather). Although its expressed purpose is for baseball and football, its 70,000 seats will also be used for concerts—more than likely rock. *Located on the south side of Front St., just to the west of the CN Tower; tel. 416/963–3513.*

The most exciting new theater is the **Pantages,** a 1920 vaudeville theater, which was a complex of half a dozen movie theaters until recently. In 1988/89, the Cineplex/Odeon people poured some $18 million into refurbishing the theater as a majestic work of art. In the fall of 1989, a Canadian company of *The Phantom of the Opera* opened, and the show should run well into the 1990s. Tickets can be ordered through Ticketmaster, 416/872–2233. *263 Yonge St., just a half-block south of Dundas, across from the Eaton Centre; tel. 416/872–2222. Performances Mon.–Sat. at 8 PM; Wed. and Sat. at 2 PM.*

The other major concert/theater halls in the Toronto area are in **Stratford** and **Niagara-on-the-Lake** (*see* Excursions).

Classical Concerts

The Toronto Symphony, now over 65 years old, is not about to retire. Since 1922, with conductors of the quality of Seiji Ozawa, Walter Susskind, Sir Thomas Beecham, and Andrew Davis, it has achieved world acclaim. Its new music director as of 1990/91 is Maestro Gunther Herbig. When the TS is home, it presents about three concerts weekly from September to May in Roy Thomson Hall and a mini-season each summer at Ontario Place. *60 Simcoe St., on King St., just west of University Ave.; tel. 416/593–4828. Tickets $16–$35.*

The **Toronto Mendelssohn Choir** often guests with the Toronto Symphony. This 180-singer group, going since 1894, has been applauded worldwide, and its *Messiah* is handeled well every Christmas (no, we couldn't resist that). *For program information, tel. 416/598–0422; for tickets, Roy Thomson Hall, tel. 416/593–4828.*

The **Elmer Isler Singers,** a fine group of nearly two dozen members, has also performed around the globe, and is a respected Toronto choir. *Tel. 416/482–1664.*

The **Orford String Quartet,** another world-class musical group, is based in Toronto at the Edward Johnson Building. *Tel. 416/978–3744.*

Tafelmusik ("table music") is a local orchestra that goes for baroque music on original instruments. *St. Paul Centre at Trinity Church, 427 Bloor St. W, near the Spadina Ave. subway stop; tel. 416/964–6337.*

Music at Sharon is a marvelous concert series, that takes place on weekends every July in the Sharon Temple, located in a small town about a 45-minute drive north of downtown Toronto. The old temple has wonderful acoustics. For 10 seasons, concerts have ranged from flute offerings and humor in music to Haydn afternoons (and evenings). Tickets cost $15–$20. *Sharon is 4 km north of Newmarket, which is just above Hwy. 9, after taking the Don Valley Parkway/Hwy. 404 north from the 401. Tel. 416/478–2431, or write to Music at Sharon, Box 331, Sharon, Ont., L0G 1V0.*

Popular and Rock Concerts

Most major international recording companies have offices in Toronto, so it's not by chance that the city is a regular stop for top musical performers of today, whether Frank Sinatra, Billy Joel, Whitney Houston, Sting, Michael Jackson, or Bruce Springsteen. Tickets ($15–$40) can usually be booked through **BASS** *("Best Available Seating Service"), tel. 416/972–2262 or 416/972–2277.*

Major venues include the **SkyDome,** just west of the CN Tower, on Front Street, tel. 416/963–3513; **Maple Leaf Gardens,** 60 Carlton Street, a block east of Yonge Street and the College Street subway stop, tel. 416/977–1641; the **O'Keefe Centre,** Yonge and Front streets, tel. BASS, 416/872–2262; and **Exhibition Stadium,** at the CNE grounds, tel. 416/393–6000.

Ontario Place (tel. 416/965–7711) has pop, rock, and jazz concerts throughout its summer season, at no cost above that of admission to the park. This is one of the loveliest and least expensive places to see and hear a concert in all of Toronto.

Kingswood Music Theatre, next to Canada's Wonderland, also has important rock and pop concerts during the warmer months. *Located along Hwy. 400, 10 min north of Hwy. 401; tel. 416/832–8131. Admission usually only $7 above the cost of Canada's Wonderland.*

Superstars Niteclub is a new venue for popular concerts. Opened in March 1989, this 1,700-seat club is the largest in the Metro Toronto area, presenting comedy, pop, rock, jazz, and more. Shows are Monday–Wednesday, with weekends dedicated to dance. *6435 Dixie Rd., 1 mi. north of Hwy. 401, just west of the airport, tel. 416/670–2211. Open Mon.–Sat. 7 PM–2 AM; closed Sun., except for "unlicensed" (aka no-booze) events for teens. Shows cost $10–$25, with dance nights in the $7–$8 range.*

Opera

Since its founding in 1950, the **Canadian Opera Company** has grown into the largest producer of opera in Canada and the fifth largest company on the continent. From the most popular operas, such as *Carmen* and *Madama Butterfly*, usually performed in the original language, to more modern or rare works, such as *Jenufa*, and the erotic success of 1988, *Lady Macbeth of Mtsensk*, the COC has proven trustworthy and often daring.

Each year, at Toronto's O'Keefe Centre, over 150,000 people attend their season of seven operas, which have included such memorable productions as Canada's first presentation of Benjamin Britten's *Death in Venice*, the North American premiere of Tchaikovsky's *Joan of Arc*, and the continent's second presentation of the complete three-act *Lulu* by Alban Berg.

Like all important companies, the COC often hosts world-class performers such as Joan Sutherland, Grace Bumbry, Martina Arroyo, Marilyn Horne, and Canada's own Louis Quilico and Maureen Forrester. The company also pioneered the use of surtitles, which allow the audience to follow the libretto in English in a capsulized translation. The COC also performs mini-operas in a tent during the summer, down at Harbourfront, on the shores of Lake Ontario. *Tel. 416/363–8231 or 416/393–7469.*

Dance

The Bolshoi is two centuries old; the **National Ballet of Canada** can trace itself all the way back to November 12, 1951, when it made its official debut on the cramped stage of the old Eaton Auditorium on College Street. In less than four decades, the company has done some extraordinary things and reaped some revered awards, with such principal dancers as Karen Kain, Frank Augustyn, Kevin Pugh, and Owen Montague all wowing the Russians at the Moscow competitions. Today, Canada's premier dance company has 70 dancers; it is the third largest troupe in North America and the fifth largest in the world. *Performances Nov., Feb., and May at the O'Keefe Centre, at the corner of Front and Yonge Sts.; in summer at Ontario Pl. Office, tel. 416/362–1041;* BASS, *416/872–1111 or 416/872–2277; O'Keefe Center, 416/872–2262. Tickets $10–$40.*

Toronto Dance Theatre, its roots in the Martha Graham tradition, is the oldest contemporary dance company in the city. Since its beginnings in the 1960s, it has created close to 100 works, over a third using original scores commissioned from Canadian composers. It tours Canada and has played major festivals in England, Europe, and the United States. After a decade of steady success, it purchased a beautiful renovated church, St. Enoch's, built in 1891, and a neighboring hall in the heart of Cabbagetown. They serve as home for its school and over three dozen full-time students. *Most performances are in the Premiere Dance Theatre, at Harbourfront, 235 Queen's Quay W; tel. 416/869–8444.*

Dancemakers is another important Toronto modern dance company, drawing on everyone from Martha Graham to Jose Limon and Merce Cunningham. It performs at both the Premiere Dance Theatre and Solar Stage (First Canadian Pl., on King St. near Bay St.; tel. 416/368–5135 or 416/535–8880).

Theater

There are over four dozen performing spaces in Toronto; we will mention only a handful of the most prominent.

The **Royal Alexandra,** the **O'Keefe,** and the **St. Lawrence Centre** are described in our Historic Buildings and Sites section.

The **Young People's Theatre** is the only theater center in the country devoted solely to children. But unlike purveyors of much of traditional children's fare, this place does not condescend or compromise its dramatic integrity. *165 Front St. E, near Sherbourne, 8 blocks east of Yonge St. Take the Yonge St. subway to King St. and then the King St. streetcar east, and walk down one block. Tel. 416/864–9732.*

The **Tarragon Theatre,** located in an unpleasant area of railroad tracks and old factories, is the natural habitat for indigenous Canadian theater. Almost anything worthwhile in this country's drama first saw the light of day here. *30 Bridgman Ave., 1 block east of Bathurst St. and north of Dupont St.; tel. 416/531–1827.*

Le Théâtre Française du Toronto, until recently known as Le Théâtre du P'tit Bonheur, has been providing French-language drama of high quality for many years. Its repertoire has ranged from classical to contemporary, from both France and French Canada. Recently it has moved to a marvelous location at Harbourfront, next door to the stunning Queen's Quay Terminal. In 1988, the theater performed a bilingual play, so English-speaking theatergoers could follow along. *The Du-Maurier Centre, 231 Queen's Quay W, tel. 416/534–6604.*

Théâtre Passe Muraille, in the unfashionable area of Bathurst and Queen streets, has long been the home of fine collaborative theater—very Canadian, very good, very innovative. *16 Ryerson Ave., running north from Queen St. W, 1 block east of Bathurst St.; tel. 416/363–2416.*

Toronto Free Theatre, although no longer free (and recently joining forces with the major Canadian Stage Company, which operates out of the St. Lawrence Centre), remains freewheeling and fascinating. This space has seen most of Canada's finest performers and playwrights showing their wares. *26 Berkeley St., just south of Front St. and 1 block west of Parliament St.; tel. 416/368–2856.*

Toronto Workshop Productions is the oldest established alternate theater company in the city and is the one with the most accessible location—two blocks north of Carlton/College streets, just east of Yonge Street. Over the years, it has presented very important, highly creative Canadian work, as well as providing space for similarly dynamic work from visiting companies from South Africa, the United States, and elsewhere. *12 Alexander St., tel. 416/925–8640.*

Bathurst Street Theatre, almost at the corner of Bathurst and Bloor streets (another unfashionable address!), is a church converted to theater space, but the gods have remained. The premises are used by dance groups and many of the more interesting theater groups in the city. The pews aren't terribly comfortable, but now they don't stop in the middle of the plays and pass the hat. *736 Bathurst St., just south of Honest Ed's, and around the corner from Mirvish Village; tel. 416/535–0591.*

Factory Theatre is another major alternate theater devoted to original and experimental work. *125 Bathurst St., at Adelaide St. W; tel. 416/864–9971.*

Hart House Theatre is smack in the middle of the University of Toronto campus and is the main theater space of U of T. Amateur, student, and occasional professional productions have been presented here for a half century, many of them controversial (and uncommercial). *Just off Queen's Park Crescent W, about one block west of the Parliament buildings, and a few blocks south of the Royal Ontario Museum; tel. 416/978–8668.*

Two interesting new companies, **Nightwood Theatre** (tel. 416/961–7202), which is a feminist collective, and **Buddies in Bad Times** (tel. 416/593–0653), which presents poetic, musical, and often gay productions, both appear frequently around town. They often use **The Annex,** *730 Bathurst St., just south of Bloor St. and next door to the Bathurst Street Theatre; tel. 416/537–4193.*

Second City, the Toronto version of the famous Chicago company, is the place where the inspired SCTV series had its genesis. Its revues tend to be the brightest, most reliable comedy in town. *The Old Firehall Theatre, 110 Lombard St., downtown, just east of Yonge St; tel. 416/863–1162.*

Two of the most entertaining presentations of the past few years are free and take place in two major parks each July and early August: Skylight Theatre and Dream in High Park, the latter named after its original production of Shakespeare's *A Midsummer Night's Dream.*

Since the summer of 1988, **Skylight Theatre** has had a new amphitheater. And they deserve it; some of their productions over the past few years—*The Little Prince, Frankenstein, Twelfth Night*—have been better than many in Stratford. Top-notch theater. *Earl Bales Park, tel. 416/781–4846. Take the Bloor St. subway to Bathurst St., then the Bathurst St. bus about a mile north of Hwy. 401. You enter the park at Bainbridge Ave., a few blocks south of Sheppard Ave. W. Admission free.*

Dream in High Park, now a half-dozen years old, presents quality productions of Shakespeare (and occasionally a musical) each July in the heart of Toronto's most glorious area, High Park. The open-air productions are usually a knockout. *Bloor and Keele Sts., tel. 416/368–2856. Take the Bloor St. subway to the High Park stop, then walk south into the park.*

There are many local productions of Broadway musicals and comedies, presented in Toronto's numerous dinner theatres. These include **Harper's East** (38 Lombard St., downtown; tel. 416/863–6223) and **Limelight Dinner Theatre** (2026 Yonge St., just below Eglinton Ave.; tel. 416/482–5200). This city just doesn't stop.

Film

Every September since 1976, Toronto has been holding a world-class film festival, called—with no great modesty—**The Festival of Festivals** (tel. 416/967–7371). Whether retrospectives of the films of Marguerite Duras, Jean-Luc Godard, and Max Ophuls, or tributes to the careers of Martin Scorsese, Robert Duvall, and John Schlesinger, this is the time for lovers of film.

Toronto is one of the film capitals of the world, and you can often catch a movie here that is not showing anywhere else—or even available on video. The Cineplex concept, which now has over 1,500 screens across North America, was created in Toronto; the multiscreened one in Eaton Centre was its genesis. Foreigners will be either delighted or disappointed to discover that Toronto is still subject to the strange machinations of a provincial—in more ways than one—censor board, and therefore has no friendly neighborhood porno movies.

Fox Beaches (2236 Queen St. E, tel. 416/691–7330) is an old-style movie house that will flood anyone over 40 with warm nostalgia.

Reg Hartt Presents is one of the more delightful traditions of underground film in the city. On various days each month, in the Cabana Room of the Spadina Hotel, this movie-maniac maven will show such films as "The History of Animation" and "The Uncensored History of Warner Brothers Looney Tunes & Merrie Melodies." ("Warning: Many of these cartoons are sexist, racist, and as violent as a two-by-four in the face!" read his ads.) *Admission: $10–$15. Tel. 416/964–2739.*

Carlton Cinemas, part of the Cineplex chain, shows rare, important films from around the world in nearly a dozen screening rooms. *20 Carlton St., just steps east of the College St. subway; tel. 416/296–FILM.*

Ontario Film Theatre is in the Ontario Science Centre. A provincially funded film house, it is much admired for its foreign art films and retrospectives. *770 Don Mills Rd., near Eglinton Ave. E; tel. 416/429–4100.*

Other places in Toronto with regular showings of important films and film series—often free or close to it—include the **Art Gallery of Ontario** (317 Dundas St. W, tel. 416/977–0414), **Harbourfront** (235 Queen's Quay W, tel. 416/973–4000); the **Metro Toronto Reference Library** (789 Yonge St., tel. 416/393–7141); **Innis Film Society** of the University of Toronto (2 Sussex Ave., tel. 416/588–8940); **Cinesphere,** at Ontario Place (955 Lakeshore Blvd. W, tel. 416/965–7711); and the **Royal Ontario Museum** (100 Queen's Park Crescent, at Bloor St. and University Ave., tel. 416/586–5549).

10 Nightlife

Jazz Clubs

Sadly, jazz in Toronto has dried up considerably over the past few years. Some say this is due to the devalued dollar; others blame a greatly reduced jazz circuit. The two most trustworthy places for jazz on a regular basis are Café des Copains and George's Spaghetti House.

For a romantic atmosphere, **Café des Copains** (48 Wellington St. E, near Yonge St.; tel. 416/869–0148) has a different solo jazz pianist every two weeks, playing every night but Sunday, from 8:30 PM to 12:30 AM. Two can enjoy the French-American cuisine for under $25. There is a bar, but this is no pickup place; people generally listen while the music is being performed. There's no dress code, and you'll see people in jeans, but it's an attractive place, and you may feel more comfortable if you're well-dressed.

A few blocks east of the Eaton Centre is **George's Spaghetti House** (290 Dundas St. E, corner of Sherbourne St.; tel. 416/923–9887), the oldest continuously running jazz club in the city. The music starts at 8:30 PM, with the world-famous Moe Koffman (of "Swinging Shepherd Blues" fame) performing one week each month. (For Moe, and on weekends, you'll need reservations.) George's has a modest cover charge and a decent Italian menu. Closed Sundays.

Meyer's Deli has two locations, both convenient to downtown and midtown hotels (185 King St. W, near University Ave., tel. 416/593–4189; and 69 Yorkville Ave., near Bay and Bloor Sts., tel. 416/593–4189). Both are attractive delis, with solid, Jewish-style food, cheesecake worth killing or at least maiming for, and some of the better jazz to be experienced in Toronto. Here is where you can hear late-night sets Friday and Saturday from 1 to 3 AM. This being Toronto, there's no alcohol served at those times.

Also in the downtown area is **Beaton's Lounge,** within Loew's **Westbury Hotel** (475 Yonge St., tel. 416/924–0611). Most evenings, the Lounge has top-40 bands and dancing, but on Sunday there's a jazz brunch from 11 AM to 3 PM. No jeans. The brunch costs about $18 for adults, $6.95 for children.

A recent jazz hangout is **East 85th Restaurant** (85 Front St. E, tel. 416/860–0011). Its gray-and-pink interior and brick walls suggest the old-style building in which it's housed. The Caribbean-style food ranges from chicken roti to jumbo shrimp, and two can eat for $20, without wine. Wednesdays through Sundays, the place features live jazz, of the modern, upbeat variety. And on Saturday afternoons, there is a jazz matinee brunch, with old jazz movies, featuring the likes of Louis Armstrong. Reservations are recommended on weekends. No cover.

Rock

Since March 1989, **Superstars Niteclub** has been packing 1,700 people nightly into its giant room. Mondays through Wednesdays, it has highly professional acts, on the line of The Fixx, k.d. lang, and comedian Howie Mandel, with prices ranging $10–$25. Thursdays to Saturdays are for dancing, with a cover of around $7. Hamburgers, chicken fingers, etc., provide the fuel. Laws banning liquor from being served on Sundays have freed the owners to use the place for children's and teen's concerts, featuring acts such as the brilliant Sharon, Lois and Bram. *6435 Dixie Rd., 1 mi. north of Hwy. 401, and just west of the airport; tel. 416/670–2211. Open Mon.–Sat., 7 PM–2 AM.*

For many years, **The Bamboo** has been providing the most bohemian atmosphere in Toronto. The Jamaican bar serves Caribbean-Indonesian food. (The decor—bamboo, Indonesian masks, etc.—goes well with the curry.) The bands are very, very *loud*. It's a funky spot, where casual dancing is not just a spectator sport. The Bamboo is wall-to-wall people on Thursday, Friday, and Saturday nights—very intense and hyper. The clientele is mixed; neighborhood Queen Street artsies and business types who want to let it all hang out mingle with Third Worldly people. And the summer welcomes an outdoor terrace upstairs. *312 Queen St. W, tel. 416/593–5771.*

Not far away is **Cameron Public House,** a small, eclectic kind of place. The music here alternates from jazz to hard rock to new wave; "alternative music," they proudly call it. Because it's close to the Ontario College of Art, the Cameron gets a creative crowd, with many regulars. The suburbanite scene gets heavy on weekends, as do the crowds. *408 Queen St. W, tel. 416/364–0811.*

The **El Mocambo Tavern** became nationally famous some years ago, when the Rolling Stones performed here and were joined by a certain Canadian prime minister's wife, who will remain nameless for the first time in her life. It's historic, but not at the forefront of the rock scene, as it once was. The age range depends on the band performing, but it's usually 19–24. The downstairs, recently christened "Bullwinkle's," has become a mainstream dance bar. The Ozark Mountain Daredevils, Rough Trade, Downchild Blues Band—they've all played here. Phone to see who's playing this week. No dress code, of course; this **is** rock. *464 Spadina Ave., just south of College St.; tel. 416/961–8991. Cover charge.*

Pop rock reins at the famous **Horseshoe Tavern,** also along the Queen Street strip. Good bands perform here, six days a week, with no food but lots of booze and a cover charge. It's a real tavern, with a pool table, lots of flannel-shirt types, mostly blue collar. Rock nostalgia lines the walls, and far more men than women line the bar. On weeknights, the ages range 25–40; on weekends, it's younger. For over four decades, the Horseshoe was known across the city as the tavern with entertainment, especially country music. (Charlie Pride, Tex Ritter, Hank Williams, Loretta Lynn all played here.) Today, it's rock, with a dance floor, too. *368 Queen St. W, corner of Spadina Ave.; tel. 416/598–4753. Closed Mon.*

A major showcase for more daring arts in Toronto has long been **The Rivoli,** along the Queen Street "mall." A place for new, local artists not yet established enough to have their own gallery showings, the back room functions as a club, with theater happenings, "new music" (progressive rock and jazz), comedy troupes providing very funny improvisations twice a month, and more. Try to catch the "Poetry Sweatshop" every fourth Wednesday, in which local, nonliterary personalities judge various poets. Dinner for two, without alcohol, runs about $25. *332 Queen St. W, just west of University Ave.; tel. 416/596–1908. No dress code. Cover charge: $3–$6. Closed Sun.*

There's alternative music provided by a DJ at the **Silver Crown,** in the heart of the downtown business district. It's a small, very busy place, filled with the sounds of the '60s, disco, even Sex Pistols music. The age range is 23–35, with suits and ties miraculously vanishing after 9 PM. By day, it's a meeting spot for local business types. By night, it's a dark, loud, sweaty dance hall, catering to an older crowd than other clubs of this sort (which usually draw 20–25 year olds). It's really a Queen Street bar on Richmond Street, with lots of artists and starving musicians. The building used to be the city hall library, so the decor is English Tudor—which the Sex Pistols were decidedly not. *25 Richmond St. W, tel. 416/868–1532.*

New Wave Music

The bartender claims that **Nuts 'n' Bolts** is the oldest dancing club in the city, edging into its second decade of existence, and who are we to argue? It's a basement dive, just steps from Eaton Centre—grimy, dark, with different colored walls to keep you awake into the wee hours (it is everything the Eaton Centre is *not*). The crowd is very, very young, and the downstairs club is packed on Saturday nights. Upstairs is a sports bar/restaurant with such classy offerings as hamburgers and fries. Open Saturday nights to 4 AM. No liquor Sunday, so it's open to "all ages," even children. *277 Victoria St., above Dundas St., just east of Yonge St.; tel. 416/977–1356.*

R & B (Rhythm and Blues)

The undisputed champion of R & B in Toronto is **Club Bluenote,** a few blocks north of the Yorkville area. It's quite unique, with many world-class musicians and singers frequenting it, and occasionally getting up and doing their stuff. A small dance floor, but who cares, with so much talent hanging around? The age range is 25–50, and the clientele is upper class. And this is no hit bar; people come here to listen to music in a serious way. When Whitney Houston, Sugar Ray Leonard, et al, are in town, this is where they go. *128 Pears Ave., just north of Davenport Rd. and west of Avenue Rd.; tel. 416/921-1109. Usually closed Sun. Cover charge: $5–$6.*

Right next door is **Network,** an entertainment lounge specializing in name acts of the quality of The Stylistics, Junior Walker, and Goodman and Brown. It's a supper club and show, with the cover and buffet combined at a reasonable $15 or so. The only dress code is "No Jeans," and there is a dance floor. The clientele is urban professionals in their early 30s; the decor is modern—brass, black, polished oak. *138 Pears Ave., near Davenport Rd.; tel. 416/924–1768.*

Blues **Albert's Hall** has been called one of the top 25 bars in all of North America, in spite of its shabby decor. It features top blues bands. The crowd's older and more laid-back than downstairs, in the Brunswick, but it's still noisy and friendly—and loud. *481 Bloor St. W, near Spadina Ave., tel. 416/964–2242. Cover charge.*

Up in the Eglinton Avenue and Yonge Street area is the very popular **Charley's,** a place with character. The clientele seems to be more down to earth than in most hangouts; more blue-collar and person-next-door. There's dancing and a big screen for sporting events. A variety of ages and types, including some students. Live entertainment Sunday–Wednesday. A reasonably priced finger-food type dinner is available after 8 PM. "Wing Eating Contests" and other special events provide some of the fun. *44 Eglinton Ave. W, near Yonge St.; tel. 416/486–6665. No dress code, no cover.*

The famous **Chick 'n Deli** was one of the great jazz places in Toronto. Now it's top 40 and a bit of everything else as well. A casual atmosphere prevails, and the lack of a dress code helps with the neighborhood-bar feeling. There's a dance floor and dark wood everywhere—kind of like a pub. It's also famous for wings and live music, both of which take flight every night of the week. *744 Mount Pleasant Rd., near Eglinton Ave.; tel. 416/489-3363.*

Bars

There is something to be said for the province's liquor laws. Having a legal drinking age of 19 and a police force that regularly stops cars (whether driven suspiciously or not—something unconstitutional in the United States) to check the driver's sobriety with a breathalyzer has cut down on drunken driving considerably. All the police have to discover is a greater amount than .08% of alcohol in the blood level of a driver and it's jail.

For a European atmosphere and a friendly, relaxed place to meet people, one of the most popular bars is **The Amsterdam.** It was recently voted "the most crowded bar," and although its busiest night is Thursday, it's jammed every business day at 5. Expect a 20- to 60- minute wait Thursday–Saturday evenings. The clientele is Bay Street—up-and-coming stockbrokers and business types. On weekends, suburbanites come out, and the population turns younger. The fixed menu is a low $10, and reservations are a must. The extensive beer list includes three homemade brews. *133 John St., near University Ave. and Queen St.; tel. 416/595–8201. No cover.*

In the middle of the ever-popular Yorkville area is the **Bellair Cafe,** *the* meeting place in Toronto. The outdoor patios are lovely in the summer, and the upstairs lounge has been converted to the "Club Bellair," an ever-so-trendy, glitzy dancing spot, with a DJ spinning the top 40. The dress code is "upscale casual to evening attire." It's a moneyed crowd, ages 25–55 and *très* sophisticated; if you wear gray, you might vanish into the ultramodern surroundings. *100 Cumberland St., tel. 416/964–2222. No cover.*

In the unfashionable Bathurst Street/Spadina Avenue area is the ever-popular **Brunswick House,** where "Rocking Irene" has been singing for centuries. Doctors and lawyers keep coming back to visit their old favorite watering hole, to hear the same songstress of their university days. (It's near the University of Toronto.) Irene's repertoire is of the "Roll Out the Barrel" variety, and everyone sings and drinks along. Loud, raucous, and fun. *481 Bloor St. W, tel. 416/964-2242. No cover.*

One of the most crowded singles' bars in Toronto is **Hemingway's,** also conveniently located in the Yorkville area. Three-quarters are regulars, middle-to-upper-class professionals, and not as pretentious as the bar's name. The atmosphere is sort of homey here, and it's less tense than at other Yorkville hangouts. The stand-up bar has a nice and easy atmosphere, and the decor is not glitzy, but literary, with a green interior, comfortable high-back chairs, mirrors, artsy posters, and real, live books lining one wall. Entertainment is piano with vocals. Dress is casual—just as Ernest would have wanted. *142 Cumberland St., near Avenue Rd. and Bloor St.; tel. 416/968–2828. No cover.*

The mirrors, aluminum, and fluorescent lighting at **Noodles** creates a very interesting modular feeling. It's frequented by stockbrokers, business people, and other locals who enjoy the pasta bar and the dinner served at the bar. (It's an Italian restaurant with a purist philosophy towards fresh ingredients.) The atmosphere is lighthearted and relaxed, and it's fun to people-watch here. The staff is attentive, and the background music is never too loud. *60 Bloor St. W, with entrance on Bay St.; tel. 416/921–3171. Closed Sun.*

Remy's seems to top the list of places for successful people to go in the late 1980s: Being right next door to the elegant Four Seasons Hotel means that Jane Fonda and nearly everyone else filming in Toronto seems to end up here. It's very elegant, so if you see casually attired men at the bar, you can be sure they can afford to look scruffy. The decor is European-inspired, all brass and shiny. There's an outdoor patio, three bars, and a restaurant where two can eat from the Italian menu for $50, including wine. *115 Yorkville Ave., near Avenue Rd.; tel. 416/968–9429.*

Comedy Clubs

A multipurpose restaurant and entertainment spot along the ever-popular Queen Street strip is **Garbo's.** The fixtures are from the original Grand Hotel in Brussels, which burned down. (Ms. Garbo was one of the stars in the classic film *Grand Hotel.)* The decor is art nouveau—all pinks and greens. A Continental dinner for two will cost about $30, excluding wine. There's live piano during dinner. Monday evenings, there's an improvisational troupe; Tuesday, jazz; Wednesday–Saturday, stand-up comedy. Wednesday is amateur night. The clientele ranges from university students on up. *429 Queen St. West, near Spadina Ave.; tel. 416/967–6425. No dress code. Cover charge: $5–$10.*

Second City, just east of the heart of downtown, has been providing some of the best comedy in Toronto—and North America—since its owner Andrew Alexander bought the rights to the name from its Chicago godfather, Bernie Sahlins, for one dollar. Interestingly, Alexander recently bought the original company and has since opened other clubs in London, Ontario, and Los Angeles—Canadian imperialism in action. This converted fire hall has given much to the world, through both *Saturday Night Live* and the inspired *SCTV* series. Among those who have cut their teeth on the Toronto stage are Gilda Radner, Dan Aykroyd, Martin Short, Andrea Martin, Catherine O'Hara, and John Candy. Shows can be seen alone or as part of a dinner-theater package. Try to catch the free improvisations, Monday–Thursday at 10:30 PM, when the troupe works out new material for future shows. *110 Lombard St., corner of Jarvis St., just a few blocks northeast of Front and Yonge Sts.; tel. 416/863–1111.*

Every Wednesday at 8 PM, would-be actors and comics get together for a night of improvisational work at **Theatresports,** down in the Harbourfront area. Two "teams" compete at different exercises, with three judges grading each sketch. Audience participation is the key, because it must dictate the character/situation of the various skits. Sometimes it's wonderfully funny, and you can catch fresh talent before it's discovered. *Water's Edge Cafe, 235 Queen's Quay W, on Lake Ontario; tel. 416/231–3611. Cover charge: $5.*

Next to Second City, **Yuk-Yuk's Komedy Kabaret** has always been the major place for comedy in Toronto. This is where the zany comedian Howie Mandel and the inspired impressionist Jim Carrey got their starts, and where such comic luminaries as George Carlin, Rodney Dangerfield, Robin Williams, and Mort Sahl have presented their best routines. Down on Bay Street, Yuk Yuk's has its amateur night on Monday. Up on Yonge Street and Eglinton Avenue, new talent pipes up on Tuesdays. A dinner-show package can run $15–$25 per person. *1280 Bay St., just above Bloor St., and 2335 Yonge St., just above Eglinton Ave.; tel. 416/967–6425. No dress code. Cover charge: $3–$10. Closed Sun.*

Dancing

Berlin quickly became one of the most popular spots in Toronto, within a year of its opening in early 1987. There's no dress code, but people dress up for this upscale, European-styled multilevel club. There is a Continental menu for dining and a seven-piece band for jazz, pop, and R & B. The crowd is 25–35 and very rich, and the club radiates a feeling of exclusivity. A classy cross between the Bamboo and the Imperial Room, Berlin is one very hot/cool place. *2335 Yonge St., north of Eglinton Ave.; tel. 416/489–7777. Open Wed.–Sat., to 2 AM or 3 AM on weekends. No cover.*

DJs play '60s music (downstairs) and '80s music (upstairs) in a four-story century-old funhouse named **Big Bop.** Drinks Wednesday nights cost $1.99; Thursday nights are Ladies' Nights, with no cover for women. The decor is early bizarre and late weird; you walk in and feel as though you've already had two drinks. In rebellion against the New York School of Glitzy, there is no chrome or mirrors—just a deliberate effort to be campy, vibrant, and unpretentious. The clientele is 18–25. It's a true meat market, but it doesn't pretend to be otherwise. Capacity is 800, and jeans are de rigueur. Many international stars walk in, but the owner insists that it's no big deal. (No big deal? Jack Nicholson. William Hurt. Matt Dillon!!) One DJ is a grad of the Wolfman Jack School of Strangeness. You can see why the kids love it here. *651 Queen St. W, tel. 416/366–6699. Open weekends to 3 AM.*

An important after-hours club is **Club Z,** which is open weekends only for a young crowd that doesn't mind staying up way past its bedtime. Hours are 10 PM to sunrise. No alcohol is served; music and dancing are the attractions. The music is funk, the crowd is young, and the soda pop flows like water. *11a Joseph St., one block north of Wellesley Ave. and Yonge St.; tel. 416/963–9430. Cover charge: $6–$8. Dress casual, but no sneakers or jeans on Sat.*

In the heart of Yorkville is **The Copa,** which has to be seen to be believed. The former warehouse is gigantic, with a capacity of 1,100! The crowd is in the 20–25 range and on the prowl. There's a zillion-dollar light show, with lasers and video screens. Tina Turner played for its grand opening; B.B. King and Ray Parker, Jr., have also performed here. The dance music is top 40; on Sunday nights, it gets funkier. (And this spot is busy on Sundays, unlike anywhere else.) Dress code? No torn or tattered jeans, please! *21 Scollard St., entrance off Yorkville Ave.; tel. 416/922–6500. Cover charge: $5–$7.*

The Diamond is an Art Deco restaurant and dance club that continually brings in big acts, such as Kris Kristofferson and Pink Floyd. Acts range from jazz to country to rock; newcomers to the record scene will often showcase their talent here. Wednesdays, Fridays, and Saturdays are for dancing. The crowd is mostly early 20s; lots of students and young professionals. The many fashion shows appeal to the trendy downtowners. And do note: People tend to come here in groups or couples; this ain't Single City. *410 Sherbourne St., east of Yonge St.; tel. 416/927–9010. Cover charge. Line-up on weekends.*

Earl's Tin Palace has been described as the star attraction of the Yonge/Eglinton/Mt. Pleasant singles scene, and it does its job well: The fashionable, affluent people have made this place their home, and many arrive in groups. The decor is stunning: a big, airy tin palace with elaborate props, such as stuffed birds. The restaurant has real cuisine, not just fries. (Dinner and drinks for two, $35.) The clientele dresses very well, with men even in (gasp) suits. The 35–40 crowd is better represented here than in most other clubs. *150 Eglinton Ave. E, not far from Yonge St.; tel. 416/487–9281. No cover.*

Back on Yorkville Avenue is **P.W.D. Dinkel's,** which has been attracting the trendies of the area for many years. The age range is 20–40, and regulars make up much of the crowd. The ratio of men to women is 50/50; the two stand-up bars are where the action is. A black-and-white-tile dance floor has the usual mirrored ball and flashing disco lights nearby. No jeans! Live bands play top-40–style, yet original, music. There's finger food and dinner at about $50 for two, with wine. *88 Yorkville Ave., tel. 416/923–9689. Open Thurs.–Sun. to 2 AM. Cover charge: about $6.*

Platters is a high-tech '50s diner, with neon and lots of kitsch. There's a full menu and specialty cocktails. Expect lots of action at the bars, especially on weekends, when it's crowded. *160 Eglinton Ave. E, tel. 416/482–9888.*

RPM, down at Harbourfront, is a psychedelic dance palace with light shows, go-go girls, and more. (Time warp, anyone?) There's a shuttle-bus service from Union Station for the young (19–25), blue-collarish, meat-market crowd. Lots of funk and pop tunes to dance to, and it's very *loud.* On Sunday, there's no alcohol, and it becomes an all-ages dance party. Wednesday is Student Night, with free admission and a complimentary buffet. Upstairs, there's a nice quiet bar with lovely views of Lake Ontario. *132 Queen's Quay E, tel. 416/869–1462. Cover charge.*

A restaurant/bar/club called **StiLife** recently opened downtown and is very popular. It caters to an older (25–35) crowd and to rapidly aging 40-year-olds. The decor is metallic and modular, with all the furnishings custom-made. The art is aided by sophisticated lighting. No jeans or sneakers. A DJ provides dancing music, and the clientele is Yorkville-ish, with many clothing designers, people who own other restaurants, etc. The food is gourmet, and the menu varies. Check out the bathrooms —you'll find out why. *217 Richmond St. W, tel. 416/593–6116. Closed Sun. Cover charge: $7–$10.*

The most exciting '50s-type place is **Studebaker's**, in the University/King area. It's bright and colorful, with memorabilia, a jukebox, and a DJ. During the week, it attracts a business crowd, with far more males than females. On weekends, a younger, suburban crowd gathers after 8 or 9; expect a 60-minute wait. No jeans or T-shirts. Celebs spotted here include actor Steve Guttenberg, Darryl Hall (the rock star), and G.W. Bailey (of "M*A*S*H"). *150 Pearl St., tel. 416/591–7960.*

Tazmanian Ballroom is a late-night place that rebels against the current understanding of what a dance club should look like. The decor is "chic Victorian"—chandeliers, red-velvet drapes, gold-painted brick walls. But the music is young. The owner brags of a "discriminating dress code": no suits, or anyone who "doesn't fit in." Most are 22–30; few business folk. Alternative music (and punk crowd) on Wednesdays. There's no name on the building; this is a low-key place whose popularity results mostly from word of mouth. *99 Jarvis St., east of Yonge St.; tel. 416/363–7117. No cover weeknights or before 10.*

Supper Clubs

Known as Toronto's "last elegant supper club," **The Imperial Room** of the **Royal York Hotel** is where you can experience Tony Bennett, Tina Turner, Ella Fitzgerald, Lena Horne—you get the idea. The decor is regal red, and dinner will run around $25 per person, plus a $20 cover charge. *100 Front St. W., opposite Union Station; tel. 416/368–2511. Book at least a week ahead. Show times Mon.–Wed. 9 PM; Thurs.–Sat. 11 PM.*

Cafés

Chapter's Bookstore Cafe is a wonderful Idea Whose Time Has Come. A sophisticated professional crowd (mid-30s–60s) fills the bar area, especially on weekend nights—although this is no pickup joint! The café upstairs is a cozy "bookloft," with a fireplace and reasonably priced food. There's an extensive magazine collection, which people at the bar sit and read. Every week a prominent author speaks in the upstairs café, followed by an informal conversation in the bar area. Major philosophers, fiction writers, and poets have done readings here. *2360 Yonge St., a block above Eglinton Ave.; tel. 416/481–2474.*

The **Free Times Cafe** is a showcase for folk music, where singers often perform their own original work. The menu is "Kensington Canadian Cuisine," with both vegetarian as well as meat dishes; it's licensed and modestly priced. The decor is white stucco with stained-pine edging; the bar has café chairs with upholstered seats. *320 College St., near Spadina Ave., on the edge of the University of Toronto campus; tel. 416/967–1078.*

Lounges

Up on the 51st floor of the ManuLife Centre, **The Aquarius Lounge** is the highest piano lounge in the city, even before you take your first, expensive drink. The busy time in the summer is Thursday–Saturday after 8:30 PM, but there's a high turnover, so the wait is never too long. In the winter, the lines begin as early as 8 PM. This is not a place to meet people, and it is not trendy in the way that most bars in the Yorkville area are. But its romantic atmosphere makes this a marvelous place for a date. No shorts, but jeans are allowed. *55 Bloor St. W, at Bay St.; tel. 416/967–5225.*

In the Brownstone Hotel is **Notes,** an intimate bar/restaurant with a grand piano and a grand bar around it. It's done up in pink-and-beige tones, with black-lacquer furniture and antiques. You'll find no windows here, and the lighting is dim, but it's a good, quiet place to get to know someone. Dinner for two runs about $40–$50, including wine (their fresh sole is fine). Paul Drake, one of the city's great entertainers, plays Tuesday –Saturday, 9 PM–1 AM. *15 Charles St. E, tel. 416/924–7381.*

In the classy Four Seasons Hotel is **La Serre,** which looks like a library in a mansion: plush and green, with lots of brass and dark wood. It has a stand-up piano bar and a pianist worth standing for. Drinks, coffees, and teas are all expensive, but what can you expect in one of the costliest hotels in the country? Weekdays attract a business crowd, weekends bring out the couples. *Avenue Rd. and Yorkville Ave., tel. 416/964–0411.*

The **Park Plaza Roof Lounge** has been used as a setting in the writings of such Canadian literary luminaries as Margaret Atwood, and Mordecai Richler. The decor is plush, in an older European style, with chandelier, marble tables, and waiters in red jackets. It remains an important hangout for the upper-middle class, business people, professionals, and, *bien sur*, literary types. *In the Park Plaza Hotel, Avenue Rd. and Bloor St.; tel. 416/924–5471.*

The Twenty-Two has been a quiet meeting spot for Torontonians and tourists for over a quarter-century. There's no dress code or cover, yet one can count on lovely live piano music nightly, 5–8, and piano with singing, 9 PM–1 AM. There are free hors d'oeuvres at 5:45; if you're still hungry, dine at the excellent Courtyard Cafe, in the same building. Big deals and hot affairs go on here, but it's very discreet, possibly because of the dim lighting. Probably 90% are regulars who have good rapport with the staff. The decor is mostly tables for two, with beige-and-green chairs and walls and lots of wood. A sidewalk café has good seating capacity. If you've got something important to say to someone, this is one of the most pleasant places in the city to say it. *22 St. Thomas St., 1 block east and south of the Royal Ontario Museum; tel. 416/979–2341.*

Pubs

The best pub in town in 1989 is **The Madison,** right next door to Ecology House, on the edge of the U of T campus. It has the atmosphere of an English pub, with lots of brass, burlap lamps, solid oak bars, ceiling fans, exposed brick, and dart boards. Most important, it offers 16 brands of beer on tap, as well as a large selection of imported draft. It serves finger food, and its chicken wings, prepared literally from scratch, are famous. There is nightly piano entertainment at the second floor bar; the bar in the basement has a fireplace and is dark and cozy. The clientele is students, yuppies, and a strong British/Scottish/Irish contingent. The patios are lovely in the summer. *14 Madison Ave., 1 block east of Spadina Ave., just steps north of Bloor St.; tel. 416/927–1722.*

On the edge of Cabbagetown, a few miles east of the downtown core, is the **Queen's Head Pub.** Very quaint and typically English, it has a good lineup of imported beer and may remind you of the attic on an antique farm: fireplace, oodles of oak, and mahogany. Flowers on the wallpaper, pâté sandwiches on the plate, chandeliers on the ceiling, beer in the belly. And tiny Union Jacks all over the dart boards. It's attached to a pleasant restaurant—Pimblett's. *249 Gerrard St. E, west of Parliament St.; tel. 416/929–9525.*

The Unicorn, in the very hot area of Yonge/Eglinton/Mt. Pleasant, has a friendly, young (20–25) crowd. The atmosphere is very British, with a six-foot TV screen. It has a nice, homey atmosphere that is missing from too many singles bars. Indeed, that often-unpleasant pressure just doesn't exist here; you can talk to other people without feeling as though you're about to be picked up. On one side, there's a seating area for quiet conversation; on the other, everyone sings along with the piano. Both snack food and complete dinners are served. Live guitar or piano Wednesday–Saturday nights. *175 Eglinton Ave. E, a few blocks east of Yonge St.; tel. 416/482–0115.*

11 Excursions

Stratford, Ontario

Ever since July 1953, when one of the world's greatest actors, Alec Guinness, joined with probably the world's greatest Shakespearean director, Tyrone Guthrie, beneath a hot, stuffy tent in a backward little town about 90 minutes from Toronto, the Stratford Festival has been one of the most successful, most widely admired theaters of its kind in the world.

The origins of the town of Stratford are modest. After the War of 1812, the British government granted a million acres of land along Lake Huron to the Canada Company, headed by a Scottish businessman. When the surveyors came to a marshy creek surrounded by a thick forest, they named it "Little Thames" and noted that it might make "a good mill-site." It was later christened Stratford, which purportedly means a narrow crossing. The year was 1832, 121 years before the concept of a theater festival would take flight and change Canadian culture forever.

For many years Stratford was considered a backwoods hamlet. Although it had the highest elevation of any town in Ontario—1,150 feet above sea level—it was too swampy to grow anything. In 1871, "Muddy Stratford" was made a division point for a major railway, attracting both industry and population. Though the river was renamed Avon, it was a stump-filled, filthy disaster, bordered by a livery stable, a junkyard, and the city dump.

Then came the first of two saviors of the city, both of them (undoubting) Thomases. In 1904, an insurance broker named Tom Orr transformed Stratford's riverfront into a park. He also built a formal English garden, where every flower mentioned in the plays of Shakespeare—monkshood to sneeze worse, bee balm to bachelor's button—blooms grandly to this day. When Tyrone Guthrie compared an aerial photograph of Stratford's, park with a photo of the park in Stratford-on-Avon, England, he was stunned to find the two nearly identical.

Then came Tom Patterson, a fourth-generation Stratfordian born in 1920, who looked around; saw that the town wards and schools had names like Hamlet, Falstaff, and Romeo; and felt that some kind of drama festival might save his community from becoming a ghost town. (The diesel was coming in, and all the steam-engine repair shops that had kept Stratford alive for generations were soon to close down.)

The story of how he began in 1952 with $125 (a "generous" grant from the Stratford City Council), tracked down the directorial genius Tyrone Guthrie and the inspired stage and screen star Alec Guinness, obtained the services of the brilliant stage designer Tanya Moiseiwitsch, and somehow pasted together a world-class theater festival in a little over one year is almost unbelievable. It is told in its entirety in Patterson's memoirs, *First Stage—The Making of the Stratford Festival*.

The festival is now moving into middle age—1990 marks its 38th season—and it has had its ups and downs. Soon after it opened and wowed critics from around the world with its professionalism, costumes, and daring thrust stage, the air was filled with superlatives that had not been heard in Canada since the Great Blondin walked across Niagara Falls on a tightrope.

The early years also brought giants of world theater to the tiny town of some 20,000: James Mason, Siobhan McKenna, Alan Bates, Christopher Plummer, Jason Robards, Jr., and Maggie Smith. But the years also saw an uneveness in productions, a dreadful tendency to go for flash and glitter over substance, and a focus on costumes and furniture rather than on the ability to speak Shakespeare's words with clarity and intelligence. Many never lost faith in the festival; others, such as Canada's greatest critic, the late Nathan Cohen of the *Toronto Star*, once bemoaned that "Stratford has become Canada's most sacred cow."

Sacred or not, Stratford's offerings are still among the best of their kind in the world, with at least a handful of productions every year that put most other summer arts festivals to shame. The secret, of course, is to try to catch the reviews of the plays, which have their debuts in May, June, July, and August in the festival's three theaters, and then book as early as you can. *(The New York Times* always runs major write-ups, as do newspapers and magazines in many American and Canadian cities.)

In recent years, the famous thrust stage at the Festival Theater witnessed *Richard III*, *The Taming of the Shrew*, *The Merchant of Venice*. *Kiss Me Kate*, and *The Three Musketeers*. Be warned that due to the great faithfulness of the stage to its Shakespearean original, it is imperative to have seats that are fairly central in the audience; otherwise, words and even whole speeches can be lost.

There is also a traditional proscenium stage, the **Avon,** where *All's Well That Ends Well*, T. S. Eliot's *Murder in the Cathedral*, and the musical *Irma La Douce* have recently been presented. Connoisseurs of more daring theater—as well as the budget-conscious—should not miss **The Third Stage,** a more recent space that allows plays in the round and in experimental modes. In the last few years, *Twelfth Night* and *King Lear* were seen here. This is often the most exciting place to see plays, so don't panic if you can't get seats at the two larger theaters.

Arriving and Departing

By Car "Who's going to drive from Toronto to Stratford to see Shakespeare?" was almost a mantra in the early 1950s, when the festival was struggling to get off the ground; you don't hear it much anymore. The town is only about 90 miles southwest of Toronto, and it takes but 1½ hours to drive there. Take Highway 401 west to interchange 35, then 90 north on Highway 8 and west again on the combined Highways 7/8.

By Train This is probably the most pleasurable way to go, especially in the fall, when the leaves are doing their quick-change act. **Via Rail** (tel. 416/366–8411) leaves Union Station at least five times a day during Stratford's high season. The trip takes about two hours.

By Bus Six buses leave the Dundas and Bay streets terminal each day, beginning as early as 6:30 AM. The trip can take up to three hours, though, and stops at places you never knew existed. Tel. 416/979–3511.

Guided Tours

Stratford Tours Inc. arranges a variety of tours, including dining and theater. *Box 45, Stratford N5A 6S8, tel. 519/271–8181.*

The Avon Historical Society conducts charming one-hour tours of the city, July 1–Labor Day, daily except Sunday at 9:30 AM. Meet at the tourist information booth at Lakeside Drive and Ontario Street. Tel. 519/271–5140.

Exploring

The Gallery Stratford has regular exhibits of local and Inuit art, as well as design sketches and costumes of the present year's productions. *54 Romeo St., just northeast of Festival Theatre; tel. 519/271–5271. Admission is nominal during the Festival's run; free at other times. Open late May–early Sept. Mon. 10–5; Tues.–Sun. 10–8. Closed Mon. and shorter hours the rest of the year.*

There are many tasteful shops in the downtown area, including antique stores, arts and crafts studios, galleries, and new and rare bookshops.

The Stratford Festival For tickets and information from late February 1989, phone from Toronto, tel. 416/363–4471; from Detroit, 313/964–4668; from elsewhere 519/273–1600. Or write the Festival Theatre, Stratford, N5A 6V2.

The **Festival Theatre** (55 Queen St.) and the **Avon Theatre** (99 Downie St.) are open from early May to late October. They have evening performances Tuesday–Sunday, with matinees Wednesday and Saturday. Tickets $20–$35. Rush seats are as little as one-third the cost. The **Third Stage** (Lakeshore Drive) has a shorter season, from late May to early September. Prices are always under $20.

Don't forget that **rush seats** are always available on the day of a performance, either at the **Five Star ticket booth** in Toronto or at the various box offices, beginning at 9 AM. Tickets can also be ordered by telephone after 10 AM, but they are usually in the lowest price category.

Wheelchair seating and a mobility bus are available if requested in advance (tel. 519/271–4000). A Phonic Ear F.M. Transmitting System for the hearing impaired is available at the two larger theaters at a nominal fee; book when ordering your tickets.

The **Stratford Summer Music** runs during the same period as the theater festival and features classical, jazz, pop, and folk music, usually at the City Hall Auditorium and Knox Presbyterian Church. *38 Albert St., Stratford N5A 6T3, tel. 519/273–2117.*

Meet the Festival is a series of informal discussions with members of the company. *Kiwanis Centre, next to the Third Stage. Admission free; no reservation required. July–Aug., Wed. and Fri., 11 AM–noon.*

Thirty-minute **post-performance discussions** take place at the Festival Theatre Tuesday and Thursday nights, late June to early September. *Meet at Aisle 2, Orchestra Level, after the performance. Admission free; no reservations required.*

Backstage tours are offered Sunday morning from mid-June to late October. Tours depart from the Festival Theatre every 15 minutes from 9 to 10:30 AM. Admission: $5 adults, $2.50 students and senior citizens. Book in advance through the Festival Box Office, although some tickets are usually available at the door.

Dining

Reviews by Joanne Kates

There is a certain inevitable mania to the Stratford dining experience. Everyone arrives in a great rush at 6 PM, eats rather quickly, and is at the theater for curtain time. We could be, in this instance, the perfect marks for lazy restaurateurs who might enjoy the financial results of quick patron processing. Other theater towns, which shall remain nameless, are guilty of this. But not Stratford. All three of the major players (The Church, sold in the summer of 1988; Rundles; and The Old Prune) tread the fine line between haste and grace, and they do so with enormous generosity of spirit. You could sling overcooked vegetables and precooked entrees our way in that situation, and few of us would have the time or the heart to complain. But these restaurants do not. They succeed at the challenge of a seasonal business that requires that the staff miraculously perform at peak levels, beginning in June, after a winter out of the saddle.

Now if someone would just open a fine hotel in Stratford, all would be well on the creature-comfort front. After a night of magic, who wants a breakfast of coffee and doughnuts in the lobby?

The following credit-card abbreviations are used: AE, American Express; CB, Carte Blanche; DC, Diners Club; MC, MasterCard; V, Visa. The most highly recommended restaurants are indicated with a star ★.

Category	Cost*
Expensive	over $50
Moderate	$30–$50
Inexpensive	under $30

**for two, not including tax, tip, or drinks*

Expensive

The Church. Ever since it opened its Gothic doors 12 years ago, this has been Stratford's gastronomical prima ballerina. Certainly it remains the seat of grandeur, with flowers and wine on the high altar, stained glass in the windows, and the high vaulted ceiling. The Church is still impeccable. Of the three important Stratford restaurants, it remains the only one with perfectly polished service. But things have calcified slightly. Its excellence, while indisputable, is dated. Tastes in food change. Today we look more to California and the Mediterranean for our food news than we do to Paris. Stronger flavors are in ascendance. The news is garlic and peppers, sauces that are reductions rather than being cream-based, and food that is grilled rather than baked or stuffed. The Church, it seems, has not quite gotten the message.

Vichyssoise, no matter how excellent, has seen its day. Shrimp-filled ravioli are certainly competent, but their cream sauce seems bland. Steak tartare? Ho hum. The famous Church chicken stuffed with zucchini, cream cheese, and herbs is still very fine, but, the menu tells us, it was selected by *Gourmet* magazine in 1979. It was au courant then. The Church steams salmon trout and scallops perfectly, but I want some pizzazz in the sauce instead of cream. *70 Brunswick St., tel. 519/273-3424. Dress: informal, but most wear jackets. Reservations required even months in advance. AE, MC, V. No lunch Tues., Thurs., Fri.; closed Mon.*

★ **Rundles.** It has traditionally played underdog to The Church, but the roles have reversed. It is, of course, a less consequential dining room—smaller, simpler, less formal. The terrace overlooks Lake Victoria, the windows stream with summer light, the napkins, the lamps, and the funny wood mobiles are a cheerful chorus of summer colors.

Rundles and The Church are equally expensive (about $100 for dinner for two with a modest wine), and in past years, while Rundles had its growing pains, The Church has seemed the better deal. But Rundles has splendidly, deliciously matured. There are some who snicker at the trendiness of a menu that features peppers, goat cheese, eggplant, cabbage, and wild mushrooms, all the culinary catchphrases of the '80s. But Rundles is doing it so beautifully that one would be a fool to say no. The roasted redpepper and eggplant terrine is a stunner, a savory layer cake iced in black-olive puree. Perfectly grilled salmon sits on mustardy *beurre blanc*. Pink roast lamb is scented with rosemary and served with a fine surprise of cabbage and white beans. The cold poached lobster comes with zingy red-pepper sauce this year; the duck melts in your mouth. *9 Cobourg St., tel. 519/271-6442. Dress: informal. Reservations required many weeks in advance. AE, MC, V. No lunch Tues.; closed Mon.*

Moderate **The Old Prune.** This could be considered a junior Rundles—a little cheaper and a little less mastery in the kitchen. The Old Prune's vocabulary is like Rundles: goat cheese and peppers, raw fish, the grill rather than the oven, mustard and garlic rather than butter and cream. The ideas are fine, but Rundles does it with more flavor. But this is also a charmer: delightful to look at, with gray walls and exotic flowered tablecloths, theatrical prints on the walls, and perfect posies scattered on the Royal Albert teacups. It does well on light meals, quiches, terrines, pâtés, and salads. *151 Albert St., tel. 519/271-5052. Dress: informal. Reservations recommended weeks in advance. MC, V. No lunch Tues.; closed Mon.*

Picnics Given the swans and the Avon River, a Stratford picnic is a delightful preamble to the play. You can do well for under $20 for two by stopping in Toronto at a delicatessen like **Yitz's** (346 Eglinton Ave. W, at Avenue Rd.) or a fine dairy takeout like **United Baker's** (Lawrence Ave. W, at Bathurst St.). One rung up the inflationary ladder is the **Danish Food Centre** (Bloor St., just east of University Ave.), which will make up nice little boxes of open-face sandwiches, complete with an irresistible almond pastry for dessert. Or, for those who like their alfresco exotic, there are picnic boxes of raw-fish delights from **Taiko-**

Sushi (Yonge St. at Wellesley Ave.). For those whose idea of roughing it is a day with caviar, picnics ought to be purchased from the **David Wood Food Shop** (1110 Yonge St., south of St. Clair Ave.; 417 Spadina Ave., south of Eglinton Ave.; and his latest, at 2637 Yonge St., about halfway between Eglinton and Lawrence Aves). All three sell very expensive salads and pâtés that will put a smile on your taste buds.

Lodging

Because Stratford is not a hotel city, visitors with the most savvy like to stay at B&Bs. Write to the **Stratford and Area Visitors' and Convention Bureau** (38 Albert St., Stratford N5A 3K3, tel. 519/271–5140) and ask for the latest *Discover Stratford Guide*.

The following credit-card abbreviations are used: AE, American Express; CB, Carte Blanche; DC, Diners Club; MC, MasterCard; V, Visa. The most highly recommended hotels are indicated with a star ★.

Category	Cost*
Very Expensive	over $100
Expensive	$75–$100
Moderate	$50–$75
Inexpensive	under $50

**prices are for doubles*

Expensive

Festival Inn. An Old-English atmosphere has survived modernization and the installation of Jacuzzi waterbeds in some rooms. Located on the eastern outskirts of town, just a brief ride to the theater. *1144 Ontario St., Box 811, Stratford N5A 6W1, tel. 519/273–1150. 151 rooms with bath. Facilities: restaurant, coffee shop, baby-sitting services, tennis, indoor pool, whirlpool, golf nearby. AE, MC, V.*

Queen's Inn. Built in 1914 to replace an earlier inn that was destroyed by fire, this 30-room inn has been gutted and turned into an elegant, if still quite small, hotel. The walls are a pleasant two-tone gray and white; the large, curved windows and bright, floral chintz sofas will charm any visitor. The dining room can be quite inventive, and next door stands a "brewpub," where homemade beer can be sold only on the premises. *161 Ontario St., Stratford, N5A 3H3, tel. 519/271–1400. 30 rooms with bath. Facilities: lounge. AE, MC, V.*

★ **Raj Guest House.** This is a beautiful and exotic place near the city center, furnished with antiques and Anglo-Indian arts from the British Raj period. Rooms vary from deluxe with whirlpool to smaller, less expensive rooms. Rates include full English breakfast. *123 Church St., Stratford N5A 2R3, tel. 519/271–7129. 14 rooms with bath. Facilities: guest lounge, outdoor area. No credit cards.*

Moderate–Expensive

23 Albert Place. This late 19th-century hotel was completely redecorated several years ago. It is conveniently located in the heart of the downtown shopping area, just a few hundred yards from the Avon Theatre. Suites and minisuites are available, and pets are allowed. *23 Albert St., Stratford N5A 3K2, tel. 519/273-5800. 34 rooms with bath. Facilities: coffee shop, restaurant, baby-sitting services, golf nearby. AE, MC, V.*

Moderate **Majer's Motel.** This motel sits on landscaped grounds, a good distance from the highway. No pets. *Hwys. 7 and 8, about a mile east of the city, Stratford RR4, N5A 6S5, tel. 519/271-2010. 31 rooms (some small) with bath. Facilities: coffee shop, outdoor pool, golf nearby. MC, V.*

Inexpensive **Swan Motel.** This motel is in a quiet country setting on generous grounds, just one mile south of the Avon Theatre. *1482 Downie St. S, RR2, Stratford N5A 6S3, tel. 519/271-6376. 19 rooms with bath. Facilities: outdoor pool, baby-sitting services, golf nearby. MC, V.*

Stratford General Hospital Residence. Students, or those traveling on a very tight budget, pay less than $20 a night for a single room. It's modern, bright, serviceable. *Housekeeping Supervisor, Stratford General Hospital Residence, 130 Youngs St., Stratford N5A 1J7, tel. 519/271-5084 or 271-2120, ext. 586. Facilities: access to lounges, kitchenettes, laundry facilities, and parking. No credit cards.*

Niagara Falls, Ontario

Cynics have had their field day with Niagara Falls, calling it everything from "water on the rocks" to "the second major disappointment of American married life" (Oscar Wilde).

Others have been more positive. Missionary and explorer Louis Hennepin, whose books were widely read across Europe, first described the falls in 1678 as "an incredible Cataract or Waterfall which has no equal." Nearly two centuries later, novelist Charles Dickens wrote, "I seemed to be lifted from the earth and to be looking into Heaven. Niagara was at once stamped upon my heart, an image of beauty, to remain there changeless and indelible."

Writer Henry James recorded in 1883 how one stands there "gazing your fill at the most beautiful object in the world." And a half-century later, British author Vita Sackville-West wrote to Sir Harold Nicolson, "Niagara is really some waterfall! It falls over like a great noisy beard made of cotton-wool, veiled by spray and spanned by rainbows. The rainbows are the most unexpected part of it. They stand across like bridges between America and Canada, and are reproduced in sections along the boiling foam. The spray rises to the height of a sky-scraper, shot by sudden iridescence high up in the air."

Understandably, all these rave reviews began to bring out the professional daredevils, as well as the self-destructive amateurs. In 1859, the great French tightrope walker Blondin walked across the Niagara Gorge, from the American to the Canadian side, on a three-inch-thick rope. On his shoulders was his (reluctant, terrified) manager; on both shores stood some 100,000 spectators. "Thank God it is over!" exclaimed the future King Edward VII of England, after the completion of the walk. "Please never attempt it again."

But sadly, others did. From the early 18th century, dozens went over in boats, rubber balls, and those famous barrels. Not a single one survived, until schoolteacher Annie Taylor did in

1901. Emerging from her barrel, she asked the touching question, "Did I go over the Falls yet?" The endless stunts were finally outlawed in 1912, but not before the province of Ontario created the first provincial park in all of Canada—Queen Victoria Park—in 1887.

The Falls alone—with a combined flow of close to three million liters per second—are obviously worth the 75-minute drive from Toronto, the 30-minute drive from Buffalo, New York, or whatever time it takes to come from anywhere else. It is, after all, the greatest waterfall in the world, by volume.

Over 10,000 years ago—long before the first "My Parents Visited Niagara Falls and All They Got Me Was This Lousy T-Shirt" T-shirts—the glaciers receded, diverting the waters of Lake Erie northward into Lake Ontario. (Before that time, they had drained south; such are the fickle ways of nature.)

There has been considerable erosion since that time: More than seven miles in all, as the soft shale and sandstone of the escarpment have been washed away. Wisely, there have been major water diversions for a generating station (in 1954) and other machinations (1954–1963), which have spread the flow more evenly over the entire crestline of the Horseshoe Falls. The erosion is now down to as little as one foot every decade, so you needn't rush your visit.

There's some interesting history to the rest of the area, as well. The War of 1812 had settlers on both sides of the river killing one another, with the greatest battle taking place in Niagara Falls itself, at Lundy's Lane (today, the name of a major street, with a Historical Museum on the site of the battle). Soon after, at the Treaty of Ghent, two modest cities of the same name arose on each side of the river—one in the United States, the other in Canada.

Only some 70,000 people actually live in Niagara Falls, Ontario, and when one considers that close to 15 million visitors come and see the Falls every year, you can get an idea of just how central tourism is to the area. Central? Try its very raison d'être.

It's true: Niagara Falls has something for everyone. For the children, there's Marineland, waterslides, wax museums, haunted houses, and more. For newlyweds, there's a Honeymoon Certificate, and free admission for the bride to everything from the giant Imax Theatre to the Elvis Presley Museum.

Sure, many of the motels and attractions are corny, even tacky, but that's really part of the charm. Three towers present their awesome views of the Falls—the **Skylon,** the **Minolta,** and the **Kodak.** The Minolta Tower has a hands-on display of high-tech camera equipment, an aquarium, and a Reptile World display. The Kodak Tower is located in **Maple Leaf Village,** which has over 80 shops, the Elvis Presley Museum, and the world's second largest ferris wheel. **Clifton Hill,** known for its rather wide selection of museums that you somehow managed to survive without experiencing until now (Tussaud's Wax Museum, the Houdini Hall of Fame, Ripley's Believe It Or Not, the Criminal Hall of Fame, and the Haunted House), had over $1.5 million worth of improvements during 1987, including a widening of sidewalks and planting of trees. A "People Mover" system has recently been introduced, so visitors can leave their cars a good distance away and ride the system all day for a single, nominal fee.

And don't allow a winter visit to the area to put you off. **The Festival of Lights,** into its seventh year in 1990, runs from late December into mid-February. The festival is a real stunner. There are 70 trees illuminated with 34,000 lights in the parklands near the Rainbow Bridge every night 5:30–11:30, plus animated tableaux of various Canadian scenes, and even a Father Frost who welcomes visitors to the Magic of Winter theme park on Buchanan Avenue in Murray Hill.

Arriving and Departing

By Plane The closest airport to Niagara Falls is **Buffalo International Airport. Niagara Scenic Bus Lines** (tel. 716/648–1500 or 416/282–7755) operates a shuttle service from the airport to both the American and Canadian Niagara Falls. Fares are about $10 one-way.

By Car Niagara Falls is about 80 miles southwest of Toronto, less than a 90-minute drive. Take the Gardiner Expressway west from downtown, which quickly turns into Queen Elizabeth Way (QEW), heading south around Lake Ontario. Exit at Highway 420, which runs straight into the downtown area.

By Train **Via Rail** (tel. 416/366–8411; in Niagara Falls 716/357–1644) runs three trains a day from Toronto.

By Bus **Gray Coach** (tel. 416/979–3511) has three buses leaving the Bay and Dundas streets terminal every morning, and then one each hour from 2 to 7 PM. The trip takes about two hours and costs about $25 round-trip.

Important Addresses and Numbers

Contact the **Niagara Falls, Canada Visitor and Convention Bureau** (4673 Ontario Ave., Niagara Falls, L2E 3R1, tel. 416/356–6061).

There is also an **Information Center** at the corner of Highway 420 and Stanley Avenue. You'll see the big TRAVEL ONTARIO sign shortly after you leave Queen Elizabeth Way, heading east into Niagara Falls.

Guided Tours

Double Deck Tours are exactly that: A double-decker bus tours the Falls and environs. During the high season, the buses operate every 20 minutes from 9:30 AM, hitting many of the major points of interest. Although the complete tour lasts 90 minutes, you may get off at any stop and grab another bus later in the day. *Tel. 416/295–3051. Cost: $12 adults, $6.50 children 6–12. A more complete tour lasting 5 hours costs twice as much. Meet at the Maid of the Mist building; no reservations required.*

The following all have air-conditioned limos: **Bluebird Tours,** 4357 River Rd., tel. 416/356–5462; **Honeymoon Motel Tours,** 4943 Clifton Hill, tel. 416/357–4330; **Niagara Clifton Scenic Tours,** 5876 Victoria Ave., tel. 357–0923.

Niagara Helicopters (Victoria Ave. at River, tel. 416/357–5672) let you see the Falls at an unforgettable angle. Yes, they do accept major credit cards, so you won't feel the cost for weeks. *Departures Mar.–Nov., 9 AM–sunset.*

Winery Tours takes you on a 90-minute walk through the vineyards, followed by a wine tasting. The tours are free, but the bottles at the recently expanded retail wine shop are most decidedly not. *4887 Dorchester Rd., off Hwy. 420; tel. 416/357–2400. Tours May–Oct., Mon.–Sat. 10:30 AM, 2 PM, and 3:30 PM; Nov.–Apr., 2 PM only.*

Exploring

Numbers in the margin correspond with points of interest on the Niagara Falls, Ontario, map.

The city of Niagara Falls, Ontario, is quite easy to picture: To the west, running north–south (and eventually east, around Lake Ontario and up to Toronto), is Queen Elizabeth Way. To the east is the Niagara River and the glorious Falls. One of the best ways to get a sense of the layout is to go up the **Skylon Tower.** It's not cheap, but the view is breathtaking. Next to the tower is the **IMAX Theater,** with its giant screen.

Clifton Hill, right near the Falls, and northeast of the Skylon Tower, is the place where most bus and boat tours begin and where many of the better attractions are located: The Oakes Garden Theater; Louis Tussaud's Waxworks; the Rainbow Carillon Tower; the Niagara Falls Museum (which is less vulgar than most); and the Daredevil Hall of Fame. In the same area is **Maple Leaf Village,** with dozens of shops, eateries, and fun-fun-fun, sell-sell-sell. (The word "souvenir" comes from the French, meaning "remember." The big question is, "Do I *really* want to remember my trip to Niagara Falls with this ugly beer glass that has a giant, drenched gorge etched into its side?")

To the north, past Robert Street, is where the Via trains pull in. Here is where you go for the Great Gorge Trip, the Spanish Aero Car, and the helicopter tours.

Just west of the Skylon and the Falls is **Lundy's Lane,** where the rows of motels and hotels look like a Monopoly board run wild. Nearby is the fine **Lundy's Lane Historical Museum.** To the south and east of the Falls is **Marineland.** Along the river is the very beautiful **Queen Victoria Park,** which also has an attractive greenhouse and even a modest-size golf course.

1 ***Maid of the Mist*** boats are surely an unforgettable experience; they sail right to the foot of the Falls, and you'll be thankful for the raincoats they give out and for the exciting trip itself. *Boats leave from the foot of Clifton Hill St. Tel. 416/358–5781. Cost: $6 adults, $3.20 children 6–12. Daily from mid-May to late-Oct. From late June through Labor Day, trips leave as often as every 15 minutes, from 9:45 to 7:45; off-season boats leave every 30 minutes from 9:45 to 5:45.*

2 At **Table Rock Scenic Tunnels,** you don a weatherproof coat and boots, and an elevator takes you down to a fish-eye view of the Canadian Horseshoe Falls and the Niagara River and a walk through three tunnels cut into the rock. *Tours begin at Table Rock House, in Queen Victoria Park. Tel. 416/358–3268. Cost: $3.75 adults, $1.90 children 6–12. Open mid-June–Labor Day*

9 AM–11 PM; 9–5 the rest of the year. Closed Christmas and New Year's Day.

3 **Skylon** overlooks the Falls and is more than just a tower; there are amusements for children, entertainment, and shops. Rising 775 feet above the Falls, it does, indeed, have the best view of both the great Niagara and the entire city. There is also an indoor/outdoor observation deck and a revolving dining room. *Tel. 416/356–2651 or from Toronto, toll-free, 800/364–1824. Cost: $4 adults, $3 children 6–18 and senior citizens. Open 8:30 AM–1 AM. Go when the Falls are illuminated, especially during the Winter Festival of Lights.*

4 The **Niagara Spanish Aerocar** (the Whirlpool Aerocar) is a cable car that carries you high over the Niagara Gorge—and back, one hopes—on a 1650-foot-long cable. Far, far below, you watch the river and Whirlpool Basin. *Located on River Rd., about 2 mi north of the Falls, tel. 416/354–5711. Cost: $3 adults, $1 children 6–12. The ride runs from May 1–Labor Day, 9–5; and from then until mid-October when the weather permits.*

5 **Marineland** is, after the Falls themselves, the highest quality attraction in the area. The 4,000-seat aqua theater has the world's largest troupe of performing sea lions and dolphins, as well as two killer whales, Kandu and Nootka. The Hot Air Fantasy consists of various animated, singing characters suspended in balloons above the aquarium. The children will be ecstatic (and so will the adults).

There are rides for all ages, as well, including the world's largest steel roller coaster, spread over one mile of track and traveling through 1,000 feet of tunnels, double spirals, and giant loops. The Game Farm is also a delight, with its herd of buffalo, sloth of bears, and over 400 deer to be pet and fed. *Located 1 mi south of the Falls; follow the Marineland signs along the parkway by the falls, or exit the QEW at McLeod Road (Exit 27) and follow the signs; tel. 416/356–9565. Admission: approximately $17 adults, $12 children ages 4–9 and senior citizens. In the winter, prices fall to less than half, because the rides are closed. Open summers 9–6, off-season 10–4:30.*

6 **Niagara Falls Museum,** at the Rainbow Bridge, includes everything from shlock to quality. Here you'll find the Daredevil Hall of Fame, dinosaurs, and a very solid collection of Egyptian mummies dating from before the Exodus from Egypt. There are also Indian artifacts and zoological and geological exhibits. *5651 River Rd., tel. 416/356–2151. Admission: $5 adults, $4 students and senior citizens, $2 children 6–12. Open June–early Oct. 9 AM–midnight; other months, weekdays 10–5, weekends 11–5.*

7 **Lundy's Lane Historical Museum,** dating back to 1874, is on the site of a savage battle in the War of 1812. There are displays of the lives of settlers of that era, as well as military artifacts. *5810 Perry St., a little over 1 mi west of the Falls, on Hwy. 420; tel. 416/358–5082. Admission: under $1. Open May–Nov. 9–4; other months, weekdays noon–4 PM.*

8 The **Minolta Tower-Centre** has its own attractions, beyond its rising some 665 feet above the gorge. There's an indoor observation deck and three more open ones overlooking the Falls , and the aquarium and reptile exhibit will ease the pains of children who might be denied a day at Marineland. There's an

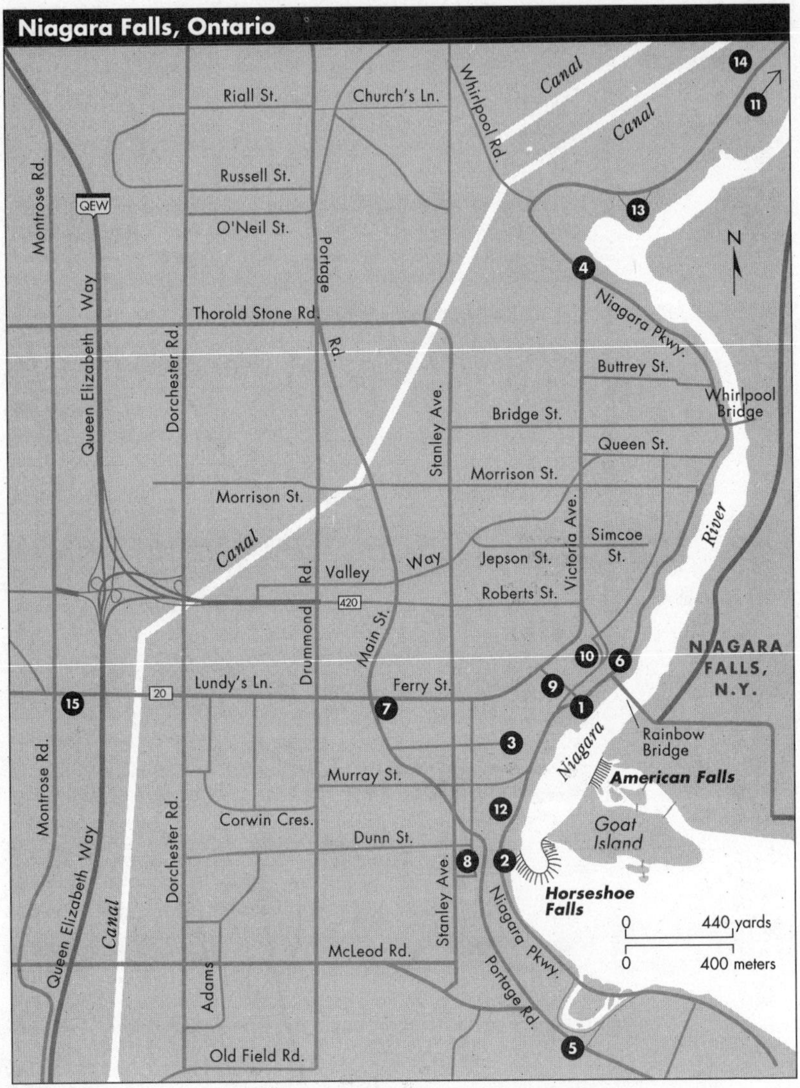

Clifton Hill, **9**
Floral Clock, **11**
Lundy's Lane Hist. Mus., **7**
Maid of the Mist, **1**
Maple Leaf Village, **10**
Marineland, **5**
Minolta Tower-Ctr., **8**
Niag.Falls Mus., **6**
Niag.Glen Nature Area, **13**
Niag. Parks School, **14**
Niagara Spanish Aerocar, **4**
Queen Victoria Park, **12**
Skylon, **3**
Table Rock Tunnels, **2**
Whitewater, **15**

Incline Railway that will take you to and from the brink of the Falls, and its Top of the Rainbow dining rooms have won at least four restaurant awards during this decade. *6732 Oakes Dr., tel. 614/356–1501. Admission to exhibits or tower: $4.50 adults, $3 children 5–18 and senior citizens. Combination tickets: $7 adults, $5 children or senior citizens. Tower open summers 9 AM–9 PM, other times: 10 AM–10 PM. The aquarium and reptile exhibit are open May–Nov.*

Children, and adults with great patience, will get a kick out of
9 **Clifton Hill** (tel. 416/356–2299), where you can visit the Movieland Wax Museum, The Haunted House, The House of Frankenstein, The Funhouse, The Guinness Museum of World Records, Louis Tussaud's Waxworks, Ripley's Believe It or Not Museum, and the Super Star Recording Studio, where you can make a tape/video of your fabulous voice/face. This is tourism at its most touristy.

10 **Maple Leaf Village** is a 350-foot observation tower with rides, games, shops, shows, and one of the largest Ferris wheels in captivity. This is where you'll find—if you dare—the That's Incredible Museum and The Elvis Presley Museum. *Clifton Hill and Falls Ave., at the Canadian terminus of the Rainbow Bridge; tel. 416/357–3090. Prices vary for various rides; admission to the village itself is free. Attractions are open mid-June–Labor Day 10 AM–midnight. The tower is open year-round.*

11 The **Floral Clock** is less than six miles north of the Falls, along River Road. Nearly 20,000 plants that bloom from earliest spring to late autumn make up one of the world's biggest, bloomin' clocks. Chimes ring every quarter-hour, and it actually keeps the right time. *Admission free.*

12 **Queen Victoria Park** (tel. 416/356–4699) runs along the Niagara River for 24 miles. The Niagara Parks Greenhouse has four major horticultural displays each year, and there is an outdoor fragrance garden for the visually handicapped.

About four miles due north of the Falls, along the Niaga-
13 ra Parkway, you can visit the **Niagara Glen Nature Area,** another free and most attractive attraction. You can actually work your way down to the gorge, observing the plant life. And just a
14 bit north, along the parkway, is the **Niagara Parks School of Horticulture,** with 100 acres of free exhibits. *Tel. 416/356–8554.*

15 **Whitewater** is a water park with everything from mini-slides and mini-pools to five giant slides and a wave pool. *7430 Lundy's Lane at the QEW; tel. 416/357–3380. Open mid-May–mid-September. Special rates after 6 PM.*

Dining

Reviews by Allan Gould

We hope you came here for the Miracle of Nature, not for any taste-bud magic. What Niagara Falls offers is mainly fast foods, faster foods, and fastest foods, with a handful of modest exceptions. You'll find all your old family friends—the King (of the Burger), the Baron (of Beef), Harry (of Char Broil fame), the Colonel (still frying that greasy, finger-lickin' chicken), and Mr. Ronald McDonald, whom we sense needs no introduction whatsoever. Still, there are respectable restaurants at rather moderate prices, considering what a tourist mecca this place is.

The following credit-card abbreviations are used: AE, American Express; CB, Carte Blanche; DC, Diners Club; MC, MasterCard; V, Visa.

Category	Cost*
Expensive	over $50
Moderate	$25–$50
Inexpensive	under $25

**for two, without tax, service, or drinks*

Expensive

Reese's Country Inn. A real cut above the other restaurants in the area, if a bit off the beaten track. It offers international cuisine in a country setting, complete with an open patio, fresh flowers, fireplace, and greenhouse. The most popular meal is rack of lamb. *3799 Montrose Rd. (Exit 32B from the QEW, then west about ½ mi on Thorold Stone Rd., and north on Montrose Rd.), tel. 416/357–5640. Tie and jacket recommended. Reservations requested. AE, MC, V. No dinner Sun.*

Moderate

Capri Restaurant. One of the better Italian places in the area, offering ethnic dishes as well as steak and seafood. Its most popular dish is a huge Maritime Platter, piled high with lobster, shrimp, scallops, salmon, and more, at about $60 for two. There are three rooms, and the owner has won the "Restaurateur of the Year Award" several times. *5438 Ferry St. (Hwy. 20), about ½ mi from the Falls; tel. 416/354–7519. Dress: informal. Reservations not necessary. AE, MC, V.*

Hungarian Village Restaurant. Family-owned for a half-century, it offers classic Eastern European dishes, as well as traditional Hungarian specialties—and a "famous Gypsy trio from Budapest" entertains in the evenings. There are three rooms, one of them more elegant and formal than the others. *5329 Ferry St. (Hwy. 20); tel. 416/356–2429. Dress: informal, but jacket welcome. Reservations recommended for weekends.*

The Minolta Tower Dining Room. This is on the top of you know what, and the food—veal Oskar and other meaty dishes—is trustworthy. The 26th-floor dining room is in pink and burgundy; the 27th-floor dining room is a more formal white and navy blue. *6732 Oakes Dr., tel. 416/356–1501. Dress: informal. Reservations recommended. AE, CB, DC, MC, V.*

Rolf's Continental Dining. The French and German menu features rabbit, filet of lamb, Dover sole, and Chateaubriand. Meals are served in three small rooms in an old house, with candlelight, fresh flowers, and sparkling china. The full-course "early dinner," served between 5 and 6 PM, costs under $15 a person. *3480 Main St., tel. 416/295–3472. Tie and jacket recommended. Reservations recommended. AE, DC, MC, V. No lunch; closed Mon.*

Table Rock Restaurant. Standard American and Canadian dishes in the pink-and-green dining room. As they love to advertise: "If you were any closer, you'd go over the Falls." It's true. *Located just above the Scenic Tunnels; tel. 416/354–3631. Dress: informal. Reservations advised. AE, MC, V.*

Victoria Park Restaurant. Like the Table Rock, it is run by

Niagara Parks. Located directly opposite the American Falls, and all done in yellows and earth tones, the eaterie offers breakfast, lunch, and dinner on a patio overlooking the crashing waters. It is known for its fresh salmon, prime ribs, and generally competent dining—but the view is the best of all. *On the corner of River Rd. and Murray St.; tel. 416/356–2217. Dress: informal. Reservations not necessary. AE, MC, V.*

Ye Olde Barn. You don't get a view of the (nearby) Falls, but the antiques and the decor of a real country barn may charm the family. It's cozy and quiet. The ribs are the most popular dish, and the food leans heavily toward barbecue, seafood, and steaks. *Lundy's Lane Motor Inn, 7280 Lundy's La., tel. 416/356–7075. Dress: informal. Reservations not necessary. AE, CB, DC, MC, V.*

Lodging

There are so many hotels and motels in the area that you can take your pick from almost any price range, services, or facilities. Heart-shape bathtubs, waterbeds, heated pools, Jacuzzis, baby-sitting services—the choice is yours. Prices are for doubles. The following credit-card abbreviations are used: AE, American Express; CB, Carte Blanche; DC, Diners Club; MC, MasterCard; V, Visa.

Prices fall by up to 50% between mid-September and mid-May, and less expensive packages for families, honeymooners, and others are common.

Category	Cost*
Very Expensive	over $100
Expensive	$75–$100
Moderate	$50–$75
Inexpensive	under $50

* *for doubles*

Very Expensive

Michael's Inn. Located by Rainbow Bridge, there's a view of the Falls from several balconies. *5599 River Rd., Niagara Falls L2E 3H3, tel. 416/354–2727. 130 rooms with bath. Facilities: wading pool, heated indoor pool, sauna, whirlpool, waterbeds, sexy tubs, theme rooms, restaurant, baby-sitting services, golf and tennis nearby, tours. AE, MC, V.*

Old Stone Inn. Its charm comes from the renovated mill at its heart. Many suites have fireplaces. No charge for kids under 14. *5425 Robinson St., Niagara Falls L2G 7L6 (by Skylon Tower), tel. 416/357–1234. 114 rooms with bath. Facilities: restaurant, baby-sitting services, outdoor pool, whirlpool. AE, MC, V.*

Expensive

Lincoln Motor Inn. A pleasant landscaped courtyard gives this motor inn an intimate feeling. The Falls are within walking distance. Connecting family suites sleep up to a dozen. *6417 Main St., Niagara Falls L2G 5Y3, tel. 416/356–1748. 57 rooms with bath. Facilities: extra-large heated pool, 102-degree outdoor whirlpool spa, restaurant, baby-sitting services, beach, golf nearby. AE, MC, V.*

Quality Inn Fallsway. Located very near the Falls on nicely landscaped grounds with patio. Pets allowed. *4946 Clifton Hill, Box 60, Niagara Falls L2E 6S8, tel. 416/358–3601. 265 rooms with bath. Facilities: indoor and outdoor pool, lounge, restaurant, baby-sitting services, golf nearby, whirlpool. AE, MC, V.*

Moderate

Canuck Motel. Located a few blocks from the Falls, this motel has fancy tubs, waterbeds, and yet a family atmosphere. Housekeeping units are available. It was recently remodeled and enlarged. *5334 Kitchener St., Niagara Falls L2G 1B5, tel. 416/358–8221. 79 rooms with bath. Facilities: heated outdoor pool, baby-sitting services, golf nearby. AE, MC, V.*

Vacation Inn. Only two blocks from the Minolta Tower, this hotel offers easy access to the bus terminal and highways. Some rooms have waterbeds. *6519 Stanley Ave., Niagara Falls L2G 7L2, tel. 416/356–1722. 95 rooms with bath, some family-size. Facilities: heated outdoor pool, restaurant. AE, MC, V.*

Inexpensive

Alpine Motel. This is a disarmingly small place, set back from the road. Rooms have refrigerators, and housekeeping units are available. *7742 Lundy's La., Niagara Falls L2H 1H3, tel. 416/356–7016. 10 rooms with bath. Facilities: heated outdoor pool, patio, golf nearby. MC, V.*

Detroit Motor Inn. It's five miles to the Falls along Highway 20, but the spacious grounds, reasonable rates, and family facilities help make up for the drive. No pets. *13030 Lundy's La., Niagara Falls L2E 6S4, tel. 416/227–2567. 38 rooms with bath or shower; some family units. Facilities: heated pool, miniature golf, playground, coffee shop, lounge. AE, MC, V.*

B&Bs

Contact the **Niagara Region Bed & Breakfast Service** (2631 Dorchester Rd., Niagara Falls, L2J 2Y9, tel. 416/358–8988).

Niagara-on-the-Lake

Since 1962, Niagara-on-the-Lake has been considered the southern outpost of fine summer theater in Ontario—the Shaw Festival. But offering far more than Stratford, its older theatrical sister to the north, this city is a jewel of Canadian history, architectural marvels, remarkable beauty, and, of course, quality theater. Though the town of 12,000 is worth a visit at any time of the year, its most attractive period is from late April to mid-October, when both the Shaw Festival and the flowers are in full bloom.

Being located where the Niagara River enters Lake Ontario has both its advantages and disadvantages. Because of its ideal placement, it was settled by Loyalists to the British Crown, who escaped north when most other Americans opted for independence. Soon after, it was made the capital of Upper Canada by John Graves Simcoe. When the provincial parliament was later moved to York—today, Toronto—it changed its name from Newark to Niagara. But that, too, was wisely changed since it was continually confused with a more spectacular town of the same name, just 12 miles to the south.

The downside of its location came in the War of 1812 when the Americans came calling, but not as tourists. They captured nearby Fort George in 1813, occupied the town itself that summer, and burned it to the ground that December. The fort is now open for touring mid-May to October. Like so many other heritage sites in Ontario, it is staffed by people in period uniform, who conduct tours and reenact 19th-century infantry and artillery drills.

Some of Niagara-on-the-Lake's best days were in the 1850s, when it was connected to Toronto by steamer and to Buffalo, New York, by train. But that era soon passed with the opening of the Welland Canal and the transfer of the county seat to St. Catherines. It remained a sleepy town until the last quarter-century, when the plays of Bernard Shaw and his contemporaries began to be performed in the Court House. Today, Niagara-on-the-Lake is one of the best-preserved 19th-century towns on the continent, with many neoclassical and Georgian homes still standing proudly—and lived in, too!

The three theaters used by the Shaw Festival do indeed present quality performances—the 10 productions in the summer of 1989 ranged from epics to murder mysteries, musicals to comedies, even lunchtime theater—but what's also special is the abundance of orchards and flower gardens, sailboats, and the utterly charming town of Niagara-on-the-Lake.

Arriving and Departing

By Car Take the QEW south and west, around the lake, to St. Catherines. At the very first exit past the Garden City Skyway, drive back north about 2½ miles to Highway 55, then turn right for 7 miles. It's a 90-minute drive.

By Bus Most buses demand a change in St. Catherines, which can be a drag. Call **Gray Coach** in Toronto, tel. 416/979–3511.

From Niagara Falls When you recall that Niagara-on-the-Lake is but 45 minutes from Buffalo, and less than 20 minutes from Niagara Falls, you may be wise to consider hooking your trip to this sparkling town with a visit to the Falls. Contact **Blue Bird Buses** (tel. 416/356–5462).

By Limo from the Airports **Laskey's Airport Transportation Service of St. Catharines** (tel. 416/685–8323 or 800/263–3636) offers door-to-door ground transportation to and from the Toronto and Buffalo airports, and from Niagara-on-the-Lake.

Important Addresses and Numbers

Festival schedules, lists of hotels and restaurants, and a Historic Guide are available from The Festival (Box 774, Niagara-on-the-Lake, Ont., L0S 1J0, tel. 416/468–2153 or from Toronto 361–1544. Also contact the Chamber of Commerce, Court House Theatre, Queen and Victoria Sts., tel. 416/468–2326).

Guided Tours

The **Niagara Foundation** visits local homes and gardens every spring. Phone the Chamber of Commerce (tel. 416/468–2325).

Hillebrand Estates Winery (Hwy. 55, Niagara Stone Rd., tel. 416/468–7123) offers free tours, followed by a free sampling of their award-winning products.

A much larger, more established firm is **Inniskillin Wine,** which offers tours and has numerous displays that illustrate the wine-making procedure inside a 19th-century barn. *Off the Niagara River Pkwy., just south of town; tel. 416/468–2187. Tours*

July–Sept., Mon.–Sat. 10:30 AM; *May, June, and Oct., Sat. only.*

Exploring

This is a very small town that can easily be explored on foot. Queen Street is the core of the commercial portion of this thriving mini-opolis. Walking east along that single street, with Lake Ontario to your north, you encounter many pleasures.

At **209 Queen** is the handsome Richardson-Kiely House, built around 1832 for a member of Parliament, with later additions at the turn of the century. At **187 Queen** is an 1822 house, with later Greek Revival improvements. **165 Queen** is an 1820 beauty, once lived in by a veteran of the Battle of Lundy's Lane, which took place in Niagara Falls in 1814. **157 Queen,** built in 1823, is still occupied by descendants of the Rogers-Harrison family, prominent since the early 19th-century in church and town affairs. **McClelland's West End Store** (106 Queen St.) has been in business on this same site since the War of 1812, and with good reason: Its local jams and cheeses are top notch. The huge "T" sign means "provisioner."

Across the street, but facing Victoria Street, is **Grace United Church,** built as recently as 1852. (It began as a congregation of "Free" Presbyterians, who later sold it to the Methodists.) Also at the corner of Queen and Victoria streets is the **Royal George Theater,** one of the three showcases of the Shaw Festival.

The **Court House,** on the next block, still going east, served until 1969 as the municipal offices of the town of Niagara; it recently underwent an award-winning restoration. It is another of the three theaters of the Shaw Festival.

Across the street (5 Queen St.) is the **Niagara Apothecary,** built in 1820 and moved here in 1866. The oldest continuing pharmacy in Upper Canada, it was restored in 1971. Note the exquisite walnut fixtures, crystal pieces, and rare collection of apothecary glasses. *Admission free. Open daily noon–6, mid-May–Labor Day.*

Behind the Apothecary is the **Masonic Hall,** also known as the Old Stone Barracks. It went up in 1816, possibly from the rubble of the town after the War of 1812. It still houses the first Masonic Lodge in Upper Canada, and some experts believe that the first meeting of the first Parliament of Upper Canada took place on this site in 1792, when it was used as a church as well.

Continue along Queen Street to Davy Street, and turn right (south) for two blocks. At 43 Castlereagh Street is the **Niagara Historical Society Museum,** one of the oldest and most complete museums of its kind in Ontario, with an extensive collection relating to the often colorful history of the Niagara Peninsula from the earliest Indian times through the 19th century. *Tel. 416/468–3912. Admission: $2 adults, $1 students and senior citizens. Open daily May–Oct., 10–6. Other times weekdays 1–5, weekends 10–5.*

Two blocks east, and a few steps north is the handsome **Shaw Festival Theatre.** Just beyond it, on a wide stretch of parkland, is **Fort George National Historic Park.** Built in the 1790s to replace Fort Niagara, it was lost to the Yankees during the War of

1812. It was recaptured after the burning of the town in 1813, and largely survived the war, only to fall into ruins by the 1830s. It was reconstructed a century later, and visitors can explore the officers' quarters, barracks rooms of the common soldiers, the kitchen, and more. *Tel. 416/468–4257. Admission: $2 adults, $1 children 5–16, $6 families. Open mid-May-late June, 9–5; July 1–Labor Day, 9–6; Labor Day–Nov., 10–5.*

The Shaw Festival. The festival began modestly back in the early 1960s with a single play and an unpromising premise: To perform the plays of George Bernard Shaw and his contemporaries. Fortunately, Shaw lived into his 90s, and his contemporaries included nearly everyone of note for nearly a century.

The Shaw season now runs from April into October and includes close to a dozen plays.

Box office tel. 416/468–2172 or from Toronto 416/361–1544. Tickets in the Festival Theatre run from $20 to nearly $40; in the Court House and Royal George, from $18 to $30. Lunchtime Theatre, usually a 1-act play, costs less than $10 per seat during its July and August run. Half-price tickets are available at the Five Star Ticket Booth, near the Eaton Centre in Toronto, and there are always half-price Rush Seats available on the day of performance, on sale at the Festival Theatre Box Office. There are performances in all 3 theaters Tues.–Sat. evenings, and matinees on Wed., Fri., Sat., and Sun. Dining

Reviews by Allan Gould

The food in Niagara-on-the-Lake is not at the level of the finest dining in Toronto, or even of Stratford. But meals are usually decent, and served in romantic, century-old surroundings.

The following credit-card abbreviations are used: AE, American Express; CB, Carte Blanche; DC, Diners Club; MC, MasterCard; V, Visa.

Category	**Cost***
Expensive	over $50
Moderate	$30–$50
Inexpensive	under $30

**for two, not including tax, tip, or drinks*

Expensive

The Luis House—Bella's Great Food. This family-owned restaurant features seafood and prime ribs. The ambience is homey. *245 King St., tel. 416/468–4038. Dress: informal. Reservations recommended. AE, MC, V.*

The Oban Inn. This is an elegant country inn where you can lunch on the patio and enjoy a superior view of the lake. The fare is standard—steak, beef, duck, and lobster—with a very solid Sunday brunch. The fresh poached salmon is popular in the summer. Fresh-cut flowers from the inn's own gardens. *160 Front St., tel. 416/468–2165. Dress: informal. Reservations required. AE, DC, MC, V.*

The Prince of Wales Hotel. Continental cuisine is served in a handsome Victorian setting. Lamb, fresh Atlantic salmon, and pickerel are the summer specialties. The luncheon buffet and

Sunday brunches offer good value. *6 Picton St., tel. 416/468-3246. Dress: informal. Reservations required. AE, MC, V.*

Moderate

Angel Inn. This is an English dining pub, located in the oldest operating inn in town. Specialties are steak, duck, and seafood, with an emphasis on the latter. Lots of antiques make this a handsome place to dine. *224 Regent St., tel. 416/468-3411. Dress: informal. Reservations recommended. AE, MC, V.*

Buttery Theatre Restaurant. Meals are served on a cozy terrace. On Fridays and Saturdays, there's a 2½-hour feast, "Henry VIII," that will have you looking like him when you finish. *19 Queen St., tel. 416/468-2564. Dress: informal, but jacket more proper for dinner. Reservations recommended. AE, MC, V.*

Lodging

There are few accommodations in Niagara-on-the-Lake, but the ones that are here have unusual charm.

The following credit-card abbreviations are used: AE, American Express; CB, Carte Blanche; DC, Diners Club; MC, MasterCard; V, Visa.

Category	Cost*
Expensive	over $100
Moderate	$70–$100
Inexpensive	under $70

**for a double room*

Expensive

The Pillar & Post Inn. This hotel, six long blocks from the heart of town, was built early in the century and restored in 1970. Most rooms have wood-burning fireplaces, hand-crafted pine furniture, and patchwork quilts. Wake up to free coffee and a newspaper. *48 John St., Box 1011, Niagara-on-the-Lake L0S 1J0, tel. 416/468-2123. 91 rooms with bath. Facilities: restaurant, baby-sitting services, hair dryers in rooms, outdoor pool, sauna, whirlpool, tennis, golf nearby. AE, MC, V.*

The Prince of Wales Hotel. First built in 1864, this charming Victorian hotel is in the heart of town and has been tastefully restored. Deluxe and superior rooms are worth the extra price. The Prince of Wales Court, adjacent to the main hotel, has many larger, newer rooms at higher prices. *6 Picton St., Niagara-on-the-Lake L0S 1J0, tel. 416/468-3246 or from Toronto 800/263-2452. 104 rooms with bath, some with fireplaces; housekeeping units available. Facilities: restaurant, lounge, coffee shop, heated indoor pool, saunas, whirlpool, health club, tennis courts, baby-sitting services, massage, golf nearby. AE, MC, V.*

Moderate–Expensive

The Oban Inn. Built about 1824 for a sea captain from Oban, Scotland, it was restored in 1963. The charming inn, centrally located, has broad verandas and beautifully manicured gardens. It also enjoys a waterfront view. Pets are allowed. *160 Front St., Box 94, Niagara-on-the-Lake L0S 1J0, tel. 416/468-2165. 23 rooms with bath; housekeeping units and rooms with fireplaces available. Facilities: restaurant, pub, patio bar, baby-sitting services, golf nearby. AE, MC, V.*

Moderate **Moffat Inn.** This is a charmer, with individually appointed rooms, some with original 1835 fireplaces, outdoor patios, brass beds, and wicker furniture. Enjoy breakfast fritters on the outdoor patio. *60 Picton St., Niagara-on-the-Lake L0S 1J0, tel. 416/468–4116. 22 rooms with bath. Facilities: restaurant, baby-sitting services, golf nearby. AE, MC, V.*

Inexpensive **The Angel Inn.** Each of the 10 rooms has antiques and beds with canopies. Built in 1823, this English-style inn even claims to have a resident ghost. *224 Regent St., Niagara-on-the-Lake L0S 1J0, tel. 416/468–3411. 12 rooms with bath. Facilities: restaurant, English tavern, golf nearby. AE, MC, V.*

B&Bs

Contact the **Niagara-on-the-Lake Bed & Breakfast Association** (Box 1515, Niagara-on-the-Lake L0S 1J0, tel. 416/358–8988).

Index

Personal Itinerary

Departure *Date*

Time

Transportation

Arrival *Date* *Time*

Departure *Date* *Time*

Transportation

Accommodations

Arrival *Date* *Time*

Departure *Date* *Time*

Transportation

Accommodations

Arrival *Date* *Time*

Departure *Date* *Time*

Transportation

Accommodations

Personal Itinerary

Arrival *Date* *Time*

Departure *Date* *Time*

Transportation

Accommodations

Arrival *Date* *Time*

Departure *Date* *Time*

Transportation

Accommodations

Arrival *Date* *Time*

Departure *Date* *Time*

Transportation

Accommodations

Arrival *Date* *Time*

Departure *Date* *Time*

Transportation

Accommodations

Personal Itinerary

Arrival *Date* *Time*

Departure *Date* *Time*

Transportation

Accommodations

Arrival *Date* *Time*

Departure *Date* *Time*

Transportation

Accommodations

Arrival *Date* *Time*

Departure *Date* *Time*

Transportation

Accommodations

Arrival *Date* *Time*

Departure *Date* *Time*

Transportation

Accommodations

Personal Itinerary

Arrival *Date* *Time*

Departure *Date* *Time*

Transportation

Accommodations

Arrival *Date* *Time*

Departure *Date* *Time*

Transportation

Accommodations

Arrival *Date* *Time*

Departure *Date* *Time*

Transportation

Accommodations

Arrival *Date* *Time*

Departure *Date* *Time*

Transportation

Accommodations

Addresses

Name

Address

Telephone

Name

Address

Telephone

Name

Address

Telephone

Name

Address

Telephone

Name

Address

Telephone

Name

Address

Telephone

Name

Address

Telephone

Name

Address

Telephone

Name

Address

Telephone

Name

Address

Telephone

Name

Address

Telephone

Name

Address

Telephone

Name

Address

Telephone

Name

Address

Telephone

Name

Address

Telephone

Name

Address

Telephone

Fodor's Travel Guides

U.S. Guides

Alaska
Arizona
Atlantic City & the New Jersey Shore
Boston
California
Cape Cod
Carolinas & the Georgia Coast
The Chesapeake Region
Chicago
Colorado
Dallas & Fort Worth
Disney World & the Orlando Area
Florida
Hawaii
Houston & Galveston
Las Vegas
Los Angeles, Orange County, Palm Springs
Maui
Miami, Fort Lauderdale, Palm Beach
Michigan, Wisconsin, Minnesota
New England
New Mexico
New Orleans
New Orleans (Pocket Guide)
New York City
New York City (Pocket Guide)
New York State
Pacific North Coast
Philadelphia
The Rockies
San Diego
San Francisco
San Francisco (Pocket Guide)
The South
Texas
USA
Virgin Islands
Virginia
Waikiki
Washington, DC
Williamsburg

Foreign Guides

Acapulco
Amsterdam
Australia, New Zealand, The South Pacific
Austria
Bahamas
Bahamas (Pocket Guide)
Baja & the Pacific Coast Resorts
Barbados
Beijing, Guangzhou & Shanghai
Belgium & Luxembourg
Bermuda
Brazil
Britain (Great Travel Values)
Budget Europe
Canada
Canada (Great Travel Values)
Canada's Atlantic Provinces
Cancun, Cozumel, Yucatan Peninsula
Caribbean
Caribbean (Great Travel Values)
Central America
Eastern Europe
Egypt
Europe
Europe's Great Cities
Florence & Venice
France
France (Great Travel Values)
Germany
Germany (Great Travel Values)
Great Britain
Greece
The Himalayan Countries
Holland
Hong Kong
Hungary
India, including Nepal
Ireland
Israel
Italy
Italy (Great Travel Values)
Jamaica
Japan
Japan (Great Travel Values)
Jordan & the Holy Land
Kenya, Tanzania, the Seychelles
Korea
Lisbon
Loire Valley
London
London (Great Travel Values)
London (Pocket Guide)
Madrid & Barcelona
Mexico
Mexico City
Montreal & Quebec City
Munich
New Zealand
North Africa
Paris
Paris (Pocket Guide)
People's Republic of China
Portugal
Rio de Janeiro
The Riviera (Fun on)
Rome
Saint Martin & Sint Maarten
Scandinavia
Scandinavian Cities
Scotland
Singapore
South America
South Pacific
Southeast Asia
Soviet Union
Spain
Spain (Great Travel Values)
Sweden
Switzerland
Sydney
Tokyo
Toronto
Turkey
Vienna
Yugoslavia

Special-Interest Guides

Health & Fitness Vacations
Royalty Watching
Selected Hotels of Europe
Selected Resorts and Hotels of the U.S.
Shopping in Europe
Skiing in North America
Sunday in New York

Help us evaluate hotels and restaurants for the next edition of this guide, and we will send you a free issue of Fodor's newsletter, TravelSense.

Title of this guide:

1 **Hotel** ❑ **Restaurant** ❑ *(check one)*

Name

Number/Street

City/State/Country

Comments

2 **Hotel** ❑ **Restaurant** ❑ *(check one)*

Name

Number/Street

City/State/Country

Comments

3 **Hotel** ❑ **Restaurant** ❑ *(check one)*

Name

Number/Street

City/State/Country

Comments

General Comments

Please complete for a free copy of TravelSense

Name

Number/Street

City/State/Zip